KING PAWN OR BLACK KNIGHT?

KING PAWN
OR
BLACK KNIGHT?

GWYNNE THOMAS

MAINSTREAM
PUBLISHING

EDINBURGH AND LONDON

First published in 1995 by
MAINSTREAM PUBLISHING COMPANY (EDINBURGH) LTD
7 Albany Street
Edinburgh EH1 3UG

ISBN 1 85158 784 5

A catalogue record for this book is available from the British Library

Typeset in Sabon
Printed and bound in Great Britain by Butler & Tanner Ltd, Frome

*To my late mother who, all
those years ago, tried to explain
why the King gave up his
throne, and planted the doubt
that has taken almost half a
century to assuage*

Contents

ACKNOWLEDGMENTS

THE AUTHOR WISHES to thank the staff of the various archives who have painstakingly produced much of the often obscure information that has enabled this story to be told. In particular to those in Ireland where the search began. Brian Donally and Catrina Crow of the National Archives in Dublin, and Father Ignatius Fennessy, the Librarian at the Franciscan Library in Killiney, Co. Dublin, where the De Valera State papers are housed. I am grateful for the help received from Horst Bredow, founder of the U-Boat Archiv at Cuxhaven, who has provided incontrovertible evidence about the voyage of U-65 including its original war diary and photographs of the boat and its crew taken before leaving for Ireland.

I welcome this opportunity to thank John Burns of *The Sunday Times* in Dublin whose report, written in conjunction with Maurice Chittenden in London, which appeared in *The Sunday Times* of 3 January 1993 proved the starting point of this story. John generously agreed to meet me to discuss the story and his unstinting help and encouragement since has been a great help; it is much appreciated. My thanks are also due to John Parker for revealing some of the original sources of the material he used for his highly acclaimed book, *The King of Fools*.

My thanks are due to the staff at Mainstream; to Bill Campbell, the managing director, whose initial enthusiasm for the project has ensured the whole thing has proceeded smoothly, and to John Beaton, the editorial director, who has painstakingly checked the book for accuracy.

The publishers and author wish to thank the following copyright owners who have given permission for the extracts reproduced in the work: Weidenfeld and Nicolson: *The Duke of Windsor's War*, Michael Block; *Wallis and Edward Letters 1931–1937*, edited by Michael Block; *Operation Willi*, Michael Block; *Edward VIII*, Frances Donaldson; *Eminent Churchillians*, Andrew Roberts. Secker and Warburg: *The Rise and Fall of the*

Third Reich, William L. Shirer. Sidgwick and Jackson: *Last Days of Hitler*, H. Trevor-Roper; *The Secret Lives of the Duchess of Windsor*, Charles Higham and R. Moseley. Robert Hale: *Errol Flynn A Memoir*, Earl Conrad. Poolbeg Press: *The Secret Army of the IRA 1916–1979*, Bowyer Bell. Sheil Land Associates: *Modern Ireland 1600–1792*, R.E. Foster. Transworld Bantam Press: *Ribbentrop*, Michael Block. Hodder and Stoughton: *The Game of The Foxes*, Ladislas Farago. Little Brown and Co.: *Spies in Ireland*, Enno Stephan; *King of Fools*, John Parker. Lowenstein Associates: *American Swastika*, Charles Higham; *Trading With The Enemy*, Charles Higham.

Finally, my thanks are due to my wife Joyce who has carried out the unenviable task of reading and re-reading the manuscript with commendable fortitude and without whose help the final result would not have been achieved.

INTRODUCTION

IF IT CAN BE SAID that there was a precise moment when the nation's affection for the British Royal Family began to change, when the problems of the past were forgotten and the country found a new respect for the institution of Royalty, one that was to develop and grow stronger over the next four and a half decades when the monarchy was to become closer and more identified with the people, that moment was on 13 September 1940. During a daylight raid on London the pilot of a lone German bomber, using The Mall to guide him, dropped six high-explosive bombs on Buckingham Palace. Later in the day as she inspected the damage the Queen gave a smile and said: 'I'm glad we've been bombed. It makes me feel I can look the East End in the face.'[1]

This remark will always be associated with her, and will inevitably form part of her epitaph. That one chance comment was to endear the Queen Mother, as she was to become, and form the bond between the people and the throne that was to make the House of Windsor the most popular and best-loved monarchy in the history of the nation, reflecting a genuine affection that was to last more than half a century until once again the Royal Family was plunged into crisis following revelations of an adulterous relationship between the Prince of Wales and a married woman.

It had been a close call: one bomb could have changed the whole course of the war, and with it history. The King and Queen were standing at the window of an upstairs sitting-room when two of the bombs burst in the quadrangle about 30 yards from where they stood, a third destroyed the chapel injuring three workmen, while another failed to explode and the remaining two fell harmlessly in the grounds. While there is no doubt that the Queen's remark was spontaneous – she was simply expressing her thoughts – it showed her desire to identify with the people of London who were nightly facing continuous air-attack, in a German effort to sap their morale, force them into submission and call upon the Government to sue for peace. It is interesting to speculate what the

Queen would have said had she known that the decision to bomb London had come from a suggestion by her brother-in-law the Duke of Windsor during the time he was in Spain plotting with his Nazi associates. *(see footnote on page 17)*

When the war was over and the German records became available, a telegram dated 11 July 1940, sent by Hoyningen-Huene, the German Foreign Minister in Lisbon, to Berlin, was discovered. It recorded a conversation he had with the Duke of Windsor and it concluded: '. . . The Duke is convinced that if he had remained on the throne of England, war would have been avoided, and he characterised himself as a firm supporter of a peaceful arrangement with Germany. The Duke definitely believes that continued severe bombing would make England ready for peace.'[2]

The British Government later tried to cast doubt on the authenticity of this and other captured Nazi documents, but this telegram was unquestionably genuine and can be relied upon; Hoyningen-Huene was a brilliant and distinguished diplomat who would have had no motive other than to report what he had been told.

It is generally accepted that the former Duchess of York, when she was unexpectedly called to become Queen following the Abdication of Edward VIII, by force of her strong personality and with a sure touch in understanding the mood of the ordinary people, did more to restore the confidence in the monarchy than anybody. She is a formidable woman (Hitler was to call her shrewd) whose influence on George VI was considerable. Coming to the throne at a time when all of Europe was in turmoil, when all across the Continent the old order was collapsing and when it was evident that things would never be the same again, was no easy task, but she accepted the challenge with fortitude.

However, there is another aspect to her strength of character. She was harsh and unyielding over certain matters, as is more evident in her attitude towards the former Edward VIII and his wife, Wallis. There seems little doubt that the initial hostility shown by George VI came from his mother. Several sources have described how Queen Mary could never forgive her eldest son for his behaviour and had great influence on the new Queen. What many have described as the 'Windsor Women' were a formidable influence that militated against the Duke's interests. Wallis had no doubt: she once said, 'The reign of George VI is a split level matriarchy in pants. Queen Mary runs the King's wife and the wife runs the King.'[3] This antagonism was to drive him to involve himself in several treacherous intrigues masterminded by Hitler and aimed at destabilising the elected Government of Britain.

There remains little real dispute that much of what happened could have been avoided had the Royal Family shown a modicum of compassion and, instead of regarding the Duke of Windsor as a threat, had discovered some way to employ his talents to support the monarchy rather than regarding him as its enemy. This does not excuse the Duke's outrageous behaviour; he seemed destined to be a rebel and, as King, Edward would almost certainly have proved a disastrous monarch. Had he not abdicated, he would have found himself constantly at odds with the Government of the day based on his refusal to accept that his role was to rule, and not to govern.

Time did little to heal the wounds. The Queen's attitude towards the Duke and Duchess of Windsor remains unchanged – her opposition was total. It is an attitude in many ways hard to imagine from a woman whose dedicated and unstinting service earned her the affection of the people and gained for herself the title of the nation's 'favourite grandmother'. Her opposition and refusal to forgive inevitably gives rise to speculation. Most informed opinion believes that her hostility was directed towards the Duchess, whom she believed to be an adventuress responsible for the weak Edward's decision to abandon the throne and desert his family, the effect of which was to thrust the burden of state on to Elizabeth's husband, a man ill-fitted to the task, who sacrificed his health to carry out what he clearly saw as his duty and who, despite his shortcomings, acquitted himself with a calm dignity that made him increasingly popular with his subjects. While this remains the conventional view and has much basis in truth, there are those who have sought to suggest that the animosity went much deeper, and may well have stemmed from an incident that occurred even prior to her marriage to the Duke of York and which may well have had a profound effect on her attitude towards the Duke of Windsor.

It is well known that Elizabeth was a particular favourite of George V, but what is less well known was the speculation that he and Queen Mary were in favour of her becoming the bride of the dashing Prince of Wales.[4] Most of the newspapers of 5 January 1923 carried a headline that the Prince of Wales had found himself a Scottish bride, a story that was hastily denied by Buckingham Palace, but the truth is that while his family regarded her as an ideal choice, the Prince of Wales rejected her. This account is given additional support when it was later learned that Queen Mary had travelled to Scotland to discuss arrangements with the Bowes-Lyon family. The story has persisted for many years, and the idea that 'Nor hell a fury like a woman scorn'd' might lie at the root of her fierce opposition to Edward, and more particularly Wallis. David Sinclair in his book *Queen and Country* suggests that while the visit by Queen Mary to Glamis Castle did take place and proved to be the subject of much press speculation at the time, the press misread the purpose of the visit. It seems more likely that the meeting with Elizabeth's family was to discuss her suitability as a future bride for the King and Queen's second son, Albert, whose engagement to her, when it came, was a great surprise to everybody. Whatever the truth behind her determination not to allow the Duke to return and overshadow his less charismatic brother George VI that was to continue until both were dead, her conduct during the Thirties and early Forties has been entirely vindicated by the revelation that the overriding reason for her apparent intransigence was that the Royal Family were fully aware of the Duke of Windsor's activities during the war. Their motives were then clear: they did not want the enviable reputation they had developed while leading the nation to victory to be sullied by the knowledge that they had protected a traitor and failed to bring him to justice. They believed their best interests would be served by allowing the truth to be suppressed, confident in the knowledge that the Duke would never speak out and that the affairs of the late Thirties and early Forties would soon be forgotten.

However, there was a moment of anger and despair when the King and Queen learned that the Duke intended to break with the convention that prevented members of the family from writing their autobiographies. He produced his *A King's Story* that was to prove a bestseller. The Duchess also wasted little time in publishing hers. Each gave their version of events surrounding the Abdication and the way they had been treated by the family and the British Establishment but they studiously avoided any reference to the dealings they had with Nazi Germany. Lady Hardinge, the wife of the King's secretary, was to describe the Duke's memoirs as 'a highly colourful one-sided account of the Abdication'[5] and accused him of selling his version of the truth for a very large cheque.

The King and Queen had moved quickly. Even before the war was over they embarked on what was to prove a controversial strategy to suppress the details of the exchanges between the Duke and the family and to conceal his treachery. They sanctioned a daring plot to hide from the world the details of his crimes.

INTRODUCTION

Even after Hitler had retreated to his bunker he continued to fight, but now it was a make-believe war: his last days were spent moving non-existent reserves to reinforce those phantom armies already defeated and whose troops were either already dead or in captivity. Living in a world of self-delusion, Hitler made lavish plans for a mighty counter-offensive which existed only in his tortured mind. Finally, on 30 April 1945, for a brief moment he faced reality. He shot his dog, helped Eva Braun, the mistress he had married only a few days before, to take poison, then he blew out his brains. He was unable to face the world he had created. The dream of a 'Reich that would last a Thousand Years' was dead, having lasted for little more than two decades, though in that time it had been responsible for more destruction and carnage than in any other period of history. With news of his death the free world heaved a sigh of relief: the great Fascist experiment was over.

As the war drew to a close there were many who wanted to change history before it was written, and to conceal the part they had played in many appalling crimes. This is natural at the end of any large conflict, but never more so than in 1945. The terrible acts of savagery carried out against millions of innocent people made it necessary for those responsible to move fast to destroy the evidence. Frantically they tried to hide the truth about the death camps where the more perverted members of the Nazi SS had carried out their appalling crimes, euphemistically referred to as the 'Final Solution of the Jewish problem'. The murders of millions of ordinary men, women and children were so terrible that even those sadists responsible found it necessary to use a macabre jargon with each other to describe the horrors in which they were engaged. The evidence revealed by the advancing British, American and Russian armies as they overran these camps stretched the credibility of those who did not actually witness for themselves the horrors of Belsen, Auschwitz, Treblinka and many others. These were not crimes of war, but a deliberate attempt to murder a race of people, a form of brutality against humanity itself.

While it is understandable that those responsible for such crimes should want to destroy the evidence and disappear before the advancing troops, it comes as some surprise to discover that their ranks were swelled by agents acting on behalf of the popular British Royal Family which had led a nation in the fight to remove such tyranny. That they should have plotted to conceal the truth of some of what happened during the war and make sure it was never exposed to public examination seems incredible, but there is irrefutable evidence that George VI did, and this begs the question: what was so important that he was prepared to run the risk of exposing himself to a charge of theft of documents that were rightfully the property of the Allied Governments and to make sure that only a sanitised version would be recorded by future historians?

During the last week of April 1945 a British army lorry drove into the village of Kronberg and drew up at the Schloss Friedrichshof, the ancestral home of the Hesse family, relatives of the British Royal Family who had collaborated with the Nazis and who were believed to be in possession of many of the Duke of Windsor's secret papers. Such an event, in the turmoil of the last days of the war in Europe, should not have been that remarkable but it was to provide the motive behind many years of speculation by those who still strive to unravel the greatest unsolved mystery of the Second World War and it forms the basis for a cover-up carried out by the nations involved.

However, the King and Queen were unfortunate in their choice of the man entrusted to carry out this difficult mission. On the face of it he should have been ideal, a member of the British secret service with cover as an art expert and a distant member of the Queen's family. His mother was the second cousin to her father, the Earl of Strathmore. What they did not know was that he was a dangerous traitor. His name was Anthony Blunt. He was accompanied to the Schloss Friedrichshof by Owen Morehouse, the Royal archivist in charge of the records housed in the Round Tower of the castle whose name the family bear.

This clandestine mission was intended to remain forever a secret and would have done so had the Royal Family and the British Government not had the misfortune to have selected Blunt to lead the mission. When Margaret Thatcher, under pressure from America and the CIA in particular, unmasked Blunt in the House of Commons on 15 November 1979 she unwittingly allowed details of his part in the conspiracy to emerge. Peter Wright, later of *Spycatcher* fame, worked for MI5 and was detailed to interrogate Blunt. In his book he reveals that he found to his astonishment that 'the Queen had been fully informed about Sir Anthony, and is quite content for him to be dealt with in any way that gets at the truth', except for, as her private secretary Michael Adeane added, 'an assignment he [*Blunt*] undertook on behalf of the palace – to visit Germany'. Wright was to conclude: 'In the hundreds of hours I spent with him I never did learn the secret of his mission at the end of the war,' adding that 'the palace is adept in the difficult art of burying scandals over several centuries while MI5 have only been in business since 1909'.6

King Pawn or Black Knight? sets out to explain much of what took place and to reveal why the Royal Family and the Government have been determined that it has remained a secret.

The King was badly shaken by the attack on Buckingham Palace which he believed was directed at him personally, suspecting the pilot had 'local knowledge'. The man he suspected was his cousin twice removed, whose mother Princess Beatrice was a granddaughter of Queen Victoria and whose father was the former Duke of Edinburgh and Saxe-Coburg. The pilot's father, Infante Alfonso was a General in the Spanish Air Force and, the King had been told by British Intelligence, was spending a great deal of time with the Duke of Windsor in Madrid. It was believed that the Nazis were planning to assist the Duke and Duchess to return to the British throne. The King was wrong, the navigator of the ME 109 was Prince Christopher of Hesse, whose family were to prove instrumental in handing over the incriminating evidence about the King's brother to Anthony Blunt and Owen Morehouse.

Chapter One

The Prelude to War

THE PEOPLE OF GERMANY were quick to recognise that the rise of Hitler and his Nationalist Socialist Party offered a realistic chance to escape much of the misery that had become their lot since the end of the Great War. Galvanised by his dynamic oratory, they recognised his promise to address the social ills and restore the country's fortunes as exactly the sort of message they so badly wanted to hear. The German national spirit has always been characterised by an overwhelming desire to find expression in a fierce, almost fanatical, pride in what they hold as the Fatherland, but this desperate need for self-respect had been denied them following the Armistice of 1918 which had left the ordinary German in no doubt that they had been humiliated and were a beaten people. Hitler's arrival on the political scene was the spur, an awakening, a chance to rediscover hope, and it pointed the way forward by providing an opportunity to recapture the dignity and sense of national identity that they so desperately sought. There is no doubt that his message struck exactly the right note with a nation suffering from the ravages of hyper-inflation caused by raging unemployment which he promised to sweep aside. His message was that full employment and the financial stability that would transform their lives could only be achieved through a revitalisation of German manufacturing potential. It was to prove heady stuff, deliberately designed to inflame nationalistic feelings among those who came to listen as he described his vision of a powerful, resurgent Germany.

Come they did; the Nazi rallies of the 1930s were a magnet for crowds of fervent supporters who flocked to hear his message. On several occasions crowds of more than a million turned up to hear Hitler explain how his policy would transform their mundane, wretched existence. The picture he painted of a future under his much vaunted 'new order' must have seemed idyllic. Inevitably anything that offered a cure for rabid inflation fell as sweet music on the ears of a nation weary of a seemingly endless struggle against a plummeting currency, whose value had continued to slide until, at its lowest point, it would require 71 billion marks just to mail a letter. Hitler not only promised that a strong Germany would allow them to hold their heads high, but also he offered a panacea for the ills of the past and a reason for the current depression.

Astutely, he absolved the German people of blame; instead he convinced them that the principal reason for the national weakness lay with the infiltration of all levels of society by those of non-Germanic origin who had gained control of the country's financial services and who were prospering while the remainder of the country starved. His target was the Jews, the race for which he had an obsessional hatred; he was able to foment and direct antagonism against the Jewish bankers and businessmen who, he could demonstrate, were not suffering the fate of the ordinary German. By directing the blame towards them, skilfully he appealed to the base instincts of his audience and played the cards of racialism and envy which enabled him to whip up and exploit the anger of the masses towards those he intended to destroy, expanding his attacks to include the gypsies and others he wished to dispossess. In time this would include the sick, the old and those suffering mental and physical infirmities; in short, anyone who could not serve his military ambitions. The policy opened up the way for his fanatical followers to carry out their terrible atrocities without attracting any real opposition, and thus having salved the German conscience, he showed them the way forward, a future that promised hope and prosperity, but most of all a chance to make Germany great again. It was not therefore surprising that Hitler and his accomplices were swept into power in the election of 1928. His position as leader was confirmed when he was elected Chancellor in 1933 and from this point onwards his power became unassailable. From the beginning, members of Goering's SA police, the dreaded brownshirts, moved swiftly. Ruthlessly they eliminated all political opposition, leaving few who dared raise their voice against the new regime. The fear of reprisals proved a powerful deterrent to dissent.

A turning point came in 1933 when a disastrous fire destroyed the Reichstag, the German Parliament building. Wasting no time, Hitler and his fellow conspirators rushed to the scene and declared this to be the start of a Communist revolution. His timing was perfect: not only did it allow him to order the round up and arrest of over 4,000 Communists, but it also gave him an excuse to close down the independent newspapers. All this happened several days before the March elections which gave the National Socialists an overwhelming victory at the polls. It would be some years before it was discovered that it had been the Nazis themselves who had fired the Reichstag. With considerable political foresight, despite their ruthless methods, the Nazis continued to hold elections even when the result was beyond doubt, thus avoiding the charge of creating a dictatorship. Most observers outside Germany still regarded the country as a democracy, so by the time the rest of the world woke up to what was really happening, it was too late.

Hitler's stirring speeches, his seductive oratory, too often dismissed by those outside Germany as the ranting of a madman, breathed new life into the nation. Many world politicians dismissed him simply as a 'rabble rouser', for indeed he was, a skill he used to great effect, his words producing an hypnotic effect on those who gathered to hear his powerful rhetoric. Hitler was a master at sensing the tenor of his audience, adept at providing the message they wanted to hear. Often speaking without prepared notes he drove his audience wild by painting them a picture of a utopian future. Today some of these promises seem rather strange, even bizarre; on several occasions he promised that he would find every German woman a husband, but it must be remembered that this was a time when the effects of the Great War were still being felt, there was a real shortage of men of marriageable age and this promise, more than anything, demonstrates how closely Hitler was in touch with his audience. His oratory and promise for the future drove the German people to follow him; their blind devotion elevated him to a status beyond that of an ordinary mortal. Not only in Germany, but far further afield he was regarded by a great many people as a visionary who would change the world.

Initially Hitler was careful not to spell out how he proposed to make Germany strong, but all those who attended his rallies and who found themselves in the grip of an enthusiasm that bordered on mass hysteria had no need to be told that he was advocating rearmament to restore the country's military might, explaining that natural justice demanded that Germany reclaim the territories it had been forced to hand over at the end of the war. Millions gathered every time he spoke, they cheered his every word; few outside Germany bothered to listen to what he was advocating.

Sadly, politicians throughout the world watched developments in Germany with little apparent concern; in fact it is fair to say that almost all were encouraged by Hitler's rise to power. Clear-thinking people were already beginning to realise that a weak, defenceless Germany was in nobody's real interest. The humiliation and stripping of Germany's wealth following the end of the war had been too severe. Although few would admit it publicly, secretly many welcomed the prospect of a German economic revival.

Germany represented a vast potential market for raw materials and manufactured goods and with the prospect that the stability of its currency was returning, the rest of the world suddenly wanted to trade with her, particularly the businessmen of America. The huge manufacturing capability of the United States made it necessary for them to seek new markets; most of the large multinationals were looking for an opportunity to form links with Germany or to expand their already existing operations there. Many of the large American companies became involved, and were instrumental in, assisting the German industrial revival. While some British companies traded with Germany, generally there was less interest. The Empire still provided a vast market for British exports; in the Twenties and Thirties the Empire had a population of several hundred million potential customers and the demand for goods had slowly begun to rise following the recession of the mid-Twenties. While Britain had suffered from the effect of falling world trade, this had partly been offset by a reduction in the cost of raw materials and, more importantly, imported food from the Empire. There they needed to import British goods to maintain their poor economies and balance of trade. The aim of improving its trading balance was the driving force central to every country's foreign policy.

Even before he came to power Hitler was aware that the greatest difficulty he would have to face would lie with the British, still the dominant force in world trade and undisputed leader in international politics. While eventually he was to be proved correct, events did not happen in the way he had anticipated. Looking back it seems almost impossible that it was not until his airforce was defeated at the hands of the RAF during the Battle of Britain that he finally came to realise that his cherished hope of an Anglo-German alliance was an impossible dream.

With some justification Hitler was highly contemptuous of many of the pre-war British politicians, while at the same time he was full of admiration for the British people and was correct in his belief that the peoples of both nations were so similar in temperament there was a genuine mutual respect. They had no wish to fight each other. It remained his passionate desire to see the two nations move towards closer co-operation. This was not a new idea; Hitler was merely reiterating what had long been regarded as desirable by many in Germany. The idea of an alliance between the two countries had first been advanced by Kaiser Wilhelm I, who tried to interest his cousin Edward VII in a similar idea in 1901 when Edward ascended the throne on the death of Queen Victoria.

Hitler was deeply committed to this concept. He tried desperately to avoid war with Britain: even when conflict became inevitable and the two nations found themselves at war, still he refused to abandon it and continued to work towards his dream of an alliance until September 1940 when, following the Battle of Britain, with great reluctance he was forced to accept that the enemy under its existing leadership would never support his ambitions.

Apart from an admiration for the working classes and a genuine belief that a strong Germany partnered with the British Empire would achieve the dominant force in world trade that would provide political stability and ultimately lead to his much vaunted new world order, there had been another, more pragmatic, reason behind his determination not to find himself at war with Britain. Hitler harboured a deep-seated fear of the power of the Royal Navy. His only experience of conflict came from his time spent in the trenches during the First World War where he rose to the rank of corporal. There he and his deputy Rudolf Hess had fought, the latter being wounded in action. The time spent in the mud of the killing fields of Flanders had a profound effect on both men and was later to determine the way in which they conducted the war. The sea formed no part of Hitler's strategic thinking. Hitler's fears were profound; he made several references to them in *Mein Kampf*. These were later justified and reinforced during the first major action of the war that involved the German navy. While the land actions at the time of the invasion of Norway in April 1940 were highly successful, the weakness in the German navy was exposed. It was given a severe lesson. A dozen Nazi destroyers and the heavy cruiser *Blücher* were sunk. The cruiser *Emden* was severely damaged as were the battle cruisers *Scharnhorst* and *Gneisnau* and the pocket battleship *Lützow*, all having to return to Germany for extensive repairs. A large number of cargo ships were also sunk. This was accomplished by a single squadron of Royal Navy destroyers, a greatly inferior force, and gave a welcome boost to British pride and morale at a time when good news was in very short supply. When word of the naval battle fought off Narvik reached Berlin, Hitler was reported to have become hysterical.

Some historians would have us believe that Hitler was a military genius, others prefer to believe he was an audacious gambler who initially proved successful before, ultimately, his luck ran out. There is no doubt what Hitler believed; he never tired of boasting about his brilliant achievements and his grasp of military tactics. Whatever view is taken, one thing cannot be denied: his single-minded determination made him highly effective at controlling the army. Initially the German generals mistrusted and opposed him, they became horrified at his dangerous foreign policy decisions which they dismissed as simply 'sabre rattling' since Germany did not have the might to defend the outcome. However, as his success began to grow the opposition began to dissolve; they became willing, enthusiastic and finally fanatical in their support of the Führer's aims. It was only when defeat after defeat stared them in the face that the officer classes, mostly aristocratic high-born Prussians who had previously been a powerful force in German life, turned on him and tried to destroy him. There is no doubt that having successfully convinced his generals to wage war in the manner he advocated, his strategy during the early days of the war was highly successful. Whatever the outcome of the argument about his abilities, there is no question that he understood the value of the fast pre-emptive strike and not allowing his army to get bogged down in the sort of nullifying battles that characterised the First World War. In this his thinking was highly advanced; unlike most of the British and French generals, he had learned the lessons of the war in Flanders. It was not until his army was brought to a halt in the snow outside Stalingrad that this strategy collapsed and memories of the trench warfare of the First World War returned to haunt him.

Fortunately for the rest of the world, and in particular Britain, Hitler failed to understand the basic concept of sea power. In permitting the German navy under Admiral Raeder to build capital ships Hitler allowed vast resources to be poured into impressive, prestigious but already obsolete battleships like the *Bismark* and *Tirpitz*, ships that were eventually destroyed by relatively inferior forces. More importantly, by allowing the German navy to dissipate its energy on these grandiose vessels he kept Admiral Doenitz short of U-boats, a massive blunder that almost certainly cost him ultimate victory in the Atlantic, and a policy that saved Britain when she stood alone in the early days of 1940. Hitler simply refused to believe that the Royal Navy with its similar, largely ineffective capital ships could be beaten. He remained convinced that the Royal Navy would always turn the war in Britain's favour. In this we must not be too harsh on Hitler, he was not alone: almost all the British admirals of the day thought similarly. They believed that the war at sea, if it came, would be a re-run of the Battle of Jutland. They too failed to understand that the day of the capital ship had passed. The funds employed in building a George the Fifth class battleship, five of which were completed between 1940 and 1942, would have built a vast fleet of corvettes, which, had they been employed on convoy duty would have saved many valuable merchant ships and their life-supporting cargoes. The evidence shows that apart from one, all the other British capital ships lost during the Second World War were destroyed by either U-boats or aircraft. The naval staff in both Britain and Germany were slow to realise that air-power had changed the war at sea forever. Hitler not only failed to understand this, but his fear of defeat at sea was another powerful reason for his wanting to effect an alliance.

To understand Hitler's entire policy and intentions it is necessary to study *Mein Kampf* which he published in 1922. Looking back it seems almost incredible that his entire 'game plan' was set out in this boring book. Never before in history has a potential dictator and warlord outlined so clearly his intentions towards his future enemies. A study of *Mein Kampf* reveals that Hitler harboured great bitterness over the treatment of Germany following the signing of the Treaty of Versailles. His desire to go to war is explained by his desire for vengeance and a deep-seated fear of the spread of Bolshevism. The feelings of revenge came as a result of the very real humiliation of Germany in 1918, for which, curiously, he blamed the French. Why he singled them out is difficult to understand, but he made no secret of his hatred of France or of his avowed intention to avenge this defeat by destroying the French army. With the self-delusion that became more and more obvious towards the end of his life, he seems to have persuaded himself that the British he so admired were not responsible for the misery he attributed to the terms of the instrument of surrender.

Determined not to do battle with the British, from the beginning Hitler decided that one of the best ways of avoiding confrontation was to gain the support of the British Royal Family in the hope that he could persuade them to influence the Government.[1] As soon as he came to power he went out of his way to establish a connection with the House of Windsor. At first he selected as his emissary Baron William de Ropp, the head of an aristocratic Balkan family who for some reason that has never emerged came to live in Britain in 1910 and soon became a naturalised British subject. During the First World War he fought on the side of his adopted country, but when the war was over he returned to Germany only to discover that his family estates had been seized by the Bolsheviks. Deprived of income, he was forced to earn a living as a journalist; he returned to live in Berlin.

When Hitler came to power de Ropp soon established himself in Nazi society and the Nazi leader took an instant liking to him, particularly when he discovered that de Ropp had powerful connections among English society and was well informed about much of what was happening in London. Hitler was to consult him frequently and before long de Ropp not only enjoyed the Führer's trust but became his spokesman in dealings with the many important British people Hitler wished to influence. De Ropp also worked for German intelligence and was the main route by which the Nazis learned what was going on in Whitehall and at Buckingham Palace. In addition de Ropp arranged for many of his highly placed British friends to visit Berlin and meet with the leaders of the Nazi party: there is strong evidence that de Ropp was instrumental in raising funds in the City of London to finance several of the Nazi election campaigns which ensured that by the end of 1933 the Nazi party was totally established and in control. Meanwhile de Ropp remained in England and continued to work on behalf of German intelligence; his greatest coup came in 1935 when he reported to Hitler that he had become friendly with the political adviser to King George V and, through him, had established a direct link with Buckingham Palace. Later it was to become known that de Ropp, who was an enthusiastic advocate of Hitler's cause, held several clandestine meetings in a number of royal residences. There he met with the Duke of Kent, now believed to be the so-called 'political adviser' and instigator of these meetings. The Duke of Kent was aware that de Ropp was a German agent and it has always been believed that the Duke was acting on behalf of his eldest brother, the Prince of Wales. That the British Royal Family were anxiously studying developments in Europe and were encouraged by the rise of Fascism in Germany should come as no surprise, for both Hitler and the House of Windsor shared a common obsessive fear, the perceived danger from a spread of Bolshevism. The British Royal Family were still mourning the fate of their cousins massacred at St Petersburg and they shared Hitler's concern that Russia would not be prepared to remain within her borders, but would eventually move westward. They believed that a re-armed and powerful Germany would provide a bulwark to deter expansionist moves by Russia.

There can be little doubt that the British Royal Family felt reassured by what they saw happening in Germany. It is well known that George V viewed the prospect of another war against Germany with undisguised horror. Leaving Baldwin, the recently re-elected Prime Minister, in no doubt about his feelings, he told the Foreign Secretary: 'I have been through one world war. How can I go through another?' And in a conversation with Lloyd George, the Prime Minister during the previous conflict, he was even more emphatic: 'I will not have another war. I will not!'[2]

In this George V was simply adopting a similar stand to most of his subjects. The policy of appeasement was universally popular: it would not be until 1939, when Hitler invaded Poland, that there were any signs of enthusiasm for a war that suddenly became inevitable. While George V was encouraged by the growing military strength of Nazi Germany, there is no evidence that he was in favour of an accommodation or alliance with Hitler. He favoured the retention of a powerful army and the expansion of the Royal Navy as the best deterrent to war. The fact that he shared a common fear of the perceived danger of Russian expansion with Hitler does not mean he supported him. George V was deeply troubled by the threat from the East. He refused to give asylum in Britain to his cousins, the Russian Royal Family – which probably resulted in their death when he bowed to British public opinion. He feared that an invitation for them to settle in England would have weakened the affection the British people held for the throne. George V worked extremely hard to portray the House of Windsor as a truly British institution – no easy task, when he himself was German by descent as was his wife Queen Mary, the former Victoria Mary of Teck. They were both related to the Royal Houses of Europe. In the case of the Queen her line can be traced to the 'morganatic marriage', of the stateless and impoverished Prince Francis of Teck, her grandfather. Queen Mary, shy and retiring, remains a somewhat shadowy figure who saw her role not so much as mother and wife, but as consort of the King. Finding sex and childbearing disgusting and painful she was only prepared to endure it out of a sense of duty, believing it was part of her role to provide children to continue the monarchy. This rather formal attitude influenced, and explains her hostility towards Edward VIII, with whom she always spoke German, over the Abdication. His refusal to carry out what she saw as his duty, lay at the root of the bitter conflict that developed between them and would never be resolved. We are told the Duke lived in fear of both his parents, this unquestionably lies at the root of many of the problems during his early life. Following her death in 1953 the *Evening Standard* described her as: 'this woman who never tasted a cocktail or flew in a plane, who only spoke 24 words on the radio and never used the telephone'.

But all through his reign George V was determined to serve the people of Britain; it was George V who had changed the family name to Windsor to remove any suggestion that he was pro-German at the beginning of the Great War which had such a profound effect on his thinking. Recently it has been suggested that during the period following his Coronation and the outbreak of hostilities in 1939, George VI also advocated coming to some kind of an understanding with Hitler and this has been regarded in some quarters with surprise. This reaction seems strange: the Royal Family were not alone in thinking this way – the Cabinet, most informed thinking and a great number of influential people (including most of the proprietors of the British press) believed that an accommodation with Hitler not only offered the way to avoid war but would provide a much needed increase in world trade.

To understand almost everything that happened during the Thirties one must be aware of the scar left by the First World War and the revulsion left in the aftermath of that senseless carnage that occurred less than 20 years before. The war that cost the lives of 15 million people and robbed the countries involved of an entire generation of young men was still fresh in the minds of most people. Hailed as a 'war to end all wars' it had achieved nothing apart from an appalling loss of life so great that it left England with only one village without a memorial to those local inhabitants who fell in battle and would never return. Nobody who had lived through or witnessed the barbarism played out in the mud of Flanders, the decimation of two huge armies, the sacrifice of millions of young men for no real purpose, was likely to advocate a resumption of a slaughter on that scale.

Hitler's objectives, set out in *Mein Kampf*, published in two parts in 1925 and 1926, were written while he was incarcerated in Landsberg prison following an unsuccessful *putsch* in 1924 when he and General Ludendorff conspired to overthrow the Government. The work was dictated to the faithful Rudolf Hess who was in reality the co-author, although he never attempted to claim any recognition for his efforts, content to allow all the credit to go to the leader he worshipped. This strange book reveals that while he had no desire to find himself at war with Britain, Hitler's eyes were firmly focused on her Empire.

During the late Thirties Germany and Britain suffered from the same basic economic disadvantages. Both were highly efficient manufacturing countries with a skilled and innovative workforce, but neither possessed much in the way of natural resources. Both had coal in abundance, but while Germany had a great deal of timber and Britain had several small deposits of iron ore, neither had much else.

Britain was a maritime nation; throughout history British merchant adventurers travelled the world in search of gold, silk and other precious commodities, but with the advent of the industrial revolution those who followed in the tradition extended their search to include the raw materials of modern industry. This in turn gave rise to the establishment of the Empire and by the late Thirties Britain had secured the rights to every material known to man. The only strategic weakness lay in time of war – it relied on its vast merchant fleet to bring much of its food and practically all its raw materials home. Germany lacked this facility: it had no ready access to the supplies of iron ore, rubber and oil, vital if it was to re-arm and develop, but it possessed one crucial advantage – any material it was able to secure travelled mostly overland. Apart from the problems posed by having to purchase everything on the open market, Germany's real weakness lay in her being unable to guarantee the continuity of supply required by her expanding industry. This need for raw materials was eventually to dictate the way in which Hitler fought the war. The invasion of Norway was to secure the route for Swedish iron, and in 1939, much against his will, he was obliged to enter into a treaty with Russia in order to obtain supplies of oil, grain and other metals such as nickel and tungsten that were desperately needed; eventually this need to secure raw materials would even dictate his battle tactics. In late 1941, to the dismay and disbelief of his generals, he ordered his forces pushing towards Moscow to be diverted south in an attempt to capture the oilfields of the Caucasus. Initially Hitler's luck held: instead of the predicted military disaster the move resulted in the encirclement and capture of half a million Russian troops, adding to Hitler's reputation as a tactical genius. However, in the event, this was to prove a grave error. The failure to take Moscow before the onset of winter was to prove the beginning of the end for his Russian campaign, but oil is the life blood of mechanised warfare and Hitler needed every drop he could lay his hands on.

Recognising the need to form some sort of alliance with Britain, Hitler stepped up his attempts to influence the Royal Family and in 1935 he adopted a more overt approach. As well as de Ropp he enlisted the aid of Karl Eduard, the Duke of Saxe-Coburg-Gotha, a first cousin once removed of the Prince of Wales.

Karl Eduard was a frequent visitor to London where he based himself in a flat in Kensington Palace. He and the Prince had been firm friends since boyhood and were often seen in each other's company. Karl Eduard was a great admirer of Hitler and became active in trying to persuade the Royal Family that Hitler represented the best chance of opposing the growth of Bolshevism while at the same time posing no threat to Britain. The degree of access he enjoyed can be judged when it was revealed that Saxe-Coburg-Gotha was in England to discuss world events with George V at Sandringham, but before the meeting could take place the King died.

In the years prior to the King's death Hitler and his fellow Nazis had been delighted to discover a willing ally in the Prince of Wales. Not only did they find him full of admiration for what he saw happening in Germany, but also he seemed anxious to employ his influence to advance the cause of Anglo-German unity. If the Nazis were encouraged by his desire to co-operate in the early years, they must have been ecstatic at the increasing amount of assistance he was to provide as time went on.

Chapter Two

The Old Order Changes

THE YEAR 1935 WAS A TIME of great change in both Germany and Britain. The first signs of Hitler's eventual move towards war were evident for those prepared to look. Closer to home the problems surrounding the Prince of Wales, while still a closely guarded secret, were causing those 'in the know' growing concern, and which could eventually threaten the existence of the British Royal Family. The events that were to precipitate a crisis between the Prince of Wales and the Government had been gathering pace for some time and were now poised to explode on a world already in the throes of political upheaval.

From the beginning of the year it had become increasingly obvious that the Prince would not have long to wait before he inherited the throne. His father's health had deteriorated steadily and it was becoming clear that George V's reign did not have long to run. The relationship between the two men, sadly never close, had degenerated to a point where the divisions between them had grown even more acrimonious. For some time before his father's death, those close to the Prince were aware that, in addition to incurring his father's wrath at his involvement in international politics, particularly his close connection with people working on behalf of Hitler, there were signs that his relationship with Wallis Simpson was developing into something more sinister than just a passing fancy for yet another married woman. The Prince seemed unconcerned about keeping the relationship a secret: he was not only happy to be seen with her, but let it be known that he would refuse all invitations to social events unless she was included. He even tried to introduce her at court despite the convention that divorced people were prohibited; his parents had refused to meet her formally but the ambitious Wallis managed to get herself included in the guest list for a Buckingham Palace garden party where she was presented to the Queen. Aware of his scandalous behaviour, his close friends become convinced his conduct could inevitably only lead to problems. Several had already begun to voice their concern: what had initially been dismissed as just another infatuation four years previously was seen to have developed to the point where she had become the centre of his life. He not only worshipped her, but her influence could be seen in everything he did. Despite the fact that she was a married woman, he spent a great deal of time with her; initially her husband was included in the Royal Party, but as time went on Ernest Simpson's presence became less and less obvious. The British public had no knowledge of what was going on – they would have to wait until the following year to learn about the liaison that was to provoke the constitutional crisis. It would be the late summer of 1936 before the storm would finally break and the news would spread swiftly around the world where it would attract enormous interest, particularly in America where events were being closely followed and openly discussed. The reason was simple: Wallis was an American citizen and its press, unlike that in Britain, were under no injunction not to carry the story of the Royal romance. There 'Wally's' involvement with the King was on everyone's lips, creating such interest that it seemed hardly a day went by without some titbit of news from London making the front pages. In answer to the question being asked, why the affair was attracting such interest, dominating all else, even being discussed on the floor of the US Congress, the *Boston Herald* provided an answer proclaiming in an editorial: 'Because this is the greatest story since the Crucifixion.'

Even today, despite the millions of words that have been written and continue to be written, about the momentous events that were to become known as 'The World's Greatest Love Story', many aspects of the strange business remain unexplained. A vast array of biographies, some authorised, many not, give widely varying accounts of the affair and the couple's eventual marriage; they all leave a picture that is far from complete.

Several biographers have tried to write sympathetically about the Duke and Duchess; they have attempted to portray them as a couple who were thrown together, fell hopelessly in love and, from that point onwards, were driven by events they were incapable of controlling. This touching, romantic view certainly gained great currency at the time, but subsequently as more and more information comes to light this rather simplistic and poignant explanation cannot be supported. The romantic notion is probably about as wide of the mark as many of the less charitable views taken by other commentators who suggest that Wallis was a greedy, manipulative woman, for which no infamy was too great, a woman prepared to resort to any sort of villainy, and probably did, to get what she wanted. The fact that she was a strong, determined woman who successfully dominated the Prince, a man who admired strength in others, cannot be questioned, but those who believe she deliberately set out to become Queen and sit on the throne of England, an ambitious woman who didn't care what chaos and trouble she left in her wake to achieve her aims, have failed to understand her and have ignored the evidence. While there is some degree of truth in the suggestion that on several occasions she allowed herself to believe she might be allowed to marry the King, there is a great deal more evidence to suggest she knew it was impossible. She never expected to be allowed to become Queen and remained convinced that it would never be permitted. Despite this she came remarkably close.

The truth as far as Wallis is concerned is far more simple. Looking back at the part she played in the events that led to the Abdication it becomes clear that she was vain, self-centred and caught up in something she didn't understand, a shallow woman who became seduced by all the attention and flattery that her presence and notoriety attracted. There is clear evidence that during the period leading up to and following the Abdication she failed to understand what was going on in the King's mind. She, like so many other people at the time, incorrectly believed that the crisis was simply a trial of strength between the King and the Cabinet over whom the King should marry. However, it is the intention of this book to show that her involvement was only the catalyst that brought matters to a head between the King and the Cabinet. Unaware of the real reasons that lay behind the Abdication, she foolishly persuaded herself that initially she could use her influence to make the King assert himself and stand up to those in political power, then finally when she saw the King's cause was lost, she tried to break free from the position in which she found herself. By then it was too late.

Like so many other foreigners Wallis failed to understand the way that the British Establishment operates. This led her to believe that she was central to the argument, which is understandable. In the days leading up to the crisis she permitted all the adulation to go to her head, unaware of the fickle nature of those who called themselves friends; in truth they were simply exploiting her position with Edward VIII to further their own social position. Their affections were quickly to change. As her friendship with the Duke of Windsor grew, London society beat a path to her door, but the moment the affair turned sour most of her shallow and opportunist friends would cross the street rather than have to meet her. Shunned and left almost deserted, she was forced to fight alone. Anyone who examines her life is left in little doubt that she became trapped in something she had neither sought nor understood. It becomes clear that there would have been nobody as relieved as Wallis to have discovered some way to extradite herself from the role in which she found herself. There had already been several instances in her life when, finding herself in trouble, she had decided that discretion called for her to quickly distance herself from her problems; but on this occasion she could not go – she was caught in the spotlight of the world's stage, there was nowhere to run. The Prince, helplessly besotted by her, continued to make it clear that he would never let her go and was determined to marry her and he never appeared overly concerned about the consequences. Giving up Wallis was something he refused to consider. This was clearly demonstrated when on 13 November the new King returned from an inspection of the Fleet and found a letter from his Private Secretary, Major Alexander Hardinge.[1] The letter warned him that the press were about to break their silence about his friendship with Mrs Simpson. Hardinge informed the King that the Government were discussing what action they should take in the light of the serious situation that was likely to develop. His advice to the King was to send Mrs Simpson abroad. The King's anger and shock at the letter is recorded in his memoirs. He showed Wallis the letter on the 15th. Later she was to record that at that point she was more than ready to go. She wrote in her memoirs:

> Now it was my turn to beg him to let me go. Summoning all my powers of persuasion, I tried to convince him of the hopelessness of our position. For him to go on hoping, to go on fighting the inevitable, could only mean tragedy for him and catastrophe for me. He would not listen. Taking my hand, he said, with the calm of a man whose mind was made up: 'I am going to send for Mr Baldwin to see me at the palace tomorrow. I am going to tell him that if the country won't approve our marrying, I am ready to go.'[2]

If further evidence is required that she was prepared to leave the King, disappear from the public gaze and turn her back on all the attention her presence had caused, it is only necessary to read the letter she sent from her temporary home in the South of France four days before the King announced the Abdication. It began:

Sunday   Lou Viel, Cannes.
Darling,
I am sending this by air as I think it important you have it before. I
am so anxious for you not to abdicate and I think the fact that you
do is going to put me in the wrong light to the entire world because
they will say that I could have prevented it. Chips [*Channon*] has
telephoned that the Cabinet have decided to force an answer by 5
today so I am sending this by air. If you will just give Baldwin my
plan. If he turns it down then you have yours and the world could
know a second compromise was turned down. My plan in detail is
that you would say I [*you*] shall stand back of everything I have said
(this saves you and me in the eyes of the world because naturally if
you did not make this clear you would be a cad in the eyes of the
world and I would be a woman well you know that was turned
down – so that sentence printed in every newspaper saves that) to go
on with the main theme . . .[3]

Several writers have suggested that her conduct during this difficult
period was little more than a bluff, and that she had no intention of
abandoning the King, confident that he would never have let her
leave. However, these were private letters, they were never
intended to have been made public when they were written, it
would be many years after when events had overcome the pair
before these letters were released. What possible purpose could
they serve if they were not genuine? There is no reason to think
that they cannot be relied upon, they clearly demonstrate how her
mind was working during the most crucial time, and what must
have been a difficult and stressful period. She was clearly troubled
and realised that she was going to be cast in the role of being
responsible for the King's problems; she wanted no part of that.

Wallis Simpson, born Bessie Wallis Warfield, was certainly a
remarkable woman whose life remains, years after her death, a
strange enigma. It has often been claimed that at different times
during her tempestuous life she worked for American, Italian,
German, Russian and British intelligence, but as yet nobody has
produced any reliable evidence that she spied on behalf of anyone.
There is the incident in 1923 when she sailed to join her first
husband, Win Spencer, in Shanghai when it was known that she
was employed by American naval intelligence, but there is a simple
explanation for this. The American Navy Department has revealed
that it was the custom at the time for trusted navy wives to be used
as couriers to Europe and the Far East because telegraph messages
were being read and the US naval codes had all been broken.

Wallis's involvement was insignificant: she was nothing more than a message carrier.

As the affair with Wallis developed the Duke must have realised that he was heading for trouble. He could not have failed to have anticipated that the moment he declared his intention to marry Wallis he would inevitably be thrown into confrontation with the Government, the Church, the Establishment and his own family. From the very beginning he was prepared to run enormous risks to protect her; on two occasions he took the almost unprecedented step of issuing a writ for libel to protect her honour. Nobody knew better than he that announcing his intention to marry her was sheer madness.

When others began to realise that his relationship with Wallis was more than just another affair with a married woman of his acquaintance (there had been several before her), the Cabinet of the recently elected Government under Prime Minister Baldwin moved to find out exactly who she was and discover details of her background. Unfortunately the Cabinet papers which record the various meetings when the events leading to the Abdication were discussed are not available: it was ruled at the time that they should be classified as 'highly secret' and thus protected by the 'Hundred Year Rule'. No government since 1937 has seen fit to reverse this seemingly curious decision. Why? There is nobody left to protect, everyone who formed part of that Cabinet is long dead, as are the Duke, the Duchess and all the advisers who played a part. Despite the multitude of books about the Abdication the official story is still hidden under a cloak of secrecy. Why the Government does not allow the official version to be told seems inexplicable. On the face of it, all this secrecy defies reason. What national interest is being protected? All that it has achieved is to deny the British people the chance to learn what really happened, discover what momentous decisions were taken on their behalf by their elected representatives and to prevent serious historians from accurately recording the political history of the times.

While it can only be speculation as to what is being concealed, several matters that must have formed part of those discussions have become known and are highly relevant. They come from a variety of other sources. We know, for example, that Wallis Simpson was investigated and placed under constant surveillance by British security.[4] At the same time Baldwin tried desperately to rake up anything that would discredit her, even to the extent of attempting to discover irregularities in her 1927 divorce from Win Spencer, her first husband. The American FBI files on Wallis were made available to British intelligence and revealed her somewhat colourful past. Baldwin arranged for this dossier on Wallis to be passed to King George V and Queen Mary who must have been horrified and it probably accounts for their reluctance to meet her.

Several sources have revealed that Wallis worked in a brothel during her time in China in 1927. One of the most comprehensive accounts of this period in her life is to be found in Charles Higham's *Wallis, The Secret Lives of the Duchess of Windsor*. Higham tells us he has studied the file on Wallis which is preserved at the State Department in Washington. It contains a remarkable story. Even today such conduct, if it were to become public, would be regarded as outrageous and would provide something of a field day for today's unfettered tabloid press in much the same way as have more recent Royal revelations. The effect it must have had on the rather staid, pompous Baldwin and the elderly straight-laced King is not difficult to imagine. Higham tells us that the dossier prepared for Baldwin by MI6 reports that Win Spencer was responsible for introducing Wallis to the 'singing houses' of Hong Kong, which were luxurious brothels staffed by beautiful Oriental girls trained in the art of love to entertain their clients with erotic songs and dancing. It is believed that Wallis learnt her 'perverse practices' in these houses of prostitution. Several sources have suggested that Wallis was taught and became proficient in the art of 'Fang Chung', an ancient skill known over the centuries to help relax the male and prolong the act of intercourse. The technique, which involves the use of hot oils and massage, is especially helpful in the case of premature ejaculation. Several titled ladies with whom the Prince had previously had affairs have provided us with details of his problems in this direction. One is reputed to have said, 'he got so excited that it was all over before he could do anything'.

Charles Higham goes on to reveal that Wallis had several affairs during her time in China when, it seems, she became a 'kept woman' living with several rich and powerful men. In his book *King of Fools* John Parker offers further evidence: he reveals that following her time in Hong Kong she became a paid hostess at a house in the exclusive brothel area of Shanghai where foreign diplomats were entertained. Her arrival in Shanghai came about after she was kicked out by her husband Win following her involvement with a young naval ensign. Her time in China was closely observed by American intelligence who suspected she was carrying out spying missions for the Russians, and it was here that Roger (later Sir Roger) Hollis, who was to become head of MI5, was sent to collect information on Wallis. Charles Higham also quotes Mrs Leslie Field, who worked in consultation with the present Queen on a book about the Royal jewels, as his source. Mrs Field claimed she knew several people who have studied the 'China dossier' and they told her that it contains much to Wallis's discredit and reveals that apart from her sexual exploits, she was heavily involved in drug peddling.

It was during Wallis's time in China that she renewed her friendship with Katherine Bigelow, a young widow she had met in California six years previously and who had married Herman Rogers, the heir to an American railroad fortune. It would be an important meeting: Herman Rogers would play an important part in the future of Wallis and the Duke following the Abdication. Great mystery surrounds Wallis's life about this time and there are reports that she was admitted to hospital with a mystery illness that has been suggested was of a gynaecological nature, something Wallis always denied. Whatever it was, she returned to America aboard the *President McKinley* and was admitted to hospital in Seattle before she eventually arrived back in Washington in 1925. As an aside Higham reveals that Win Spencer was later to develop strong links with the Fascist administration in Italy, and was awarded the Cavaliere of the Order of the Crown of Italy, a high decoration, for his services in helping Mussolini organise and expand the Italian Air Force.

What now seems certain is that had much of this information become public, as would inevitably be the case today, King Edward VIII would have been publicly humiliated, made a laughing stock and his credibility destroyed. It is not difficult when looking back almost 60 years to speculate on the public's reaction. Apart from the obvious titillation all this would have caused, these revelations about Wallis would have destroyed much of the genuine affection and support there was for the King.

Inevitably there were those who were aware of the curious relationship between the Prince and Wallis, but they remained loyally silent. Few details of their relationship became known at the time, or even during the remainder of their somewhat sad and lonely life. However, since their death several people have provided us with an insight into their curious behaviour and revealed what can only be seen as strange and something of a tragedy.

Writing in the *Sunday Express* in January 1994, in an article entitled 'Dark Side of the Great Love Story', Scarth Flett quoted the Hon Charles Wilson, son of Lady Mary Thynne, daughter of the fifth Marquess of Bath, who was married to the Rt Hon Sir

Ulick Alexander, a close adviser to the Duke. Wilson reveals his mother told him: 'Edward gained pleasure from being beaten by Wallis who delivered the strokes with her own small whip . . . He needed the stimulus, I think in order to perform in the normal manner – something with which he had great difficulty in earlier relationships.' Charles Wilson goes on to say that on another occasion he was told by his stepfather: 'It was at a country house party where the then Prince of Wales and Mrs Simpson were guests that the Prince's private detective came to Ulick one morning with some worrying discoveries. He produced a pair of the Prince's underpants striped with caked blood and a small whip that he found in Mrs Simpson's underwear drawer.' The article goes on to tell us that Charles Wilson believed: 'There is no doubt that Edward loved Wallis, but he was frightened of her – this she was quick to exploit.'

What seems incredible was that in spite of this highly damaging information circulating among servants and the like, the Duke of Windsor embarked on what was an extremely dangerous venture. In April 1937, he sued Geoffrey Dennis who had suggested in his book *Coronation Commentary* that Wallis had been the Prince's mistress. Later he sued Sir John Wheeler-Bennett (his biographer) for referring to Wallis as his lover while she was still married to Ernest Simpson. It has been suggested the Duke was encouraged by Churchill who is reputed to have said: 'These people require a lesson and the only thing they appreciate is being made to pay.' The Duke's advisers were appalled at the prospect of the Duke appearing in the witness box to be cross-examined on his private life, prompting Hardinge to write to Walter Monckton, the Duke's lifelong adviser, 'this demonstrates the loopiness of our friend in Austria, does he realise the amount of muck they can rake up about him?'. Both actions were settled with a minimum of publicity.

The relationship between the Duke and Wallis was a curious one, it must have been worrying for the Cabinet and potentially damaging to the future King if details of his private life were to become public. Such knowledge would only increase the doubts of his father and the Cabinet about his fitness to inherit the throne, but there were other, more pressing, reasons for disquiet. Already his many indiscretions and pronouncements on behalf of his Nazi friends had given deep offence to the Government. The fact that he made no secret of his intention to carry on in this way after he was crowned made it difficult, if not impossible, for him to remain on good terms with those who held the political power in a country slowly becoming deeply suspicious of Hitler's motives. The King was known to have been a fervent advocate of an alliance with Germany, but what will never be known is whether, had he remained on the throne, he would have been instrumental in persuading the Cabinet not to declare war on Germany in 1939.

This raises an interesting point which previous commentators seem to have ignored but which could have been highly significant. Under the British Constitution only the monarch can declare war; it is important to remember that all members of the armed forces formally swear allegiance to the Sovereign who is the titular head of the nation's military forces. Without his, or her, direct order they cannot be deployed. In almost all other countries the prime loyalty is to the political system, only Britain retains this historical concept. In time of war the members of the armed forces are urged to fight for King (or Queen) and Country, the officers who hold a commission actually swear an oath of allegiance to the Sovereign. This patriotic loyalty cannot be ignored; the fact that they serve the Crown is taken very seriously by many of all ranks in the armed forces, especially in time of war. Additionally the forces of law and order, the police and the judges, swear a similar oath of allegiance to the Crown and are careful to avoid being seen as the instrument of Parliament. Whether this was a factor that was considered is not known, but had the Abdication not resolved the issue, there seems little doubt that the Government's decision to declare war on Germany in September 1939 would have given rise to conflict between the King and State. Had the Government of the day been determined to honour its treaty obligations towards France and Poland and had the King refused to declare war, then the constitutional problems of 1936 would have paled into insignificance in comparison. There remains little doubt about the outcome: either the monarchy would have fallen and the country would have become a Republic or Britain would have faced civil war. Prior to 1939 there was widespread support for the policy of appeasement of Hitler: there were few who wanted to fight, which is reinforced by the fact that it was thought necessary to introduce conscription for the first time in British history.

During 1935 many people were using their personal friendship with the Duke to promote the Nazi cause and in a particularly shrewd move Hitler had given orders to recruit Wallis Simpson to assist in bringing pressure to bear. MI5 had become aware that Wallis was a friend of Joachim von Ribbentrop who, posing as a champagne salesman, had previously integrated himself in fashionable society before being appointed to head the German Foreign

Office. In the late Thirties he had become a frequent visitor to London.

Reports also reached Baldwin that Wallis was in contact with monarchist circles in Germany. It was believed that Otto von Bismarck and his wife, Princess Anne-Marie, played an important part in maintaining this connection. The Bismarcks were attached to the German Embassy in London where they became very friendly with the Prince and Wallis and were often seen at the lavish parties at Carlton House hosted by the German Ambassador, Leopold von Hoesch, who was under instruction from Berlin to make sure that Wallis was included in all invitations. There is little doubt that Wallis was the main route by which the Nazis obtained vital information about the Government's discussions regarding Germany, but this does not make her a spy. Her source of information was Edward and she was simply passing on information that he was providing. Eventually this was recognised, and the information passed to the King in the 'Red Boxes' was carefully screened when it was realised where some of the information was heading. Rather than establishing Wallis as a spy, this simply provides additional evidence of Edward's treason. To have passed sensitive and secret information to an American citizen amounts to much the same as passing it to anyone else, particularly as he was perfectly aware that it was being transmitted to a foreign power. As a result of all this, it is not surprising that the Prince's sympathies towards the Third Reich, already firmly in place by the beginning of 1935, became more open, causing him to become indiscreet. The most notable 'gaffe' came in a speech he made to the Royal British Legion in June when he said: 'I feel that there could be no more suitable body or organisation of men to stretch forth the hand of friendship to the Germans than we ex-servicemen who fought them and have now forgotten all about it and the Great War.'

The response was immediate. The Prince was sent for by the King and severely reprimanded, probably at the instigation of No 10 Downing Street. His father left him in no doubt that not only were his remarks contrary to Government policy, but were seen as an unwarranted attempt to involve himself in politics without the permission of the Prime Minister.[5]

Predictably, Goebbels seized on the Prince's remarks to use as welcome propaganda. All the German newspapers carried accounts of the speech and their headlines proclaimed that the Prince of Wales had put his seal of approval on the friendship that existed between the two countries. While it is unlikely that the timing of this speech was deliberate, it was more likely to have been one of a series of unguarded remarks that he was prone to make. However, it caused the maximum embarrassment to the British Government and delighted a German delegation who were in London at the time trying to negotiate a naval treaty that would permit an increase in the size of the German navy.

The British Government's problems were further compounded when, in 1935, the Italians were about to invade Abyssinia. The Foreign Office was applying maximum pressure to try to diffuse a dangerous situation by sending a destroyer to the Mediterranean when the Prince suddenly announced that he was taking Mrs Simpson on holiday to the Mediterranean.

In making this trip the Prince revealed his true hand; it showed that when he became King he would never be content to carry out his Royal duties in the way that Parliament would expect or demand, making no secret of his intention to involve himself in world politics. The old King, learning of his heir's intention to cruise off the coast of Italy, sent for him and, in an acrimonious meeting, pointed out the damage such a cruise would have on world opinion. With his father's angry condemnation ringing in his ears, the Prince left, going first to Cannes where the couple enjoyed an endless round of parties, spending their days swimming and generally enjoying a life in the pursuit of pleasure. Reports of his behaviour were greeted at the Palace with disquiet: his conduct would not be forgotten and would come back to haunt him later. However, the gay, carefree life was soon to take on a more sinister aspect. After cruising off Corsica, a clear snub to his father, the Prince and Wallis travelled to Budapest where he discussed the worsening international situation with leading Government figures. It was while the Prince was in Hungary that Hitler made his infamous anti-semitic speech at a rally in Nuremberg, publicly declaring his hatred of the Jews that was to translate into official Nazi policy. Moving on to Vienna, and later Munich, the Prince continued to have meetings with leading politicians, finally going to Paris where he lunched with Armand Gregoire, a lawyer who had previously acted for Wallis and Ernest Simpson and was a Nazi agent who was responsible for channelling funds to Sir Oswald Mosley, the British Fascist leader, on behalf of Hitler and Mussolini.

All this was bad enough but then the Prince went on to meet Pierre Laval, the French Premier, a sworn enemy of Britain. It seems the Prince was not only prepared to openly discuss political matters, but he declared his support for Laval's pact with

Mussolini, thereby providing the Italians with the encouragement they needed to invade Abyssinia.

It is difficult to imagine a more embarrassing series of incidents for the British Cabinet. To sit back and watch helplessly as the heir to the throne, accompanied by another man's wife whom everyone suspected of being his mistress, travelled around a Europe in the grip of political tensions openly meeting politicians and enemies of Britain during one of the most difficult periods in history.

Sadly, there was worse, much worse, to come. Baldwin and the Cabinet had already begun to realise that even if they were successful in persuading the Prince to abandon this dangerous woman (whom they were already beginning to suspect of being in the pay of the Nazis and who they correctly believed was passing information to them), the problem of his interference in foreign affairs and his friendship with Nazi Germany would remain. They were not alone, their disquiet was shared by his father. The King's health was beginning to fail. George V would soon die in despair; everything he had worked for, his life devoted to making the monarchy popular and generally more acceptable to the British people whom he totally supported and whose respect he had gained, now seemed in danger of collapse. This caused him to record in his diary shortly before his death: 'When I am gone, he will ruin himself within a year.'[6]

George V was proved correct, except that it did not take the new King that long to fulfil his father's prophecy.

Chapter Three

The Affairs that Led to the Abdication

IT HAS ALWAYS BEEN popularly believed that the principal reason behind the crisis that developed between Edward VIII, the Cabinet and powerful members of the Establishment opposed to him centred on his stubborn determination to marry Wallis and that it was this that ultimately cost him his throne. While it cannot be denied that in declaring his intention to marry a woman who still had two husbands alive and was still married to one of them would inevitably bring him into conflict with those elected to run the country, the issue of the marriage alone is almost irrelevant.

Strictly speaking, Edward did not require permission from anyone to marry whom he wished, something often overlooked when considering the Abdication of 1936. It is not generally appreciated that he was not required to seek the approval of Parliament, the Bishops or anyone else for his choice of partner. In this respect he was no different from any other of his subjects with one proviso: as head of the Established Anglican Church he was not permitted to marry a Roman Catholic. The Royal Marriage Act of 1772 requires that the Sovereign approves the intended spouse of all members of the Royal Family, but it does not apply to the Sovereign. Nobody is required to approve the Sovereign's choice of partner.

Under the unwritten British constitution it has always been understood that the King can do anything provided that he does not allow himself to be drawn into public controversy. It has always been seen that by consulting Baldwin and informing him of his intentions Edward allowed Parliament to become involved, thereby taking sides on the issue. The King could be said to have created controversy that would eventually make his position so difficult that it became untenable. His greatest ally, Churchill, who issued a statement on the evening of 5 December, five days before the Abdication, seems to have fallen into the same trap:

There is no question of any conflict between the Sovereign and

Parliament. Parliament has not been consulted in any way or allowed to express any opinion . . . This is not a case where differences have arisen between the Sovereign and his ministers in any particular measure. These could certainly be resolved by the normal processes of Parliament . . . No Ministry has the power to advise Abdication of the Sovereign. Only the most serious parliamentary processes could even raise the issue in decisive form. The Cabinet has no right to prejudice such a question without previously having ascertained at the very least the will of Parliament . . . If an Abdication were to be hastily exhorted, the outrage so committed would cast its shadow forward across many chapters of the history of the British Empire.[1]

Churchill was clearly playing for time, and he either failed to understand the constitutional position or believed that by turning the matter over to Parliament it would enable them to resolve the issue. This being so no controversy could be said to remain. Churchill was wrong. Unwittingly he had handed the King's enemies victory on a plate; the die was cast, the country began to take sides. Although the next few days would see a few false dawns and a great deal of speculation, in reality the deed was done; no compromise was possible.

What is now clear and was understood by several of the King's advisers at the time was that had Edward not announced his intention to marry Mrs Simpson when he did, the Abdication crisis of 1936 would never have occurred. The King could simply have gone to his Coronation as a single man, ascended the throne with the adulation of the British and Colonial peoples ringing in his ears and been proclaimed King Emperor. There is no doubt that the Prince of Wales was extremely popular – this succession to the throne would have been universally welcomed. Had Edward followed this course that many of his friends and advisers were urging upon him, he would have been crowned King. Then, following a suitable period of calm, he could have announced his intention to marry Wallis and there was little anyone could have done about it. So why did he tell Baldwin and raise the issue? Why do it at a time when Wallis was not in a position to marry Edward or indeed anyone? She was still married to Ernest Simpson and it would be at least six months before she could be free of him and able to marry. Had Edward then announced his intention to make her his wife there was nothing Parliament or anybody else could have done to stop him. It is inevitable, even after a year or so, that had Edward announced his intention to marry a divorced woman it would have caused a public outcry, but when all the fuss had subsided the fact remains: nobody could do anything about it, and he would most certainly have got away with it. The fact that he chose to disclose his marriage plans when he did allowed them to develop into a constitutional problem; it was simply a matter of timing.

Parliament is required to pass a 'Coronation Act' and, as such, has some degree of control over an incoming monarch, but once the monarch has been crowned there is little that Parliament can do to influence the Sovereign's private life. His (or her) marriage does not require the approval of the House of Commons. 'The King of England rules by the Grace of God', and as such remains untouchable by the Government for his personal decisions. Of course, it would be naïve to suggest that his decision to marry a divorced woman would not have resulted in a huge and damaging controversy; the King would have been required to abandon his position as head of the Anglican Church – it is almost certain that the Church would have refused to have anything to do with the marriage, despite the fact that the Anglican Church owed its existence to providing marriage services to a former Sovereign whose requirements were equally less than conventional. But some way would have been found; if all else failed a civil ceremony would have had to suffice. It is interesting that had Edward opted for this course of action the discussions and debate about the so-called 'morganatic marriage' would never have occurred. Had the King married Wallis after his coronation she would have automatically become Queen. The Home Secretary of the day, Sir John Simon, speaking in the Commons against the idea of a morganatic marriage, confirmed this: 'The lady whom [*the King*] marries . . . necessarily becomes Queen. She herself, therefore enjoys all the status, rights and privileges which . . . attach to that position . . . and her children would be in direct line of succession to the Throne.'

The fact that there was a solution that was so clear-cut, that an obvious way out existed, begs the question, why he did not adopt it. This requires some explanation. There is no question that the King was unaware of this way of obtaining what everybody believed he wanted. There is evidence that it had been suggested to him by several of his close friends and advisers. They believed he could have simply toughed it out. As Churchill said at the dinner party at Fort Belvedere the night before the Abdication, while still trying to persuade the King to stay and fight, to play for time: 'We must have time for the big battalions to mass. We may win, we may not. Retire to Windsor Castle! Summon the Beefeaters! Raise the drawbridge! Close the gates! And dare Baldwin to drag you out!'[2]

In the light of all the advice he was receiving it seems clear that the King was perfectly well aware that he could have been crowned had he wished. If we return to Wallis's letter in the previous chapter urging the King not to abdicate, it is clear that she too had been advised of this solution and was trying to persuade him to consider it as an answer to the problem.

Why, then, did Edward choose to opt for what turned out to be an ineffectual fight against Baldwin? It would be to Edward VIII's eternal credit if he had refused to involve himself in this kind of subterfuge out of a sense of honour. He was reputed to have said: '[I] would not go to my Coronation with a lie on my lips.'[3] This remark has always been regarded as a reference to his refusal to be crowned knowing that he planned to marry Wallis when she became free. However, this may not have been what was troubling him. The remark might equally have been a reference to the fact that he was unhappy about swearing an oath to uphold a system that he had no intention of supporting and whose demise he had already begun to work towards.

However, all this became academic the moment he declared his intention to marry Wallis. He must have known that nothing was more likely to throw him into conflict with the politicians. In seeking their advice he was honour bound to take it, which handed Baldwin the initiative and gave him the opportunity he had been looking for. He was able to advise that he could not in all conscience place the Coronation Bill before Parliament knowing what was in the King's mind, warning that a defeat for the Bill would mean that the Government would fall and the King would have no option but to dissolve Parliament. He went on to further warn that it was unlikely that anyone else would form a new Government. This left the King with little alternative but to try and come to terms with Baldwin.

In announcing his intentions the King had deliberately presented the Cabinet with a constitutional problem of some magnitude that was bound to bring the monarchy into direct conflict with Parliament and had he not been prevailed upon to abdicate, it would have had far-reaching consequences in several other directions. The King was the head of the Established Church and while many of the bishops may have been privately sympathetic, publicly they could only maintain the official line of the Church that prohibited the marriage of divorcees. Curiously, it was the Bishop of Bradford, the Rev Dr Blunt (an academic who was totally unaware of the impending crisis), who became responsible for bringing the whole thing into the public domain. The bishop had prepared a sermon for an ecclesiastical conference using as his subject that the Church should not allow its stand on the marriage of divorcees to be eroded. Somehow the contents found their way in to several newspapers which had, up until that point, agreed not to mention the existence of the King's affair with Wallis. However, the press saw his remarks as an oblique reference to the Royal adultery and took it up without committing themselves to what course of action the King should take. The cat was out of the bag. Despite their public stance, and while giving all the appearances of trying to find a solution, the Cabinet must have been overjoyed at the King's declaration that he intended to marry Wallis. It enabled them to deal with a problem that had been growing for some time, namely the King's refusal to behave in the way they believed he should. The problem of the marriage, particularly now that it had become public, came as a welcome opportunity to resolve their other worries. The issue of the marriage was simple and clear-cut: the Cabinet had right on their side – they could adopt a sympathetic, tolerant attitude to a man who appeared to be in trouble while at the same time appearing to defend the nation's morals. They saw this as an opportunity to bring him into line by opposing his wishes. There could only be one outcome: either he should give up the woman with whom he had become besotted and behave himself or he would have to go.

The King's intention to marry Wallis has often been seen as the only problem, but there seems no reason to suppose that had the Cabinet not been so determined to get rid of him for other reasons, some way of accommodating him might well have been found. It is well known that Edward's advisers (Churchill is believed to have been the first to suggest it) raised the question of the 'morganatic marriage', which even today is regarded by many as a perfectly legal and legitimate solution to the King's marriage problem. There had been many instances where its use had been successfully adopted by many of the Royal Houses of Europe.

Sexual scandals have never been far away from the British Royal Family, never a stranger to problems caused by friendships with married women. While George V had led a blameless life untouched by scandal, there were many instances where his forbears had not behaved so impeccably. The most notable example was a previous Prince of Wales who was eventually to reign as George IV. He proposed marriage to a Mrs Mary Fitzherbert despite knowing that, had she accepted, the marriage would have been illegal under the Royal Marriage Act because his father opposed it. The lady refused and went abroad for a year to allow things to settle down, but the King pursued her, begged, wept and finally threatened suicide until she agreed to marry him in secret in 1785. Some time later, under pressure from his parents, he was forced to marry Princess Caroline of Brunswick. So when George IV went to his coronation and became the head of the Church of England he swore his oath in the full knowledge that he was a bigamist. There are several other notable examples. William IV, formerly the Duke of Clarence, lived with his mistress. There was a more recent example, Edward VII, the grandfather of Edward VIII, had a succession of mistresses, notably Lily Langtry, the music hall artist. She was followed by Mrs Keppel, who was at the King's bedside when he died. She and the Queen shared the same carriage at the King's funeral. There were several options open to Edward VIII, with no shortage of precedents. Throughout history the British Royal Family has been forced to come to terms with scandal about almost every Prince of Wales, including the present one: they all seem to have developed a penchant for the wives of other men.

What will never been known (public opinion of the time is difficult to judge even with the advantages of hindsight) is whether Edward would have succeeded in marrying Wallis whilst still holding on to his throne. Today, when attitudes to divorce have dramatically changed, it remains questionable whether the country would accept the sovereign marrying a divorced woman. Current opinion polls suggest not. But back in the late Thirties, although the country was a great deal more religious, the amount of opposition would not necessarily have been greater. Had the Government agreed, it might still have been difficult. However, Edward was popular, whereas the current Prince of Wales does not enjoy the same level of support, but more significantly the press in the Thirties was owned and controlled by powerful members of the Establishment who, had they been persuaded to throw their weight behind the idea, could have steered public opinion and made it possible. Many people regarded the alternatives to Edward with dismay; they believed that the Duke of York was far from being a suitable replacement. So the Government could have made a case, the crisis might possibly have been contained and what by any standards would always have remained a difficult situation might have been made to work. Those who showed sympathy for Edward were trying to persuade him to take more time, to be crowned alone and allow Mrs Simpson to remain in the background, hoping that time would solve the problem. They also hoped that pressure on both the King and Wallis would gradually erode the relationship and the problem would solve itself.

However, that was the last thing that the Cabinet wanted. Time was something they didn't have, they were becoming increasingly aware that there were signs of a growing movement in support of the beleaguered King and it was beginning to gain momentum. A man turned away by the police when he attempted to cycle into Downing Street was wearing a placard which read: 'WE WANT KING EDWARD THE VIII NOT BALDWIN'. On his back he carried the message: 'THE KING MUST NOT ABDICATE'. This view was shared by many and once started could have grown quickly, spread and gained strength.

The inability to examine the Cabinet papers can only lead to speculation but one is left in no doubt that the facts leading to the Abdication and the reasons for the Cabinet's opposition to the King were not necessarily those that were presented at the time. What other explanation can there be for deciding to keep the contents secret?

It seems probable that when, or if, these minutes are eventually released in their entirety they will show that the Cabinet's greatest fear was that either the King would mount a campaign of opposition to the Government or become the rallying point around which others might seek to mount such a movement. The suggestion that Edward was in favour of forming a new Government with Churchill as leader was not only rumoured, but gained currency. It seems certain that the Cabinet was taken by surprise by the amount of anti-government feeling that suddenly appeared, and became more than a little concerned that the King might marshal a significant body of support among a wide section of the community who would then persuade him not to abdicate. This would have meant defeat for the Government and would leave him with a great deal more power than hitherto and free to behave in any way he chose. There was a great deal of concern in Whitehall at the prospect of the formation of a King's or People's party. The balance of support for the existing parties was already finely divided; a split in the popular vote could have seen the electorate either turn towards Fascism or flock to a new political party. Already Sir Oswald Mosley's British Fascists (BUF) were growing in strength and were known to support Edward. Mosley himself was calling on the King not to abdicate. While the BUF had failed to get any of their candidates elected in the last election, their support was growing and they could not be ignored as a threat to the existing parties. While all this was possible, it is by no means certain, but it was something the Cabinet were not anxious to put to the test. A solution was becoming urgent. The majority of ordinary people still knew little, if anything, about what was going on. The press was still keeping to its self-imposed vow of silence, but it could not last. The American newspapers were reporting everything in great detail; they were less inhibited about running the story and hardly a day passed without some incident involving the King and 'Wally' hitting the headlines. Already some of these newspapers were beginning to find their way across the Atlantic. As the crisis reached its climax the British press allowed the news to leak out. The years of silence only added to the impact.

The idea of a People's party led by the monarch was not new: it surfaced during the reign of Edward VII, when he too found himself at odds with the Government of the day over his desire to involve himself more closely in political affairs. The threat of a new political party and the measures taken to combat it might go some way to explaining why the Cabinet was so anxious not to allow the contents of their discussions to be revealed, and might ultimately be seen as the overriding reason why the crisis was allowed to develop. To prevent the formation of a new political party is not the business of elected government. At best it is undemocratic, a flagrant misuse of executive power. To be seen to have taken steps to prevent a legitimate political party being formed would have been a blatant infringement of the powers conferred on the Cabinet by Parliament.

As we have seen, Baldwin and his Cabinet had several reasons to be concerned at the prospect of Edward VIII remaining on the throne. His determination to marry Wallis provided them with a heaven-sent opportunity to rid themselves of this troublesome monarch.

Even before his father's death there were serious misgivings about his conduct. His defiant stand over his marriage showed he was not afraid to take on the Establishment. The realisation that he could marshal large bodies of support meant that, had he remained, several other constitutional problems could have come to a head. The continual interference in political matters and his avowed intention to carry on taking an active part in international affairs were regarded as a 'ticking time-bomb'. This more than anything else ensured that when the King asked for the proposal for a 'morganatic marriage' to be considered, it gained short shrift with the Cabinet despite being seen by many as a perfectly legitimate solution. But Baldwin was not looking for a way out, he was determined to get rid of the King and saw his pathetic obsession with Wallis as the chink in the armour of the headstrong Sovereign.

Baldwin's role has been re-examined over the years. At the time it was believed he was genuinely sorry for the King's plight – the truth is that he was playing a cynical and clever role, the most difficult of his life. But play it he did. So successful was he that even the departing King believed the Prime Minister had acted honourably and in his best interests. Only a few hours before he went abroad, the Duke of Windsor, as he had become, sent Baldwin a telegram, dated 12 December 1936, thanking him for his assistance. It read:

> Mr Baldwin, 10 Downing Street.
> Sincere thanks for kind letter, so much appreciated yours and Mrs Baldwin's great understanding at this difficult time . . . Edward.[4]

It would be close on a year before the Duke and Wallis came to realise that Baldwin had not only plotted against them, but had successfully outmanoeuvred them.

Despite a certain weakness in his character, the King was very stubborn when prevented from doing what he wanted, and whatever else he wanted he was determined to marry Wallis. If the Cabinet had been using Wallis as the reason to get rid of the King, he might equally have been using Wallis as an excuse to go. We have already seen that a way out existed: all that was required was to send Wallis away, even if only for a short time, while he was crowned. But the truth was that Edward was aware that becoming crowned would only prove a temporary reprieve: in the final analysis his future did not lie with being King and he knew it. Accepting the easy solution might have solved his marriage problem but all the others would have remained. His desire to change the political system would eventually bring him into conflict with any selected government: he had to go. The supreme irony of the Abdication was that both sides in the conflict believed they had achieved what they wanted.

If we accept that the King engineered the Abdication and had no wish to be crowned, we must look for the reason. It is now known that he and Wallis had both been collaborating with the Nazis prior to his decision to abandon the crown, and this was to increase after the Duke left England. Their later co-operation is easy to understand: Wallis in particular believed they had been harshly treated by the British Establishment, the Government and Baldwin in particular, and it is generally believed that both felt little affection for Britain and blamed all their misfortunes on the Cabinet and its intransigence and the subsequent attitude of the Royal Family. However, what seems so curious and appears not to have been addressed is what possible motive Edward could have had for wanting to help a foreign power, the former enemy responsible for all the misery of the First World War? What remains so difficult to understand is the reason that lay behind his involvement with the Nazi regime prior to 1935.

The Nazis had been quick to recognise Wallis's power which amounted to virtual domination of the Duke. There is ample evidence of their considerable efforts to court her and persuade her to influence him. The advantages in this to the Third Reich are obvious, but what remains so inexplicable is what the Duke hoped to gain in return for the considerable assistance he rendered to the Nazis.

While it is true that the Duke found himself increasingly the target of the carefully orchestrated campaign by those employed by Hitler to enlist his support, it was also becoming apparent to those working for Hitler that the Duke was a more than willing helper. True, he was not alone. There were many others at the time who were advocating co-operation with Nazi Germany, appeasement was Government foreign policy designed to avoid the threat of war. Later this came to be regarded as a policy of defeatism, a desire to avoid war at all costs. But there is no doubt that it was not until 1939 that the widespread feeling of the danger from Fascism was seen by anyone other than a small minority. Up until that point the fact that the Fascist regime in Germany was building up its military strength was not seen as any real threat, and those who were aware of this imagined that it was to repel the danger from Communism.

The prospect of an alliance with Germany was gaining ground; there were many who believed it was a good thing. It is difficult, having witnessed the effect that the war with Germany had on the people of Europe, the depth of depravity plumbed by the evil Nazi regime, the genocide inflicted on its own people and those of the states it overran, to be objective about what would have been the result had the strong desire for peace on the part of many of those in power during the late Thirties resulted in some form of an alliance. Whatever advantages were perceived they are now regarded as being largely illusory. It is clear that Hitler's lofty ideas were either a cruel deceit or yet another example of his self-delusion. But at the time the idea of peaceful co-existence was tempting. The British economy was slowly recovering and the horrors of war were still fresh in the thoughts of most people.

It cannot be denied that Edward's pro-Nazi utterings seem to have been more overt as the relationship with Wallis developed, but this must be seen as coincidence rather than as any effort on her part to force the King to support Fascism. While her first husband was known to have worked for the Fascist Government of Italy, there has never been any suggestion that she was in any way politically active. Her second husband, Ernest Simpson, was a businessman who dealt internationally and does not seem to have had any political affiliations. There is no evidence to link Wallis with any political cause until she became involved with the Prince of Wales. He was the driving force.

Returning to Edward's growing enchantment with what was happening in Germany, it seems inconceivable that he could have imagined that any form of partnership between Britain and a Germany run by the Nazis could have survived. In the late Thirties the policies that would result in the destruction of millions of people by the SS had begun; rumours of ill-treatment were already beginning to filter out from Europe, mainly through the international Jewish community. The British record during its early colonial days is not without blemish: history records many instances of brutal massacres – in fact the British have been awarded the dubious honour as being the inventors of the 'concentration camp' during the Boer War – but by the late Thirties its reputation on human rights was better than most. Its colonial administrations were generally welcome in the countries of the Empire where they were regarded as even-handed towards all the people under their jurisdiction. Once Hitler's policy of genocide was discovered, such an alliance would have been short-lived.

It has previously been difficult to understand what possible advantage the Prince of Wales could have imagined such an arrangement could have had for the British Royal Family. We know that the former King George V was horrified at the prospect of another war, and it is reasonable to expect that the Prince of Wales shared his father's objections. As a serving officer in France during the previous conflict, he witnessed the futility and horror at first hand and could not have remained untouched by its terrible statistics, when, for example, on 1 June 1916, the British Army suffered 60,000 casualties, the blackest day in its long and glorious military history. Losses on both sides were equally horrendous.

The Duke's admiration for Hitler and his obvious desire to see the two countries coming together cannot be explained away simply by his wish to avoid another war. The degree of his support and determination to be involved show us that his motives are to be found in another direction.

Is there any evidence for believing that Wallis was a German spy? There are several recorded instances where it was believed that she passed information to the Nazis, information that came from the King. That she was involved with Ribbentrop is also well known. Several sources have revealed that he went out of his way to court her: he is known to have sent 17 red roses to her apartment at Bryanston Court every day and they were not returned. It is widely believed that she entertained him there, occasionally in the presence of her husband, who, incidentally, was a Jew. Charles Higham goes as far as to suggest that they had an affair, quoting as his source Mary Kirk Rafferty, a close friend of Wallis.[5] The evidence is largely circumstantial, which is not surprising. Wallis would have been more than discreet and there would have been a very real desire for secrecy on the part of Ribbentrop: he would be anxious that his wealthy wife didn't learn of the lengths he was prepared to go to carry out his Führer's wishes. Whether this allegation is correct or not, no other source has suggested it, but it was clear that Hitler was delighted at the way things were progressing. Wallis was later to deny that she had any dealings with Ribbentrop. In an interview with Helana Normanton of the *New York Times* on 30 May after she had left England, she claimed that she hardly knew him:

> I cannot recall being in Herr von Ribbentrop's company more than twice, once at a party at Lady Cunard's before he became Ambassador, and once at another big reception. I was never alone in his company, and I never had more than a few words of conversation with him – simply the usual small talk, that is all. I took no interest in his politics.

This is clearly untrue. Wallis was lying, understandably, for if she had been having an affair with the German Ambassador she was hardly likely to admit it, especially at the time when she was waiting for her divorce to be finalised before marrying the Duke. It may be of relevance that Mary Kirk Rafferty was herself having an affair with Wallis's husband Ernest at the time of the supposed affair with Ribbentrop. Later, after his divorce from Wallis, they married and Mary became the third Mrs Simpson.

Mary may have had a lot more to answer for than she suspected. Wallis, it is said, was outraged to discover that Ernest and Mary were carrying on their affair under her own roof at

Bryanston Court. It drove her into a fury and this, more than any idea that she might one day marry the King, prompted her to seek a divorce: it was only after she announced her intention to sue Ernest for divorce that the King, suddenly aware that she was about to become free, announced his plans to marry her. This more than anything tends to demolish the suggestion that she deliberately set out to trap the Prince of Wales.

Ribbentrop's attention to Wallis was well known, particularly to those in the circles in which they both moved in London. It was certainly known to Baldwin and the Cabinet – they were receiving reports from MI5 who were taking a great interest in Wallis, the Prince and the Nazis in London with whom they both mixed freely. During the whole of 1935 and 1936, up to the period when the Duke left for France in December 1937, both he and Wallis were under constant surveillance which was to continue even after they were married and went to live in Paris.

That British intelligence should have been employed to watch the heir to the throne and that it was to continue when he became King is incredible. But much of the concern about his conduct was justified; no charge of paranoia can be levelled at the Cabinet. The reports they were getting fully justified their actions. The FBI files in Washington contain a report entitled *International Espionage behind Edward's Abdication*. This reveals that certain state secrets known to Edward found their way to Ribbentrop and such was the accuracy of the information that reached him that the British Government were able to pinpoint the leak. The report concludes that Wallis was responsible for passing on the information to the German Ambassador.[6]

The revelation that the Cabinet had ordered MI5 to spy on Edward even before his father's death demonstrates that any form of trust had broken down long before the so-called 'Abdication Crisis'. What has never been revealed is whether the King and Wallis were aware that they were being watched and investigated. It seems likely: in the late Thirties members of German intelligence were active in London. They would almost certainly have kept a close eye on MI5 and must have been aware of what was going on. This information would have been reported to Ribbentrop who would in turn have told the King. Even before he came to the throne, the Prince of Wales must have known that pressure was building up. When George V had concluded that the Prince's days were numbered, he was not alone. Even before his father's death the Prince must have already arrived at that conclusion for himself.

Chapter Four

Uneasy Lies the Head that Wears the Crown

FOLLOWING A PAINFUL ILLNESS George V died just before midnight on 20 January 1936. Several sources have ascribed his death to a lethal dose of morphine administered by his long-time friend and Court Physician Lord Dawson of Penn whose intention was to bring the King's suffering to an end, but some cynics have suggested it was to enable the news to arrive in Fleet Street in time to appear in the following morning's newspapers.

By right of succession Edward VIII, King of Great Britain, Ireland and British Dominions across the Seas, Emperor of India, came to the throne to begin what was to be a turbulent if somewhat brief reign as the new Sovereign.

This was the moment Hitler had been waiting for. His emissary the Duke of Saxe-Coburg-Gotha wasted no time in rushing to his cousin's side. Already aware that George V was dying, he raced to Sandringham to offer his condolences and accompany the new King to Buckingham Palace when Edward drove there to assume his duties. Saxe-Coburg was delighted to be able to report to the Führer that the new King was determined to take a greater interest than his father in the business of government. While admitting it was an area where the new King was likely to come into conflict with Government ministers, he believed Edward would still prove a valuable ally. Saxe-Coburg was able to reassure Edward that he was acting as Hitler's emissary and was the King's direct contact with the Führer. That Edward should have gone along with this arrangement seems inconceivable. It was truly outrageous and a clear demonstration that he didn't care what the Cabinet or for that matter the public thought. Saxe-Coburg was a well-known Nazi; although born in England, he had been stripped of his peerage and had his name removed from the roll of Order of the Garter for his pro-German activities during the First World War. That the King, who knew perfectly well that Saxe-Coburg was a Nazi spy, should even have allowed him access was to send out completely the wrong signals. His presence would be seen abroad as a demonstration of British support for the Third Reich and a tacit acceptance of the atrocities the regime had begun to inflict on its own people. The Duke of Saxe-Coburg, generally considered to be something of a fool, was to cause the new King embarrassment and invite widespread public condemnation when he wore a Nazi uniform at the funeral of George V.

Just what was going on in Edward's mind in the days prior to and immediately following his father's death is difficult to imagine. At that moment he had become the most powerful constitutional ruler on earth, the sovereign head of the largest empire the world had ever seen who could count on the support and adulation of a third of the world's population spread throughout the globe. But almost from the early days of Hitler's emergence on the political scene, Edward had been steadfast in advocating that the country he was born to rule should share its incredible power with the German people. Can we really believe that he imagined that the only way to preserve peace and to increase the standard of prosperity in Britain, where, during the late Thirties, the first signs of improvement were already beginning to be felt, was to form an alliance and share these advantages with a nation plagued by inflation and raging unemployment? Why form an alliance with a country suffering the effects of defeat after starting a terrible war that had brought nothing except humiliation and poverty to its own people? Many sources have revealed that Edward was no intellectual; several have even gone as far as to suggest he wasn't very bright; but even he must eventually have come to see where Hitler's ambitions were inevitably to lead, he must have known that, if he were not curbed, Hitler's aim was nothing less than the total domination of Europe which he proposed to secure through military might. Already Hitler was making no secret of the fact that he wanted those territories Germany had been forced to give up; early in his rise to power he had hinted he had no intention of stopping there. His policy of 'Lebensraum', or 'living space', was simply a euphemism for a programme of territorial expansion only achievable through a massive increase in the German armed forces. With his eyes firmly directed towards the East, initially he wanted to change the balance of power, then he could afford to disregard the Treaty of Versailles, sweep it aside and renegotiate with his former enemies. From that point onwards the German 'master race' would move to rule the world.

So why did Edward go out of his way to support Hitler's regime? What possible motive did Edward have for giving it his unquestioned support? Was he too so seduced by the idea of a

European super state that he was prepared to sacrifice the power of the British monarchy to this utopian ideal or did he see a role for himself in the 'New Europe'?

Of course, it would be unfair to suggest that Edward was alone in thinking this way. A great many people, including those in positions of power, felt that an accommodation with Hitler was not only possible but desirable. In the years following the Abdication, in the run up to and even for a while following the events of Munich, Government policy would continue to favour appeasement. Even when a new King and Queen came to the throne foreign policy didn't change. George VI was as enthusiastic as anyone for coming to an arrangement with Hitler. Fritz Weidemann, Hitler's adjutant, is reported to have said: 'Halifax [*British Foreign Secretary*] once said he would like to see as the culmination of his work the Führer entering London at the side of the English King amid the acclamation of the English people.'[1] Halifax was a trusted confidant of the King and Queen. His stance on appeasement is well known. He remained on personal terms with the Royal couple who regarded him as a friend and adviser whose views they sought and welcomed.

Historians who have studied the policy of appeasement (official Government foreign policy in the years leading up to the declaration of war) make it clear that all the members of the Cabinet, with the exception of Churchill who was regarded as a warmonger and as being out of touch and whose opinions about most everything were not taken very seriously, genuinely believed that Hitler's aims were largely domestic and, while they were prepared to accept that he was a dangerous fanatic, they failed to recognise him as the threat he would come to represent. A united Europe had long been a dream of many; a trading partnership that would sweep away all barriers, introduce a new sense of co-operation and remove the risk of war that had ravaged Europe for centuries was clearly an attractive idea. Alas the world had yet to learn that Hitler and his crowd of self-serving megalomaniacs were the least likely to bring it about. Still, no one could deny his vision was sound, even if the brutal methods he employed lacked attraction. Europe was going to have to wait another 34 years before a referendum of the British people would vote to make Hitler's dream a reality and allow the British to sign the Treaty of Rome.

The run-up to the Second World War must be the only time in history when a potential aggressor had laid out his objectives for all the world to see, as Hitler did in *Mein Kampf*. Sadly, when he published his vision of the future it was not taken seriously, something the world would come to regret. Most people who tried to read what is a very dull, boring book (it even contains a section devoted to the dangers of syphilis) failed to realise its significance and its importance was almost entirely ignored. Queen Elizabeth sent a copy to Lord Halifax, the Foreign Secretary, in September 1939 with a note advising him not to read it: 'Or you might go mad and that would be a great pity. Even a skip through gives one a good idea of his mentality, ignorance and obvious insincerity.'[2] Her reaction seems a fair reflection of how Hitler was regarded by most people. The seeds of appeasement fell on fertile ground. Had the Foreign Office allotted the task of studying and understanding *Mein Kampf* to a panel of experts, informed opinion might well have come to the conclusion that Hitler intended to set Europe alight a decade sooner. But the painful memories of 1914 were too fresh in the minds of most people – nobody wanted to consider the prospect of another bloody conflict. The thought of war was unthinkable to a world gradually beginning to emerge from the grip of deep recession following the Great War and as a result the Government had been forced to reduce drastically the amount of money it spent on armaments. Nobody was ready to fight even had the Government wanted.

The scope of this book seeks briefly to re-examine the events leading up to the Abdication, believing that they will help to explain the part the Duke played in events over the two and a half years that followed, covering the period up to late 1940 following the declaration of a war that would eventually sweep the world. Many of the events have been examined before, but few, if any, attempts have been made to establish a reason for the way that Edward behaved. Despite a great deal of speculation, many of his reported activities have been confined to specific isolated incidents and there has been no real attempt to explain his motives. Much of what has been written about the Duke during this period has concluded that he was a man who drifted into several situations that were later to prove embarrassing. We have been conditioned to think that he was following no specific path and was less than clear where his curious actions would lead. That this version of events should have been allowed to gain acceptance to the point that it has become generally believed is not surprising. This was deliberate policy, fostered principally by the Royal Family and the Government, to allow the part played by the Duke to remain largely undiscovered. This is hardly surprising: had the degree of enthusiasm with which the Duke plotted against his country and members of his own family been revealed it is not difficult to imagine the effect it could have produced. It has not proved that difficult, looking back over all the evidence that has gradually come to light over the last 57 years, to establish the degree of treachery in which the Duke became involved during the period between the Abdication and when he left Europe to take up his appointment as Governor of the Bahamas. He had become closely involved with some of the most evil men who have ever walked this earth. Even if his motives were those of the gullible fool, and there are many who manipulated the truth and hid the evidence to persuade us he was, he was still a dangerous man. As the old saying has it: 'Those who lie down with dogs . . . get up with fleas.' The extent of the infamy he was involved in could have had devastating results.

To try to understand what he did it is necessary to go back a few years. Even during the last days of his father's reign Edward saw the storm clouds gathering over his future. The looming crisis, brought to a head by his decision to marry Wallis, would not have come as any great surprise: he had been left in no doubt about his father's and mother's views about much of his previous conduct. Declaring his intention to marry Wallis sealed his fate – he did not need to be told that his chances of hanging on to the throne were slim.

Edward has frequently been portrayed as a weak, self-indulgent man, given to being influenced by strong characters whom he admired and to whom he found himself attracted. While this seems to have been true – it explains the reason he was besotted by Wallis – it may be that history, in portraying him as lacking in determination and a certain amount of inner strength, has judged him unfairly. To dismiss him as a self-indulgent playboy who had no real desire to serve his people, who threw away his heritage and failed to shoulder the burdens of responsibility for which his life should have trained him, simply for the love and companionship of a woman with whom he could have continued to have a relationship, to have even married without giving up the throne, cannot be the whole truth.

The power struggle between the King and Baldwin led everyone into the trap of believing that the Abdication was brought about solely because of his determination to marry the woman he loved. However, there is a great deal of evidence that for some time during the later part of his father's reign the Prince of Wales was having serious doubts about his future, even as early as 1926. Hector Bolitho writing in *A Century of British Monarchy* reveals:

It is said that [*in the autumn of 1926*] on the way back to Britain from South America [*the Prince*] dreaded the discipline awaiting him so much that he sent a letter ahead to the King, saying that he had decided to renounce his rights and settle in one of the Dominions unless he were allowed his own way.

Several sources have quoted Elsa Maxwell who wrote that the Prince of Wales told her in 1927: 'I don't want to be King, I wouldn't be a very good one.'[3]

So if we accept that Edward, even while the Prince of Wales and before his obsession with Wallis developed, never wanted to become King we must try to discover his reasons. There seems little doubt that the Prince had become frustrated at the way things were going and that he recognised, more than anyone, that he was out of tune with his times. He grew deeply disillusioned with the way in which the country was being governed. He saw a nation beginning to slide close to bankruptcy, but more importantly he recognised the unmistakable signs that the Empire was beginning to disintegrate. For this he blamed, and was contemptuous of, the current politicians. Gradually, it seems, he had begun to realise that he couldn't bring himself to face a future presiding over the demise of the Empire with little if anything being done to halt its eventual break-up. Another clue to the state of his mind can be gained from the views of Lady Hardinge, wife of the King's private secretary, who wrote:

His behaviour over the death of his father was 'frantic and unreasonable', his grief was far in excess of that shown by his mother and brothers, which was strange considering the relationship he had with his father, it suggested his grief was motivated by the awareness of the hateful task he had been given.[4]

It seemed that the position for which he had been trained no longer looked attractive, he did not want to face a prospect of rule without having any real influence over the affairs of a country in the grip of a weak Government whose leaders couldn't see, or didn't care, what was happening. The Prince had always regarded himself as a German, was proud of his family roots and, more significantly, being Germanic he admired the strength and national determination so evident in the Germany of the late Thirties and so lacking in Britain. To a much lesser degree Britain had suffered the same sort of malady that had afflicted Germany, but there were few signs of a similar dramatic resurgence of national identity, no leader prepared to face up to the problems of inflation, lack of trade output and the attendant unemployment which produced the general strike of 1926. He was disappointed that no dynamic politician looked likely to emerge, one who could be hailed as a leader. With a growing sense of despair, the Prince dreaded spending the rest of his life without any real power, having to stand by and watch a great Empire, built by men of stature who ventured out and extended Britain's dominance throughout the world, slowly crumble while its politicians were prepared to humble themselves and allow Britain to take second place to a country ruled by a little painter from Austria with the drive and ambition to conquer the world.

Gradually he came to realise that there was nothing he could do to reverse this situation, he knew what his life as King would mean, the future that had been ordained for him, nothing to look forward to apart from the superficial trappings of power, knowing that in reality he himself had none. There would be the indignity of having to seek the permission of the politicians to discuss world events, whilst at the same time being obliged to carry out a life of endless ceremonial. Being ordered to attend, unable to refuse, to be used as some puppet to be paraded when the occasion demanded was not something he viewed with any enthusiasm. It was all made worse by the prospect of having to either face all this misery alone or being forced to agree to marry some suitable woman, some obscure foreign princess who would have been prepared to sit beside him and watch the country and Empire degenerate while the Royal Family become more and more impotent. He was convinced that the divisions between state and monarchy would degenerate as the Government sought to curb his involvement and that the House of Windsor would be reduced to a 'peacock throne', as proved the fate of most of the Royal Houses of Europe.

To refuse to bow before the inevitable, to accept a comfortable life of luxury with few demands on his time, able to carry on with the endless house parties that he obviously enjoyed, and able to share all this gaiety with the woman he loved either as a mistress or wife, was not the action of a weak man, but shows a remarkable strength of character of which few, given his circumstances, would have been capable.

While it has been suggested that Edward needed to be dominated, that he was a masochist who craved control by someone powerful and who it seems found in Wallis a woman who was prepared to fulfil his sexual need for domination, this does not explain his desire to give up the throne. Whatever his sexual predilections (there are some who have even tried to suggest that he was homosexual), it could have had little relevance to his position on the throne. Many men with less than conventional sex lives carry on their public life without problems. It is well known that highly successful businessmen who find the need to visit so-called 'houses of correction' to be dominated and humiliated by professional 'madames' are not prevented from holding responsible positions in the tough environment of corporate in-fighting nor distinguished members of the legal profession who adequately dispense justice in the courts of law. Whatever Edward VIII did in the confines of his private life need have had no bearing on his royal duties; the fact that his conduct before the Abdication did not become public for many years after his death confirms this. Several people have tried to suggest that his affection for Hitler was a result of his need to worship those he saw as powerful and charismatic, and that his admiration was based on a form of sexual chemistry between the two men. This can be dismissed as rubbish. His admiration of Hitler was based on the Führer's determination to make Germany powerful again rather than any need to submit to domination from afar. If any of these factors played a part, it was nominal. The facts support the contention that in 1936 he didn't want to be King and announcing his intention to marry Wallis brought the problem to a head. Considering all the evidence, and with the advantage of the knowledge of his later life, it seems clear that even had Wallis not entered his life he would not have remained as King.

The King's long-time admiration for Fascism and the prospect it appeared to offer of creating a strong, united Europe, was powerful in persuading him that he could effect change in a totally different and more efficacious way. It seems certain that he believed that, free of the restrictions of the Crown and untrammelled by any need to seek permission for his actions, he would be able to influence the tide of events towards a more socially acceptable solution to the world's problems. With this in mind, it is more than conceivable that the idea of abdicating presented him with a welcome chance to discover a new way forward. If he gave up the throne, left the country and married Wallis, he would be free to establish a power base to work for the idea of Anglo-German unity that had made such an impression on him. If this is what he had in mind, and it seems it was likely, then this provides an explanation of why he faced the prospect of abdication with equanimity. Many at the time were surprised at how quietly he went – even Baldwin recorded his relief at the King's acceptance of what the Prime

Minister saw as the end of a difficult time. The Duke did not share the view of many of his friends and supporters who saw the Abdication as defeat, rather he regarded it as a wonderful opportunity to do something about his future. It presented him with a chance to build a new Europe which he had come to believe would be the solution to all the world's problems and an opportunity to curb and eventually destroy the spread of Communism that threatened to destroy the Empire. Looking back, this seems entirely consistent with what happened. He was convinced that the only way in which he could achieve what he believed in and the salvation for both Europe and the Empire was to encourage Hitler. He could see that the current policy of appeasement would reduce Britain to a subservient role that would mean initially she would be the weak partner in a powerful alliance, but he saw a role that was unique: because of his special position with a role in both camps, he could bring all the other nations of Europe together in common cause. Edward realised that fighting for Britain from the inside was likely to prove a great deal more effective than allowing Britain to be drawn into a war it had little chance of winning.

Edward VIII's motives were not entirely altruistic. He was encouraged by Hitler's avowed intention to restore the position of the monarchy in Nazi Germany, and it is this aspect of the policy that attracted him. The German branch of the family were a pretty weak and ineffectual lot. Hitler's plan offered the chance to reunite the House of Hanover and the House of Windsor, who would between them rule over the greatest power base the world had ever seen, the might of Britain and Germany harnessed together to maintain peace. Then with the conquest of Russia (again spelled out in *Mein Kampf*), they could bring half the world under their control. The prize was irresistible.

While at first glance this might seem a fanciful hypothesis, it is entirely possible that Edward VIII and Hitler shared a common goal, a new and united Europe. Many of the events that were to occur over the next few years bear testament that this was in their minds. What we can be sure of is that both were travelling down the same road, probably not as partners, but each making use of the other to achieve dreams and fulfil ambitions.

The very last thing that George V said before he closed his eyes for the last time was: 'How is the Empire?' He was told, 'The Empire is fine, Sir.'[5] Little did they know that his heir believed that he had found a way to reverse the decline and make it even more powerful.

Chapter Five

War Becomes Inevitable

AS HAS BEEN SEEN, working through his emissaries, de Ropp and Saxe-Coburg, Hitler had been working hard to persuade the King that co-operation between the two countries offered the best way forward. They must have painted a glowing picture of the Führer's dream of how he proposed to create a super state so powerful that nobody would dare oppose it. But what Hitler and his henchmen had failed to realise, along with most of the rest of the world, was that the King had already begun to use his position to advance Hitler's plans. What is so ironic is that at the time when Hitler was confident of the King's co-operation and overjoyed that he could rely on what the Nazis regarded as a considerable asset, the King had already decided to give up his throne.

Even in his wildest dreams Hitler could not have realised that the strategy he had patiently followed for two decades was already in ruins. The Abdication came as a surprise to many in Britain but it must have come as a devastating shock to Hitler and Ribbentrop since they were forced to accept that they could no longer rely on their friend and ally in their time of need. It was a serious setback, particularly when they realised that the man chosen to succeed him was unlikely to show much in the way of sympathy, never having previously shown any interest whatever in politics.

This loss of Edward must have come as a blow in view of the King's assistance to Germany and in particular to Hitler over the affairs that surrounded the first time that the German Army went on the offensive in 1936. Edward's behaviour over the issue of the Rhineland provides powerful evidence that he was prepared to assist Germany long before the question of his abdication became public. His conduct indicates ample reason to conclude that he had decided where his future sympathies lay. While no longer wanting to be King of England he was still in favour of the monarchy, believing that a strong constitutional ruler was essential. He remained convinced that any new and powerful Europe should include the former crowned heads of Europe, believing that they had a significant part to play. The various Royal Houses of Europe had been fragmented by political divisions, any power they once held was gone, their influence was largely illusory although some were still retained for ceremonial duties. However, if restored to prominence they could again become a force with which to be reckoned. Their rehabilitation would inhibit the excesses of the politicians in their own countries; not only would their influence for peace be considerable, but they would also provide an additional tier of government. The advantages for such an arrangement to the current head of the House of Windsor were obvious, indeed if this was what Edward had in mind it explains much of what happened.

To have achieved it would have meant that the Duke would have done what no man had done before, to have brought all the Royal Families of Europe together in common cause and to have given the continent one constitutional ruler, a 'United States of Europe'. This puts the Duke's actions in a totally different light: instead of being seen by many as a weak character bedazzled byHitler and driven by his admiration for this charismatic little man, it reveals the Duke was following a vision and an agenda of his own. This fanciful, but entirely possible, explanation could explain his reluctance to oppose the demands of his abdication and provides the only logical reason for some of his later behaviour.

There is no reason to suppose that Hitler and Edward VIII were working to the same hidden agenda prior to 1937, no evidence has ever come to light. Of course, this does not mean that one did not exist, but it seems unlikely. It is more likely that the Duke was keeping his plans to himself and rather than helping Hitler, he was planning to use him to get what he wanted. Royalty has never been short on ambition: it is not the sole preserve of former painters.

This would help provide many answers and offer a theory as to why King Edward had no scruples about betraying his country. Unlike his father, Edward always regarded himself as a German.[1] He and his mother always spoke to each other in German, a language in which he was as fluent as he was in English. Had he felt any qualms about what he was eventually to do, he would have consoled himself in the knowledge that the House of Windsor was a fairly recent development, an invention of his father's to avoid embarrassment, and instigated to improve the image of the British Royal Family while the country was at war with Germany. Previously the family had rejoiced in the German name of Saxe-Coburg and Edward was proud of its Germanic ancestry: no less than 14 of his 16 great-grandparents had been born to German

Royal Houses. The loss of the British throne for a short while was a small price to pay to find himself the trusted ally of the most ambitious leader in the world. Working together they were a powerful alliance. The Duke gambled that with his German background and unquestionable charm he would soon become as popular in Germany as he believed he was in Britain. It was an attractive idea. Hitler as Chancellor would continue to remain in charge of the political life of both nations while the House of Windsor would rule over a united Europe. Later events will demonstrate that it was his intention to come to such an arrangement with Hitler. While it is speculation, the facts lead us to this conclusion. The evidence that the Prince never really wanted to rule the Britain he inherited is overwhelming, and even ignoring everything that happened previously, almost as soon as he cast off the shackles of monarchy he began to negotiate with several leading Nazis. Whatever he had in mind, he must have been following some agenda that required him to involve himself in what was going on in Nazi Germany.

If there had been any doubt that the King was prepared to act on behalf of the Nazis, and that he was not merely displaying foolish indiscretions while basking in the adulation of a collection of sycophantic Germans who deliberately set out to flatter him, it was finally dispelled in the summer of 1936 when he betrayed his country in the frenetic few days that followed Hitler's audacious invasion of the Rhineland.

Without warning on 9 August, while still telling the Reichstag and the world 'We have no territorial demands on Europe', Hitler's troops were already on the move. They crossed the border and moved into the Rhineland, which had been declared a demilitarised zone under the terms of the Treaty of Versailles. This was to prove the boldest move Hitler was ever to make. When news reached Paris, the French Government was reduced to a state of impotent shock. Hitler had predicted, based on intelligence he'd received from Admiral Canaris, that the French would not move unless they received the support of the British. Anthony Eden, the British Foreign Secretary, rushed to Paris to make sure that the French were not about to do anything rash; he need not have worried, the French were in no mood to do anything. Eden's solution was to call an urgent meeting of the League of Nations and allow them to resolve the matter. A hastily convened meeting was held in London two days later where the matter was discussed but no agreement was reached upon what action should be taken.

Curiously, the invasion caused as much concern in Berlin as it did in London and Paris. Characteristically, Hitler had acted without bothering to consult his generals. They confidently expected an Anglo-French force would be sent to the Rhineland within days. However, disagreement developed in London: the military men favoured action both drastic and immediate, the politicians were less than enthusiastic, fearing that a hasty move could see Britain and France embroiled in a war that nobody wanted. While the various shades of opinion talked endlessly and continued to vacillate, the German attachés in London frantically tried to discover the likely outcome of all these deliberations. Colonel Gayer, the German military attaché in London, was fooled by the British War Office into thinking that military intervention was imminent. He sent an urgent telegram to Berlin: 'Situation Grave. Fifty-fifty war or peace.' This produced a sense of panic among the German generals who believed Hitler had gone too far. Convinced that his action had provoked the British and French, they expected an imminent move to recapture the Rhineland and issued plans for a hasty retreat, wanting to withdraw the German troops before confrontation broke out. Everything hinged on the stance of the British Government; their decision was vital if the threatened military action was to be avoided.

Monsieur Flandin, the French Foreign Minister, arrived in London. It seemed a decision was about to be made. Desperate to learn the outcome, Germany waited with bated breath. Such was the importance of knowing that late on the evening of 9 March, Leopold Hoesch, the German Ambassador, took it upon himself to drive in great secrecy (even to the extent of using a hired car) to Fort Belvedere, where he had sought an audience with the King, who was spending the evening there with Mrs Simpson. Hoesch was confident of the King's special understanding on the course being followed by Hitler and believed he would be able to persuade the King that action by the Allies was unnecessary. After all, the territory morally belonged to Germany, the demilitarised zone had been set up originally at the insistence of the French but was no longer required. He assured the King that the Führer was prepared to enter into a new pact in which he undertook to protect the people who lived there.

The King proved very understanding and agreed to intercede with Prime Minister Baldwin. Hoesch then returned to the Embassy where he called Otto von Bismarck and Dr Fritz Hesse, the press attaché, to his office where they waited for news from the King. They had a long wait. Eventually the phone rang. Picking it up, Hoesch heard a familiar voice:

'Hello,' it said, 'is that you Leo? Do you know who's speaking?'

'Of course, Sir.'

'Listen carefully, I've just spoken to the Prime Minister,' the King said triumphantly. 'There won't be a war.'[2]

With the benefit of hindsight it is hard to overestimate the degree of damage contained in this one telephone call. It would bring misery for millions around the world and signal the start of a war that would first ravage a continent and then sweep across the entire world. This act of gross stupidity, taken without the understanding of the full implications of what he had done, was not the first time Edward had meddled in international affairs, but this example of his infamy was a forerunner of what was to come. To have transmitted highly sensitive military information, obtained by virtue of his privileged position, to a foreign power was nothing less than high treason, a crime for which the penalty was death.

While it is unlikely that the King would have realised the far-reaching consequences of his action – he was naïve enough to believe that he was simply helping his Nazi friends – instead he had made the Second World War inevitable. It would be no exaggeration to say that this was the spark that originally set Europe ablaze. When he moved against the Rhineland, Hitler was aware of the tremendous risk he ran. At that time Germany was militarily weak. Had the British and French moved swiftly and with any degree of purpose, there is little doubt that Hitler would have fled from the Rhineland with his tail between his legs, not waiting to suffer a humiliating defeat at the hands of a combined expeditionary force. Nobody knew this better than Hitler. He was aware that his entire future standing depended on the outcome of his daring bluff. Later he was to confide:

> This was the greatest risk I ever took in all the conduct of my foreign policy. During that hectic week in March 1936, I really hoped I would never have to go through another such ordeal for at least another ten years. We had no army worth mentioning, at that time it would not even have had the fighting strength to maintain itself against the Poles. If the French had taken any action, we would have been easily defeated; our resistance would have been over in a few days.[3]

Later, Hitler gave the credit for saving his skin to Edward, believing that the King had been instrumental in persuading

Baldwin that the demilitarised zone wasn't worth risking a war over. The truth was that Edward had no need to convince anyone; neither the French nor the British Government were in the mood to fight. But the King and Hitler were unaware of this, and it was to emerge later that the various British military commands had cast sufficient doubt among the German generals to cause them to openly oppose what they saw as Hitler's reckless action. Plans already in place to withdraw the troops from the Rhineland called Hitler's authority into doubt. With his entire political future at stake, it was make or break time. He found himself facing his greatest ever crisis. Then, when even his own confidence and resolve was beginning to weaken, he received news that was to save him. Some 48 hours after his troops had moved, Hitler was travelling in his train to Munich. Everyone who accompanied him was aware of the tension gripping their mercurial leader, one minute arrogant and boasting, the next in the grip of despair.The train drew to a halt, the stationmaster handed over a message that was rushed to Hitler. 'At last,' he shouted, waving the piece of paper, 'England will not intervene, the King has kept his promise, This means it can go well.'[4] Able to show he had the support of no less a person than the King of England gave his personal standing the boost he needed. Now his ego would soar to new heights.

Having suffered a narrow escape, Hitler learned a valuable lesson. He became convinced that the French and British were less than enthusiastic to get involved in military action and were unlikely to challenge any of his plans for further military excursions. Now he could show his followers, or more importantly the doubters, in Germany, that he could get away with anything. His success at occupying the Rhineland was the impetus he needed to embark on conquest – Austria, Czechoslovakia and finally Poland would fall to his advancing army before Britain and France were forced to act against him. There would be no stopping him now. As Ralph Wigram of the Foreign Office said as he watched the French delegation leave after the decision to do nothing over the Rhineland: 'War is now inevitable, and it will be the most terrible war there has ever been.'

The details for this revelation come from the Abwehr records in the National Archives in Washington and were first revealed in *The Game of The Foxes* by Ladislas Farago, published in America in 1971 and in Britain a year later. Without access to the Cabinet papers it is impossible to know if Baldwin and his ministers were aware of the King's treachery; it is difficult to see how they could have been unless MI5 were monitoring his telephone calls. This incident, the most serious so far, indicates the lengths to which he was prepared to go to help the Nazis further their ambitions.

During the period leading up to the invasion of the Rhineland, Ribbentrop was making use of every opportunity to ingratiate himself with the King and he was known to be a frequent visitor at the 'Fort'. Following his assistance over the Rhineland, Hitler decided that the King was too important an ally to be left in the hands of Leopold von Hoesch. So, despite having saved Hitler's neck, Hoesch became an embarrassment; secret plans were made to have him replaced. Hitler decided to take the unusual step of appointing Ribbentrop as Ambassador to London. Leopold von Hoesch was a career diplomat, a bachelor with homosexual tendencies whose wealth came from his family business empire. He was thought not to be totally committed to the Nazi cause, but merely caught up in Hitler's intrigues. It was decided that he had to go. Shortly afterwards he died; officially it was reported that he'd suffered a heart attack, but several sources have suggested that he was probably murdered to make room for Ribbentrop, whose appointment came as a surprise.[5]

'Chips' Channon MP, a close confidant of the King, was Ribbentrop's guest at the 1936 Olympic Games in Berlin when he learned of the appointment. He wrote in his diary: 'No one quite knows why he has been selected. Is it because his power is waning? Or is it because London is so important a post that the best man had to be sent? Or is it that there is simply no one else?'[6]

Channon had stumbled on the truth, London was the most important post at the time. In addition to keeping close to the King there was another compelling reason for his presence there. Ribbentrop was later to reveal that the reason for Hitler's decision to appoint him as Hoesch's replacement was his friendship with Mrs Simpson.

During his trial at Nuremberg after the war, Ribbentrop maintained that he had long discussions with the former Edward VIII about the formation of an Anglo-German alliance and he tried unsuccessfully to call the Duke as a witness to confirm this. Unfortunately for Ribbentrop, events had already begun to overtake him. Soon after his appointment the Abdication crisis broke. The Nazis' most important asset in Britain was soon to leave the country and settle abroad in an exile that nobody expected to prove permanent.

Chapter Six

Setback for the Nazis

WHILE THE EFFECTS of the Abdication in Britain are reasonably well known, what is less than clear is the effect it had on those in power in Germany. The news seems to have come as a terrible shock: there was little if any warning of the impending crisis which seemed certain to destroy the relationship they had so carefully developed with the King. The Nazis, it appeared, were no better informed about what was happening during the weeks running up to the Abdication than ordinary members of the British public.

No record of Hitler's reaction has survived, but it isn't difficult to imagine his disappointment at what must have been a devastating setback. The Nazis, in common with world opinion, would have found it inexplicable that an elected Government could simply remove its hereditary ruler and replace him with another without some sort of military coup or uprising having first taken place. Anyone unfamiliar with the British constitution must have wondered how the reigning Sovereign, who could in theory dismiss the Government of the day and invite someone else to form a replacement, could allow himself to be dictated to and banished by 'his' Cabinet. Hitler must have been more puzzled than most – his way of removing anyone with whom he disagreed was to have them murdered. That Edward allowed himself to be dictated to by an elected Prime Minister would have left Hitler, who had little time for the niceties of democracy, confused. If he understood them, he had never felt the need to observe them.

In the normal course of events the leader of one country should be able to rely on his ambassador to keep him fully informed about public opinion as well as the political situation in the country to which he had been appointed, but Hitler was particularly poorly served in this respect. The more that is learned about Ribbentrop, the more he is revealed as an incompetent, lazy and foolish character who managed to achieve his position more by cunning than ability, having persuaded everyone in Berlin that he was well respected and informed among those who wielded power in London. Nothing could be further from the truth. Goering believed Ribbentrop was the worst possible choice and said so. When Hitler defended the appointment saying, 'He knows Lord so-and-so and Minister so-and-so', Goering retorted: 'Yes, but the difference is that they know him, Ribbentrop.'[1] The only influence he had, which proved minimal, was amongst fashionable London society where wealth and position had enabled many to become friendly with Wallis and, through her, to move in the company of the King.

Ribbentrop's appointment as Ambassador was marked by stupidity from the moment he arrived. Stepping off the train at Waterloo station on 26 October 1936, he gave the Nazi salute and proceeded to read to waiting journalists a statement he had prepared during the stormy sea crossing on his way over. Popular convention demands that an ambassador must wait until he has presented his credentials before saying or doing anything. Not only did Ribbentrop fail to observe the normal demands of etiquette, but this ill-timed gesture proved foolish in the extreme. His theme was a common one, it was Hitler's favourite dream. He proposed that Britain and Germany should unite to oppose the 'most terrible of all diseases, Communism'. His staff at the Embassy were horrified. At first they could hardly bring themselves to believe he had made such a diplomatic blunder that was unlikely to endear him to anyone. The British press were quick to point out and question whether there was nothing better he could do than to foster good relations between Britain and Germany other than to suggest they should unite in hostility towards a third country. This less than auspicious start was only a foretaste of worse to come. In his biography of Ribbentrop, Michael Block recalls how during his first weekend in England he was the guest of Lord Londonderry at his estate near Durham. He attended divine service in Durham cathedral where, during the singing of the hymn *Glorious Things of Thee are Spoken*, sung to the same tune as *Deutschland uber alles*, Ribbentrop gave the Nazi salute.

One of his first official engagements was to meet Anthony Eden, the Foreign Secretary, who, it seemed, was less than enthusiastic about Hitler's latest envoy. Later, Eden was to try to circumvent Ribbentrop and talk directly with the German Government.

The new Ambassador presented his credentials to Edward VIII on 30 October, still unaware that the King's private life would shortly be revealed to an astonished public. His term as Ambassador was to end abruptly little more than a year later – he was recalled to Berlin in December 1937 following a period where he had been less than effective. Ribbentrop continued to cause offence with his determination to strut about, use the Nazi salute and utter shouts of 'Sieg Heil' wherever he went to peddle his almost parrot-like message that Hitler desired peace.

Less than a month after his arrival he was back in Berlin; the records show that during the 20 months that he held his appointment less than half his time was actually spent in London; for the remainder, during nine long absences, he was in Germany. There was a good reason for this. Ribbentrop was aware that anyone who spent too much time away from the shadow of his beloved Führer ran the risk of being forgotten and was likely to lose what influence he had. In addition he couldn't have failed to be aware that Martin Bormann, Hitler's secretary, regarded Ribbentrop as a fool and had begun to plot against him. Martin Bormann was no man to fall out with – his influence on Hitler, although undervalued by everyone, was considerable. Described by Hitler as his 'most loyal party member', he was to rise from virtual obscurity to be the most powerful man in the Nazi party with hardly anyone in Germany ever knowing his name. A man hated by everyone except his leader, Bormann remained a shadowy figure who preferred to stay in the background, but later, after his mysterious death and all the rumours that grew up around it, he was recognised as not only having been the dominant influence over Hitler, but also as having effectively ruled Germany in the years prior to and during the war.

Any suspicion that Bormann was plotting his downfall was enough to keep Ribbentrop continually rushing back and forth to Germany. Bormann was a specialist in the Jewish question; he and Ribbentrop (who had many Jewish friends) were to fall out violently over their treatment. Bormann regarded Ribbentrop as a vain numbskull and an upstart who didn't understand the ideological arguments of the party. They were to remain enemies until eventually Ribbentrop's influence waned and he was sidelined.

On the night of 27 November, after a week's absence, Ribbentrop came back to London to find trouble of the worst kind. Edward VIII had signified his intention to marry Mrs Simpson; all hell had broken loose. The newspapers were still sticking to their agreement not to print the story, but it was becoming clear that things were approaching a climax. Ribbentrop completely misread the signs and refused to accept that the Führer's policy was in trouble. Prince Louis of Hesse, a grandson of Queen Victoria and another Royal Nazi collaborator who had remained in touch with the British Royal Family, tried to warn Ribbentrop of the coming disaster, but the Ambassador remained optimistic and refused to believe that the King was about to go, he retorted contemptuously: 'Don't you know what expectations the Führer has placed on the King's support in the coming negotiations? He's our greatest hope! Don't you think the whole affair is an intrigue of our enemies to rob us of one of the last big positions we hold in this country? You'll see, the King will marry Wally and the two will tell Baldwin and his whole gang to go to the devil.'

By 3 December, when the whole thing had become public, Ribbentrop still remained convinced that the business would soon blow over. He and Hitler agreed to play down the issue and prevented the German press from reporting the crisis. Both, it seems, were confident that everything would turn out all right, and it was not until the Abdication Bill was laid before the House of Commons on 10 December that people in Germany learned the truth. Ribbentrop was reduced to a state of shock. Michael Block records that on that day Ribbentrop lunched with J.C.C. Davidson, a close confidant of Baldwin, who was amazed to hear him say: 'That this is the end of Baldwin, that there would be shooting in the streets, that the King's party would eventually restore Edward VIII to the throne. Indeed, he said that he had been extremely nervous coming to lunch on a day like this! He talked more nonsense than I have ever heard from anyone in a responsible position of the level of Ambassador . . . It was quite obvious that he had been stuffing Hitler with the idea that the Bill and Government would be defeated and that a more pacifist Government would replace it . . .'[2]

Several important conclusions can be drawn from this discussion with Davidson. It shows that the Nazis, or at least their Ambassador in London, were less than fully informed, they were clearly not aware of the way in which events had been moving. Whatever had been happening over the previous week had not been reported to Ribbentrop, and this indicates that the King was not in regular contact with him, nor had he discussed matters with or sought advice from his Nazi friends. It also suggests that German intelligence was oblivious to the coming crisis, or if they knew about it, they had failed to pass the information to Hitler or Ribbentrop. There is a simple explanation for this; it must be remembered that Wallis was not in London, she was in 'purdah' in the South of France following her divorce. She had been the main route by which the Nazis had discovered what was happening at the Palace. They had probably found her so reliable that they had not bothered to set up other means of obtaining information. Wallis was not in touch with any of her old friends – and in any case she would have been more than reluctant to have been discovered making contact with Ribbentrop. Divorce at that time was handled by the ecclesiastical division of the courts; those waiting for their decree absolute had to be very careful. Anyone discovered having anything other than the most innocent of contacts with members of the opposite sex would be inviting the attention of the King's Proctor, who could refer the divorce back to the courts to have the petition rejected. This meant that the action would fail and the parties would remain married. So seriously was this taken at the time that when the Duke of Windsor suggested staying in Calais following the Abdication his lawyers considered it was too near Cannes, advising the safety of a national border between himself and Wallis until she obtained her decree absolute.

By far the most revealing part of the reported conversation, however, is his reference to the 'King's party'. That Ribbentrop should have mentioned it reveals that he was aware of its existence. Plans to establish one had clearly been discussed and the information had found its way to the Nazis. This is highly revealing and lends weight to the contention previously held. This was exactly what the Baldwin Government feared more than anything. The fact that Ribbentrop not only knew of, but expected, a movement to rise up and cause insurrection meant the possibility had been discussed among those who supported the King and that included the Nazis. It seems that most everyone in the know was aware of such a movement, and the serious threat it posed to the elected Government. What are we to make of this? If the facts outlined here are true, Britain could have come perilously close to civil war. The references that appear in reports about the possibility of the existence of a 'People's Party' suggest it was a great deal more advanced than we have been led to believe. If this were so, the reasons behind the Abdication become much clearer. The picture (as far as the rest of the general public were concerned) that this was a nine-day wonder brought about by the King's desire to marry Wallis is clearly not what it was really all about. There was a tide of intrigue ebbing and flowing under the surface that the Government was anxious not to allow to be revealed. If Ribbentrop, who was not the most politically astute person in the world, could openly discuss its existence with Davidson (expecting him also to be aware of the existence of such a movement) it shows how significant it was. All of this indicates that the chance of insurrection was a great deal more real than most people could have imagined.

There are strange parallels here with the way the Nazis had

come to power. The 'Night of the Long Knives' in 1934 removed friend and foe alike if they were opposed to the aims of the party; from that moment onwards the Nazis became all powerful. While Hitler and those who helped him to power may not have understood the reason behind the Abdication, they certainly understood insurrection and murder as political weapons. That is not to suggest that the Nazis had a hand in planning anything similar here, but there is no doubt they would have been ready to exploit the situation had the opportunity occurred.

When the war was over and the German security files were examined it was revealed that the Nazis had prepared a list of many in British public life whom they expected to be helpful to their cause. Peter Fleming's book, *Invasion 1940*, published in 1957, contains four pages of photographs of names and addresses of those beginning with the letter 'C' taken from the German files. These lists were prepared from people who had either formed contacts with Nazi Germany or who had shown sympathy for the cause through either their writing or public speeches and, while many would have remained loyal to the country, there were a large number who would have rallied behind a movement that would have united the two countries believing this was a sure way to avoid war.

If the Nazis had imagined they were about to witness civil disturbance in Britain and were about to rejoice in the overthrow of the Baldwin Government, hoping it would be replaced by one more sympathetic and supportive of the King which, in turn, would prove to be a Government that was likely to be amenable to the policy of co-operation that Ribbentrop had been slavishly peddling, they were to be sadly disappointed. Hitler would have taken cold comfort from the fact that his overtures towards the formation of an alliance were about to be dashed. However, those few remarks over lunch provide a remarkable insight into just how close Britain came to political unrest and how fortunate it was that Baldwin handled the situation with the decisiveness and effectiveness he did; but the real reason that trouble was averted remains the King's decision to step down without a fight.

Chapter Seven

Exit the Duke

AT PRECISELY TEN O'CLOCK on the evening of 10 December 1936, Edward VIII discharged his final act as Sovereign. Speaking to the nation by radio from a small apartment he maintained at Windsor Castle, he told his people, and many listening throughout the rest of the world, of his decision to relinquish the throne. The King seemed relaxed and calm but the speech seems to have evoked a mixed reaction among those who heard him. Some considered it a disappointing performance, lacking in warmth, while others found it marked a very moving and emotional moment of history.

Henceforth the former King would be known as the Duke of Windsor, a title that had come at the suggestion of his brother George VI, when it was realised that in all the confusion of the previous few days nobody had given any thought to what title he should have. Returning to Royal Lodge the Duke said his farewells to his mother and the rest of his family and later that same night slipped out of England and turned his back on his former role, little knowing that he was beginning an absence that would effectively last for the remainder of his life.

Accompanied by Walter Monckton and followed by Lord Louis Mountbatten, who rode behind in a car with the luggage, the Duke headed for Portsmouth where on his arrival he was met by Admiral Sir William Fisher, two other admirals and the captain of the destroyer HMS *Fury*. At the foot of the gangway they were joined by Ulick Alexander, Keeper of the Royal Purse and one of Edward's closest advisers, and also Godfrey Thomas and Sir Piers Legh, his equerry who had loyally served him for 16 years. The party boarded and after a farewell drink in the wardroom the former King left for Boulogne where it had been arranged that he would join the Orient Express.

It must have seemed ironic to those who saw him leave to watch a man who it was generally believed had given up everything to be with the woman he loved, walk off alone, apart from a small Cairn terrier called Slipper held under his arm for company, heading off in a different direction from where his future wife was anxiously waiting to discover what was going to happen next. It was a confusing time; we learn that when HMS *Fury* cast off and headed towards the Continent,the Duke's destination had still not been finally determined. Previously he had told Wallis that he intended to go to a hotel in Switzerland, but she was outraged and regarded this as another humiliation, an example of how the Royal Family had callously abandoned him. The Duke had wanted to stay in France but his advisers had cautioned against it for fear of upsetting Wallis's divorce proceedings. Appalled at the thought of him alone in a hotel, Wallis was instrumental in getting their mutual friend Perry Brownlow to arrange with the Baron and Baroness Eugene de Rothschild to invite him to stay at their castle, the Schloss Enzesfeld, near Vienna. The Schloss was a large baroque hunting lodge set in a huge park surrounded by beautiful gardens which the de Rothschilds had not used for some time, and which had been closed up and empty apart from the small skeleton staff retained to maintain the property. News of the hastily arranged visit of the Duke prompted a flurry of frantic activity. Extra staff were recruited and were set to work cleaning and polishing; carpets were relaid, the silver and valuable paintings were taken from storage in the cellars and the chandeliers and furniture uncovered. The whole house was filled with flowers and a string of pure white matching Lippizaner ponies was delivered to fill the once deserted stables and to complete the illusion that it was a comfortable family home.

It is not difficult to see Wallis's hand in the choice of venue for the Duke's enforced separation. Kitty de Rothschild was a fellow American whose story bore a certain similarity to her own. As Kitty Wolffe she had begun life as the daughter of a Philadelphia doctor and owed her current aristocratic status to an upwardly mobile spiral that had involved two previous marriages. She welcomed the opportunity to have a famous house guest, albeit an ex-king, but one who could still bring a great deal of social cachet and who was capable of enhancing his host's social standing. This probably explains why Kitty and the Baron went to such immense trouble and expense to make his stay as pleasant as possible.

The Duke was to spend the next five lonely months as guest of the de Rothschilds, and the frantic preparations before his arrival at the Schloss Enzesfeld tell a great deal about the Duke's attitude. It was clear that he had never given a moment's thought to the way in which he intended to spend the rest of his life; he expected that somebody somewhere would always make arrangements for his care and comfort.

The effect of the Abdication, which had occupied the press and the thoughts of most people in the days leading up to the announcement, disappeared with almost indecent haste; in the days that followed, life quickly returned to normal. It was as if the crisis had never happened. The following day *The Times* had briefly reported that the Duke had arrived in Austria but made no reference to Wallis – it seemed as if she no longer existed. The relief felt at the outcome had a settling effect on the country, which was reflected in the movement of what is generally regarded as the barometer of public confidence, the London Stock Exchange. During the crisis there had been a significant fall in share prices but almost as soon as Baldwin announced to the House of Commons that a resolution to the crisis had been found, to be followed by a formal declaration on the following day, millions of pounds began to flow back into the market. The industrial index which had stood at 122.3 at the start of the crisis had sunk to 119.1 during the week prior to the Abdication, but within days it had risen to 121.6 and more significant still was the rise in the value of sterling. which had weakened during the crisis. It responded to the settlement by reaching $4.90 with a corresponding rise in the strength of Government bonds. Such was the feeling of relief that the whole business was over that with their happy knack of putting a brave face on disaster the British people turned their backs on the Duke in much the same way as he seemed to have done to them. Inevitably there was a small minority who were unhappy at the way things had turned out, mainly wealthy friends of the King and Wallis, many of whom were Americans who had anticipated taking advantage of their position close to the new King to improve their social standing. It was left to Chips Channon to record their view; he wrote in his dairy: 'We will be out of the Royal racket, having backed the wrong horse.'[1]

What is more remarkable is the way the Duke reacted. Almost from the moment when he decided to abdicate he behaved as if a huge weight was lifted from his shoulders. His conduct was reminiscent of a man who had been reprieved rather than one who had lost an Empire. There was no suggestion that he had left the country in any sense a beaten man or one who had been rejected by his people, in fact his mood has been described as euphoric. This became apparent to everyone who met him in the few days before the Abdication. Instead of appearing depressed by what everyone else saw as his personal troubles and disappointment at their outcome, he was positively buoyant and seemed to be looking forward to leaving the country of his birth. Even Baldwin was to remark about the King's 'positively jolly mood' while his friend Perry Brownlow found him 'exalt to the point of madness'. In his first letter to Wallis following his arrival in Austria the Duke wrote: 'I am really happy for the first time in my life.'[2]

However, while the Duke was making his preparations to leave England, in Cannes his future wife was not so ecstatic at the outcome, nor was she enjoying a similar feeling of relief; she, it seems, was finding it hard to come to terms with the situation. She began to realise that everyone would blame her for allowing the crisis to develop, casting her as the villain in a catastrophe of unimaginable proportions. Her moves to persuade the King not to abdicate had failed; despite her entreaties and her offer to disappear from his life forever, her efforts were of no avail, she was trapped. Poor Wallis, no longer the darling of the world's press, quickly saw that if she continued to try to persuade him to let her go she could so easily find herself back in the headlines. She found herself driven into a corner from where there was no escape. To have deserted him, the man who had won the sympathy of the whole world because it was believed he had given up his throne and ruined himself to become an outcast from his own people just for the sake of her love, would have meant she could never show her face in public again. She would have been the victim of the world's scorn, the most hated woman in history. No longer could she think about running away – there was nowhere to run. The fashionable society she adored and where she had been the centre of attraction; London, Paris and more particularly America, would be about as hospitable as that at the South Pole. For Wallis it was now life with the Duke or nothing. Her letters during this period reveal the true extent of her anguish. As she wrote to Kitty de Rothschild: 'One felt so small not to be able to make him stay where he belonged and have the world turned against me because I fought a losing battle.'

Her unhappiness was not helped by the mountain of hate mail and threats against her life that were arriving daily. This was the very situation that Edward had envisaged when he persuaded her to leave London before news of the Abdication became known.

Wallis had tried her best to persuade the King to remain on the throne. There was only one occasion when she was said to have made her position known publicly; on 7 December she issued a statement to the world's press. It stated:

Mrs Simpson throughout the last few weeks has invariably wished to avoid any action or proposal which would hurt or damage His

Majesty or the throne. Today her attitude is unchanged, and she is willing, if such action were to solve the problem, to withdraw forthwith from a situation that has been rendered both unhappy and untenable.

We are told that she read this statement to the King over the telephone; he was unmoved and is reputed to have told her: 'Go ahead if you wish; it won't make any difference.' All this seems consistent with him wanting to give up the throne regardless of the reason that was popularly believed to lie at the heart of the crisis. The reaction of the press was to welcome her statement and announced prematurely: 'Mrs Simpson renounces the King! Crisis Ends.' It had no effect – three days later the King abdicated.

Wallis knew the game was up. There was nothing she could do but make the best of it. Her letters during this period show how she gradually became resigned to her fate, a future trapped into a marriage that the rest of the world still believed was 'the love story of the century', but which was, in reality, a loveless marriage to a man who continued to adore her until the day he died. So intense was his almost blind adoration that it has been said many times that he could never take his eyes off her whenever they were in the same room. Sadly, many sources have revealed that she did not feel the same way about him.

It was during the exchange of letters while they were apart that the name Charles Bedaux first cropped up; he was the man whose influence was to have a profound effect on their future. In this correspondence Wallis appears to have had trouble coming to terms with all that had happened. In several of her letters she continues to refer to the Duke as the King and the King and Queen as the 'Yorks'; maybe it was force of habit, but it can be seen that her failure to readjust to what had happened was a clear indication of the stress she was suffering.[3]

During January of 1937 Wallis received another shock. Her solicitor, Theodore Goddard, broke the news to her that Sir Boyd Merryman, the President of the Divorce Courts, had ordered Thomas Barnes, the King's Proctor, to investigate the circumstances of her divorce. Goddard was either not aware of the true facts or was very confident that what had been done had been well buried. He wrote: 'I do not think that you need to be worried by this, I propose to give the King's Proctor every facility in this matter as, after all, we have nothing to hide.' In her reply Wallis was equally sanguine: 'I see everything as the greatest obstacle race of all time. I shall try not to worry nor am I afraid to fight any intervention. I was surprised that one can investigate something that does not exist.' Her calmness was sheer bravado – she had plenty to hide. On the other hand, it might be that Wallis saw this, even at the last moment, as a way out, in which case her coolness is understandable. There is no doubt that had the true facts of her divorce come out she would not have been granted a decree. Eventually her divorce came through, and it is now known that the entire thing had been carefully stage-managed from the outset. Ernest Simpson was the injured party, he had been publicly humiliated but he was persuaded to allow Wallis to divorce him after he was conveniently discovered in bed with a professional co-respondent by a waiter who had arrived to serve breakfast in the Hotel de Paris in the village of Bray, a standard ploy frequently employed at the time. Divorce in the Thirties was neither easy nor cheap; later, several sources were to reveal that the Duke did not only pay Simpson's legal costs but, incredibly, compensated him for all his trouble. On 28 March, five weeks before the divorce was made absolute, the Duke gave Wallis a hundred thousand pounds, which she transferred to Ernest through a bank in Paris. For that sum the Duke had bought himself a wife. If this account is true, and there is no reason to doubt its accuracy, then the divorce was obtained without the true facts being disclosed. However, the investigation by Thomas Barnes did not reveal any malpractice or if it did it was not allowed to prevent Wallis's freedom. *(see footnote on page 92)*

Considering his mood when he arrived in Austria it must have come as something of a shock for the Duke to realise that things were not going to be quite as pleasant or as easy as he had imagined. Almost from the first day things began to go wrong. Within days his relationship with the Palace and his brother George VI became strained, and this can only be blamed on the Duke's behaviour during the first few weeks of exile. His conduct proved insensitive and arrogant. He seemed unable to understand that the Abdication had changed things. From the very moment he began his stay at the Schloss Enzesfeld he began to bombard Buckingham Palace with incessant telephone calls, behaving as if he were on holiday, conducting himself in the way he had previously done when abroad, issuing orders and making demands, and generally becoming a nuisance. Details of his behaviour even found their way into the newspapers. Several reported those endless phone calls, how his constant attempts to speak to and instruct the new King were both unremitting and unwelcome. The leader writer of the *Daily Mirror* at the time was in no doubt, nor was the Duke himself, that his return would soon follow. He wrote:

Daily the Royal Family is receiving calls from Austria. Not content with causing a pretty serious change in Coronation plans, Edward, Duke of Windsor, has been calling up members of his family to discuss revised proceedings.

Talk of years of voluntary exile for the Duke is so much rubbish. As much as he loved dashing abroad for his holidays when duties chained him here for most of the year, now that lack of duties keeps him chained abroad he is straining to return. England is dear to the Duke and already Fort Belvedere is being prepared for his homecoming, which will not be so long after the Coronation.

However, the new King, furious at being subjected to all this unwarranted interference, sent for Walter Monckton and instructed him to contact the Duke and tell him, diplomatically if possible, that it had to stop. Monckton did his best, but the Duke was left enraged. This was the beginning of a bitterness that was to develop and grow more acrimonious with time and would never be forgiven by either brother. There followed a further snub when the Duke was informed that his presence would not be welcome at the Coronation on 12 May. This so infuriated him that in an act of petulance he called a press conference to announce his engagement to Wallis in an attempt to draw attention away from his brother's important occasion. In a final show of annoyance, he told the world he would marry Wallis on 3 June, the anniversary of his late father's birthday, an act deliberately designed to upset the Royal Family further. Hardly the best way to begin his reconciliation or return to public life, but there was worse to come.

In showing that he intended to carry on in the way he always had he made a grave error of judgment. Instead, had he kept a low profile and allowed others to smooth his path there was a very real possibility that he would have soon been invited to return and take some part in the life of the nation. Those close to him were actively trying to make this possible. Winston Churchill, probably his greatest champion, worked hard in this respect. Shortly after the Abdication he wrote to Geoffrey Dawson, the editor of *The Times* newspaper and a bitter opponent of the Duke, believed by many to have conspired with Baldwin to force the Duke to relinquish the throne. Churchill began by referring to this when he wrote to Dawson about 'the hammer blows *The Times* had dealt the late King' and went on to plead:

Now, of course, the only thing is to look forward and repair the damage that has been done to the Throne. I am hoping that the

Duke of Windsor will soon be able to come back and live here quietly as a private gentleman. For this purpose the dust of controversy must be laid, and it seems very hard if he should not be allowed to do this.

May I enlist your chivalry in trying to bring this about, after a suitable lapse of time? Perhaps the Newspaper Proprietors' Association might be induced to give him the same kind of immunity as was such great comfort to Colonel Lindbergh. Perhaps you will let me have a talk with you about this later on.[4]

However, caged up in Austria, the Duke was in no mood to be patient or wait for any dust to settle. Feeling miserable and dejected, he stepped up his efforts to influence what was happening in London. The Duke's unhappiness was not helped by his enforced separation from Wallis. Fruity Metcalfe, his life-long friend who went out to join him at Enzesfeld, later wrote to his wife: 'He's on the line for hours every day to Cannes . . . I don't think these talks go well sometimes . . .' He also revealed: 'He won't pay for a thing . . . it's becoming a mania with him. It really is not too good.' In another letter Metcalfe was to record: 'He has become very foreign, talking German all the time. All he is living for now is to be with her. I have never seen anyone so madly in love. It's pathetic.' Metcalfe was also to reveal that the Duke was drinking heavily, something he was prone to do when he was depressed.[5]

The reasons for the Duke's unhappiness were several. It must have been an agonising time, gradually forced to realise that the future wasn't going to be anything like he had imagined. It is not difficult to understand his growing feeling of dejection, the increasing realisation of what giving up the throne was actually going to mean. The sense of anti-climax must have been dramatic and deeply wounding. Apart from his hosts, his few companions and servants, he was alone. His life had been transformed from one where his every word was heeded, his every whim catered for, where he was surrounded by flattery and the sycophantic attentions of those who fluttered around him. All that was over. It would have left him feeling that the world was moving on without him.

His feeling of rejection was made worse by the absence of Wallis who, up to the time she left England, had been his constant companion. Desperately he missed her – she had become the centre of his life. Knowing she was equally alone and feeling sorry for herself in the villa on the Côte d'Azur upset him deeply. Wallis meanwhile seemed to have come to terms with her fate. She was trying to cheer him up. A study of her letters shows that she was gradually beginning to return his messages of love and affection. Seemingly her mind was made up to make the best of a 'bad job'. The letters became more affectionate and ignored what had taken place, they began to talk about the future. This only made the Duke more anxious to see her. It was not an easy time for either of them.

The Duke had been warned that any contact with her could seriously prejudice her divorce so he had to make do with telephoning her several times a day. Despite this, he became impatient with the self-enforced separation. Friends and advisers lived in constant fear that he wouldn't be able to resist the temptation to rush to her side. The separation was to last until 4 May, the day following her decree absolute, when after 16 long weeks apart they were reunited near Paris. Churchill, who proved a staunch friend for most of the Duke's life, echoed the concern of those who sided with the Duke in a letter written shortly after the Duke arrived in Austria:

> I was so glad to learn that your Royal Highness had found an agreeable shelter for the moment . . . From all accounts the broadcast was successful, and all over the world people were deeply moved; millions wept. From words I had with Neville [Chamberlain] I gathered that what he attached great importance to was your living absolutely separate until everything is settled and the new Civil List is voted. He was rather grim and bleak, but I am sure he is right on that point. I suppose, Sir, you saw that the Attorney General in the debate on the Abdication Bill declared formally that there was no obligation upon your RH to reside outside the British Dominions. So I earnestly hope that it will not be very many months before I have the honour to pay my respects to you at the Fort.

Apart from the clear warning to stay away from Wallis, this letter went straight to the heart of another important matter and drew attention to another area of acrimony occupying the mind of the Duke. This was money. During the frantic discussions that led up to the Abdication, this was something that had been given scant attention. It is highly revealing that, from the moment he went into exile, the Duke became obsessed with the idea that he was practically destitute. His refusal to pay for anything during his time in Austria (which Fruity Metcalfe had reported to his wife) was a clear indication that the problem of money was never far from the Duke's thoughts. The idea that he was going to be left penniless was preposterous, but one that was to continue to haunt him and leave him convinced that he was desperately short of money. This paranoia was to be responsible for many of his future problems; it would be the reason why he allowed himself to be drawn into several dubious money-making ventures which did nothing for his reputation and produced little if anything in the way of profit.

What is so remarkable is that the Duke, who had always been obsessive about money, didn't demand from Baldwin as his price for stepping down from the throne a substantial settlement or an annual income from the Civil List. There is little doubt that he would have been awarded something. In financial terms the handing over of the Crown had cost him a great deal. There can be only one explanation for this uncharacteristic behaviour. The reason that he neglected to address his future financial position is revealed in the later part of Churchill's letter – the reference to the Civil List. He, more than anyone, would know what was in the Duke's mind. When he left England he confidently expected to return, firmly of the opinion that all that was required of him was to take a long holiday, marry the woman he wanted and then, when everything had settled down, return to England.

Despite everything that had happened the Duke never had any intention of turning his back on England. He believed, with some justification, that while he was regarded as something of a liability by those running the country, he enjoyed a great deal of support among the ordinary people. While on a visit to the Rhondda Valley in 1936, he saw for himself the terrible poverty and conditions of the unemployed miners and his concern had struck a chord with the working class. His now famous remark – 'Something must be done' – made people believe that at last somebody was about to take an interest in the conditions of those who had seemingly been abandoned by the State. They believed the future King understood and was determined to address the plight of many of his people. That one remark, which was widely taken up by the popular press, won him a tremendous amount of support. Sadly, it was all an illusion: not only did he do nothing, but it seems unlikely that he ever had any intention of doing anything. His mind was full of his other problems; once he left Wales he forgot all about the plight of the miners. Edward had never shown any concern for them previously. Up to that point his life had been an endless round of glittering parties thrown by rich, aristocratic friends, many of whom owed their opulent lifestyle and large country estates where the Duke spent his weekends with Wallis, to the efforts of the miners and others similarly exploited to create much of the nation's industrial wealth. If he was sorry for the miners he soon forgot them.

Much has been made of the incident at Brynmawr in Monmouthshire, where the remark was said to have been made. At the time it was seen as a spontaneous reaction by a caring man who had come face to face with the plight of the people. This is nonsense: as Prince of Wales, and later as King, he knew perfectly well what was happening in the country. How could he have remained unaware, when, since the early Twenties and during the early Thirties, the country had suffered the greatest period of industrial unrest in its entire history? Hunger marches and the lock-outs by the mine owners and factory owners that followed the general strike of 1926 gave rise to a series of riots that spread across the country. Long before his visit to Wales great bitterness was felt when armed troops were employed to quell riots in the Welsh coalfield and while the Government had managed to censor some of the more inflammatory incidents for fear of widespread civil unrest, reports of many of these incidents had found their way into the press. If Edward was unaware of what had been happening in the country for over a decade, it was because he chose not to know. However, his now famous remark may hold a clue to what was in his mind in the days of the run-up to the Abdication. 'Something will have to be done' could so easily have been an unguarded remark about what he was about to do. To improve the conditions of the poor and those without work was something that needed radical change. It was not going to be achieved with the present Government or by the way the economy was being run. As King he had no chance of changing anything, but maybe in thinking aloud he was simply expressing what he had already decided.

It has always been regarded as something of a surprise that the King gave up his throne without a fight. This was not understood at the time and still requires an explanation if the theory that it was simply the action of a weak man besotted by a woman is to be demolished. The King had a reputation for stubbornness and wanting to get his own way and yet he played directly into the hands of everyone who wanted to see the back of him. In providing them with all the ammunition they needed he made it very clear that he was manipulating the situation to suit himself. There remains little doubt that, given the political situation at the time, an appeal to the people could conceivably have brought the

Government down. Apart from the emergence of the so-called People's or King's Party, there was growing support for Sir Oswald Mosley and his British Union of Fascists. Mosley was playing the anti-war card, knowing that any political leader who could show a way forward without the need for another war could be sure of support from an electorate which had no need to be reminded of its horrors – the country was full of ex-servicemen, some blinded, others who had lost legs and arms or still suffering the effects of poison gas.

If the King was a long-time admirer of Fascism and saw this as a way to improve the lot of the people, why did he not show more support for Mosley? Why embrace a German Fascist dictator when a home-grown one was already in place and gaining some support? The answer is not difficult to find. Edward VIII had little confidence in Sir Oswald Mosley and his British Union of Fascists. They had become a thorn in the flesh of the Government and had they become more powerful, the Government would have been forced to move against them. Mosley's blackshirts were already carrying out marches that had already been the cause of riots in the East End of London following their attacks on the homes and businesses of the Jews. The reprisals against them could have escalated and civil unrest could have forced the use of the police and possibly the army to contain the riots and restore order. This would have placed the King in an impossible position: as head of the forces of law and order he would have been obliged to sanction the use of troops against the Fascist elements. Edward could not remain on the throne of a country which had formed an alliance with Fascist Germany if he had previously given orders to crush the British Fascists. While it is true that Edward VIII had little time for Mosley and his followers, the same cannot be said for the Fascists, who fervently hoped that the King was going to show them his support. The Fascists had held several campaigns between 1935 and 1939 such as the 'Mind Britain's Business' and had offered their support for the King when in 1936 they mounted a 'Stand by the King' campaign. They offered to support Churchill and Beaverbrook in a fight against the Establishment. Anyone who has read *My Life* by Sir Oswald Mosley is left in no doubt that Mosley, a former Cabinet Minister, was a great admirer of the dashing young Edward: he believed that the King was the ideal leader, young, unconventional, friendly with Nazi Germany and, more importantly, anti-Establishment. There is no doubt about the way that Mosley's mind was working; he had already tried to persuade the King to stay and fight. As he was later to write:

The issue is not whether or not we are pleased with the King's intentions to marry the American lady, but whether or not the King, under our constitution, has the right to choose to marry whatever woman he chose to marry, and the answer is clearly he had.

He went on to accuse the Cabinet of being 'guilty of a flagrant act of dictatorship in hustling Edward off his throne without consulting the people'.

The real explanation for the King choosing to leave quietly is easy to determine: he did not expect to be away very long. Taking comfort from the inherent handicaps of the man chosen to succeed him, the Duke had every reason to suppose that George VI would prove a weak and ineffectual ruler and many people shared this view. The former Duke of York suffered from a great many disadvantages that were expected to militate against him. Andrew Roberts, in his book *Eminent Churchillians*, published in 1994, paints a harsh, but accurate picture of the new King:

> The key to the unfortunate forays George VI made into governmental affairs is not to be found in any latent political views he may have held, but merely in his lack of cunning and intellectual ability. In his naval college exams at Osborne he came 68th out of 68 and at Dartmouth he was 61st out of 67. He had not wanted the job of King. He had a stammer and suffered from vertigo. His shyness was so acute that as a child he once sat in a darkened room rather than ask a servant to light a lamp. His various disadvantages encouraged a certain obstinacy and sometimes brought on what his family called 'gnashes' – tantrums which could blow up in a moment, often over some obscure point of dress or procedure.

Roberts also reveals that the King kept his private secretaries in the dark about political discussions he had, quoting his official biographer, Sir John Wheeler-Bennett, as telling a friend years later: 'The King was secretive and conceited. He kept things to himself as if to reassure himself that he [*the King*] knew something that you don't.'

The Duke of Windsor knew his brother's shortcomings and lack of training for the exacting role suddenly thrust upon him. He must have felt confident that when the time came to return he would have little difficulty in picking up the reins; he probably viewed his future role with a great deal of quiet satisfaction. As 'shadow King' he would be able to meet and discuss with whom he wished without incurring the direct sanctions of the politicians, who, if they felt it necessary to reprimand him, would have to do it through the King. This was hardly something likely to strike terror into the Duke's heart; his father, a strong character given to bawling out his sons in 'naval language', had little success in that direction, and his weak and pliable brother would be much easier to manipulate. The Duke could shrug off the duties and trappings of state, the ceremonial, the endless red boxes which he hated and had to be cajoled, practically forced, to deal with when he was King. All that would be someone else's problem. He could relax, enjoy himself in an endless round of parties, feel free to slip abroad whenever he and Wallis felt the mood take them. While showing all the outward trappings of a free and easy life he would retain the real power behind the throne, the head of the family of Windsor able to negotiate and work towards the future he wanted, using his trips abroad to meet with those he needed to influence and with whom he could enter into secret alliances. With that in mind there is little wonder that he failed to address the question of his future finances. He confidently expected to regain control of the family fortunes: he and his brother could arrange things between themselves. With this in mind it was not surprising that the Duke left the country in such a light-hearted mood. He was leaving on what he saw as a short holiday with his beloved Wallis and soon expected to return.

Meanwhile, in Britain things had begun to settle down, everyone was looking forward to the Coronation on 12 May, believing that a troubled period of history was behind them.

The story of Ernest's costs being paid and the handing over of £100,000 is described in John Parker's *King of Fools* and was widely believed at the time. The money was almost certainly routed through Armand Gregoire the French lawyer who acted for both Wallis and Ernest and was a confidant of the Duke. After the war Gregoire was arrested in California, extradited and sentenced by the French to hard labour for life on charges of being a Nazi collaborator. Ernest Simpson later tried to sue a women for libel when she repeated the popular story, but pressure was brought to persuade him to settle the matter quietly and not pursue it.

Chapter Eight

The Duke Joins His Nazi Friends

WHATEVER THOUGHTS were passing through the Duke's mind as he stepped ashore from HMS *Fury* when it docked at Boulogne he could hardly have anticipated the way in which the events of the next few weeks were to develop. Almost from the moment he arrived at the Schloss Enzesfeld, the burden he felt lifted from his shoulders was replaced by the great black dog of depression. His constant telephone calls to Wallis left him with a growing feeling that she was less than happy with the prospect of them spending the foreseeable future wandering around Europe with him stripped of his previous authority and much of his former prestige. Wallis had revelled in the adoration, the gaiety and, above all, the position of respect she had previously enjoyed as consort of the most powerful emperor on earth. Following in the wake of a former king reduced to the role of a country gentleman without a country held little attraction, and her unhappiness was compounded by the realisation that most of her former friends had abandoned her and, instead of maintaining contact, were busy jockeying for a position in the circle of the new King and Queen.

By the end of the 26 weeks he spent in Austria, frustration and anger had replaced any thoughts he might have had about a life free of, and away from, the affairs of state. There were a number of reasons for his misery. It was not just that time passed slowly or the fact that he and Wallis had begun to quarrel continuously, although this did little to help, it was the change in the attitude of his family and the Government in London that lay at the root of his troubles.

It quickly became apparent that the family, influenced by his mother (who, it was thought, brought her influence to bear on the new Queen), were not going to forgive him. In fact, their attitude towards him had already begun to harden. His constant phone calls convinced them that unless some way could be discovered to isolate him, he would continue to dominate events and his hand would be seen in everything they did. This was rather astute of them; they correctly anticipated the plans the Duke was harbouring and took steps to divert him. Despite Churchill's encouraging remarks, the Government, and in particular Chamberlain, who had replaced Baldwin as Prime Minister, was less than kindly disposed towards the Duke. The first blow came with the Government's decision not to grant the former monarch an income from the Civil List and thereby allowing him access to the public purse. The Duke saw this initially as a snub rather than a loss of income because he had agreed with his brother the King that he would make up any short-fall between what the Duke was voted under the Civil List and an annual income of £30,000 a year. However, when faced with the prospect of having to provide the entire amount the King began to prevaricate – a less than generous attitude considering the huge fortune he had unexpectedly inherited when he became King; indeed, it was considered rather mean and spiteful. It was believed that his mother's influence was behind the decision. The Duke decided it was time that he began to apply himself to the subject of his future finances. As King he had been one of the world's wealthiest men, and while by ordinary standards he was still rich, his fortune had been drastically reduced. The 4,000-acre ranch he owned in Canada was not much of an asset; it produced little if any income, but remained the only property he could claim to own. It was at this time that he suffered his most serious setback. His lawyers informed him that his income of £100,000 a year from the Duchy of Cornwall, which he had assumed would continue, would not in fact be made available. As Edward VIII he received nothing under the terms of George V's will, not because the late King was being vindictive but, assuming that his eldest son would inherit the income that belonged to the Crown, he left his money to others in the family.[1] Information on Royal inheritances is hard to come by (Royal wills are never published nor are they required to be lodged for probate) but there is little doubt that when Edward abdicated he was at least a billionaire. To find himself, even after the sale of Balmoral and Sandringham, suddenly worth less than £3,000,000 would have come as a great shock to a man habitually obsessed with money. With time on his hands the Duke was able to reflect on these and other problems. The frustration he suffered is clear from a study of his letters, together with the accounts of his incessant phone calls that have been allowed to become public. They mark a difficult time for both himself and Wallis during their six months' enforced separation, and forced her to call into question the wisdom of leaving England at the height of the crisis. On one occasion she seems to have let her guard drop; in a moment of weakness she wrote to a relative in America 'that leaving has probably cost me the chance of becoming Queen'.

It is highly revealing that J. Bryan III and Charles J.V. Murphy, who both met and collaborated with the Windsors (Bryan being asked by the Duchess to help write her autobiography, while Murphy worked with the Duke on his), writing in their book *The Windsor Story*, came to the conclusion that while the Duke was desperately in love with Wallis and his feelings were never to change, she on the other hand never really loved him. Certainly she never showed the sort of devotion that he lavished on her. His generosity towards her was unstinting. All through his life he acquired a reputation for meanness; it was said that during his time at the Schloss Enzesfeld he frequently played cards and, when he won, collected his winnings, but if he lost he would never offer to pay. Nevertheless his generosity towards Wallis was never in doubt and it has been estimated that during their lives together he spent, in today's value, in excess of £6,000,000 on items of jewellery for her in addition to that which he gave her from the Royal collection.

This is not likely to have been much compensation for Wallis who was trapped in a one-sided, loveless marriage. We are left with the feeling that this was a shallow woman with little in the way of foresight or understanding of where all her manipulating would lead her. She was driven by her need for excitement. She became intoxicated by the drama that her presence generated. To have to face the result of her intervention must have been a bitter realisation.

During this time, we have learnt from 'Fruity' Metcalfe that the Duke was speaking German and having constant disagreements with Wallis, a clear indication of the way things were affecting him. He was behaving badly and becoming difficult to live with and the Baron and Kitty de Rothschild had come to regret their generosity in inviting him to stay. He was an ungrateful and difficult house guest, he spent most of the day on the telephone, referring to it as his 'work', and not only contributing nothing to the cost of running the Schloss, but refusing to pay any of the bills he had run up locally. He became more churlish and ungrateful as time went on, a sure sign of his growing bitterness and unhappiness. Without question the refusal of the King to permit the Duchess to be granted the title 'Royal Highness' was the final humiliation. For many years this was regarded as the ultimate snub, a manifestation of the family's hatred for the Duchess and all that her manipulations had brought about. The Duke and Duchess certainly regarded it as such, but curiously we learn that it was not intended to be a snub directed at him, or so the Royal Family would have us believe and they have encouraged another explanation to be advanced. The person always thought of as being responsible for the title being withheld is the present Queen Mother. She has never denied this but has let it be known that the reason was not malicious, but simply pragmatic. The Duke is known to have wanted to give his new wife this honour to compensate her for all that she had given up. Several biographies of the Queen Mother, written long after the event, have attempted to explain away this seemingly vindictive reason behind the refusal to grant the title. It has been suggested that the true explanation is that the Royal Family believed that the marriage was doomed and would be short-lived and they were not anxious to allow Wallis to swan around the world being forever called Your Royal Highness, since once created the title could never have been withdrawn. While this may be true – the explanation that the title would be permanent was certainly correct – this reasoning took such a long time to emerge and seems so reasonable that if it were true it would surely have come out before. By the same token, the marriage of the Duke and Duchess was to last until his death on 29 May 1972. So surely, had the Royal Family wanted to show any compassion and remove any suspicion that there was no malice behind the withholding of the title, there would have been ample opportunity in the 35 years the couple remained married to have granted him his dearest wish. The refusal hurt him deeply and was to remain a bitter disappointment for the rest of his life.

It is clear that both the Royal Family and the State were less than generous to the Duke at this time. Parliament refused him a pension under the Civil List and the arguments with his brother George VI over money became extremely petty and did neither much credit.

While the true extent of the wranglings between the Duke and his family will never be revealed, there remains little doubt that it was during this period that the Royal Family effectively, for whatever reason, turned the Duke against his country. Whether deliberately or through mishandling the situation, they turned a man who could possibly have been working to a secret agenda aimed at social reform and world peace into a powerful enemy of the State. The fact that some of his ideas were misplaced and the ways he sought to bring about social change were mistaken (in that he sought to align himself with a corrupt and inherently evil regime) were largely irrelevant in the early months of his exile. His former assistance over the Rhineland invasion and the passing on of information to Ribbentrop via Wallis, and what can now only be seen as treason carried out on behalf of Nazi Germany, was not so far removed from official Government policy of the day. His assistance to Hitler was a grave mistake, but in the final analysis his treachery only produced the same result as if Edward had not interfered. The main reason Hitler went into the Rhineland unopposed and remained there was inaction by the British and French Governments whose refusal to act positively only encouraged him. This was at a time when those opposed to the Duke of Windsor – Baldwin, Halifax, Chamberlain and, eventually, his own family – were all speaking out on behalf of appeasement with Nazi Germany.

It cannot be coincidence that during the constitutional troubles that drove him to abdicate his two staunchest supporters were Churchill and Lord Beaverbrook, whose later records as war leaders and patriots need no defence; they were two men who correctly anticipated the events that were to follow and were never lulled into a false sense of security by the demonic Hitler. Would it be too fanciful to imagine that between the Duke and these two supporters there was a meeting of minds and a clear understanding of the way that things were heading in Europe? It is clear on balance that the Duke also recognised the danger from Hitler. His method of containing that danger until the time of his marriage was to influence by co-operation rather than outright opposition. Sadly this was all to change.

The British Establishment's humiliation of the Duke drove him into the hands of those who had formerly courted him and sought to influence him and who were still suffering the disappointment of losing what they had come to regard as a powerful ally. That period between 1936 and 1940 when the Duke and Duchess of Windsor were forced to leave Europe for the Bahamas was a time of great upheaval; there can be little doubt whatever that during the months around the time of their marriage in 1937 the Duke and Duchess were drawn into co-operation with the Nazis. Their conduct was a great deal more sinister than we have been led to believe. With devastating clarity they began to see that quitting Britain and giving up the throne had been a dreadful mistake and something they had come to live to regret. A disillusioned and disappointed man robbed of his future, the Duke was quite naturally drawn to try and re-examine and attempt to redress the mistakes that had cost him his inheritance. The British Government had also made a major error in treating him so badly;

had they found something for him to do and watched him carefully they could have neutralised a Nazi strategy that almost came off. If it had, the outcome for Britain would have been very different. Instead, they allowed the former King to wander off abroad believing that his role on the world stage was over. Those in power expected this bitter and humiliated couple to gradually retreat more and more into the background, to live out their days in France and not bother anyone. Content that they had successfully fought off a challenge to their right to govern and had acquired themselves a King who would behave and go along with all their decisions, the politicians forged ahead, whether it was in the country's interest or not.

However, even before the honeymoon was over, events had started that would overtake the Duke. He found himself drawn into a disgraceful period of his life in which he was to play a significant part. Many years later, in 1986, following the death of the Duchess at the age of 90 in the house they shared in Paris, it was discovered that, apart from photographs of their wedding, there was nothing to remind anyone of this period of their life leading up to their withdrawal from Europe in 1940. When the house was opened up following its acquisition by Mohamed Al Fayed it was discovered that, despite the thousands of photographs and memorabilia of their life together, there was no record of what they did during this period following their marriage and their leaving Europe in 1940 to remind them of their infamy. They, in keeping with the British Royal Family and British Government, wanted to pretend that what really happened never took place and went to enormous trouble to ensure that the world would never learn the truth. Fortunately for history, they failed.

Chapter Nine

The Plot is Hatched

BY 1937 THE CLOUDS OF WAR had begun to gather over Europe, and while the Governments of France and Britain were still clinging doggedly to their official policy of appeasement, there were signs that some people were slowly beginning to wake up to the threat posed by Hitler's Germany. The first indications of a change in attitude had already started to appear.

The British Government, which had moved rapidly to reduce spending on defence following the 1918 armistice, began to realise that the intelligence services, the first victims of a savage rundown, now needed to be expanded and to have their operations extended. The Cabinet became alarmed at the rumours coming out of Germany of reports of a sizeable German air force, contrary to the terms of the Treaty of Versailles. Accurate information was hard to come by and this lack of hard evidence only served to increase the pressure on the Cabinet to increase intelligence gathering. On 17 April it instructed the Ministerial Committee on Defence Policy and Requirements to investigate the claims about the numbers of pilots and planes Germany actually possessed. Predictably, and in keeping with bureaucratic tradition, the committee's first decision was to suggest that more money was needed to enable the various security services to operate more effectively. As a result, the Foreign Office and Treasury were instructed to provide funding, which in ministerial jargon meant fiddling the books to divert non-secret funds and make them available for clandestine purposes. A handful of senior ministers, without the arrangements ever coming before Parliament for approval, more than doubled the budget in the years between 1935 and 1937 and in addition a great deal of money already allocated under the general umbrella of passport control and customs and excise operations was diverted to fund intelligence gathering. One of the results of all this increased activity was to enable the various intelligence agencies to observe the movements of various people suspected of being pro-Nazi sympathisers and who were in contact with the Third Reich both

99

in Britain and on the Continent. It was during one of these routine surveillance operations that a remarkable series of incidents was observed.

Paris in the late Thirties, in keeping with other European cities, was alive with intrigue. MI5 was routinely observing the comings and goings of a number of important figures who were suspected of having links with Nazi Germany when they stumbled on an unusual meeting. British agents watching could hardly believe their eyes and when they reported their findings to London it caused those in control to begin to wonder what was going on.

The incident occurred only a few days after the Duke and Duchess of Windsor returned from their three-month honeymoon, having spent the last few weeks at a Hungarian hunting lodge belonging to their friend Charles Bedaux. The couple had now returned to Paris and moved into an apartment at the Hotel Meurice while looking for a more permanent home.

Among those being closely watched were Charles Bedaux, together with a man with whom he had been seen on several occasions, namely Errol Flynn, the film star. Both were known to have connections with Berlin and to have acted on behalf of the Nazis and while their sympathies and contact with the Nazis were known to the intelligence community, the degree of their involvement was yet to be fully realised.

There was an additional reason why MI5 was taking an interest in Flynn. They suspected (without foundation, as it turned out) that in addition to working for the Germans, he was active in raising funds on behalf of the IRA. Unbeknown to the British, American intelligence was also taking a keen interest in Flynn, who had just returned from Spain where he had been in contact with a number of Fascist organisations. In what started as a routine operation Flynn was watched as he caught a train for Berlin where it came as no surprise when he was seen in the company of a well-known Nazi agent. Arriving in Berlin, the mystery began to deepen. To the surprise of those following him, Flynn was seen three days later in the company of Rudolf Hess, the deputy Führer, and Martin Bormann, Hitler's secretary.

Before anyone in London could speculate as to what possible explanation could lay behind this strange meeting, events moved swiftly on. The agents trailing Flynn were amazed to discover that the three men boarded a train and travelled back to Paris together. Clearly something important was afoot. When the train arrived, the two senior Nazis and Flynn went directly to the Hotel Meurice where, to the disbelief of those watching, they were cordially received by the Duke of Windsor and invited into his suite.

Several sources have revealed that this meeting took place but previous writers seem to have dismissed its importance by suggesting that its purpose was to discuss the forthcoming visit by the Duke and Duchess to Germany where it was planned they would meet Hitler. This is pure supposition; there is no way in which anyone can have learned what was discussed. No record of this meeting has ever been discovered. After the war a search among the captured German documents revealed no trace. If the Duke kept a record we can safely assume that it remains safely hidden away in the Round Tower at Windsor Castle with the rest of his papers or has long since been destroyed.

However, a clue as to what was discussed has survived. The occasion clearly made an impression on Hess who asked for a private audience with the Duke following the meeting. Hess recorded his impressions of that meeting for Hitler, and from this we can gain some idea of the subject of their discussions. 'The Duke was proud of his German blood . . . was more German than British . . . keenly interested in the development of the Third Reich.' This must have given Hitler a warm glow of satisfaction, especially when his report added, 'There is no need to lose a single German life in invading Britain. The Duke and his clever wife will deliver the goods.'[1]

It isn't difficult to imagine the reaction in Whitehall or at the Palace to the reports of this curious meeting. Apart from everything else the very mention of the name Charles Bedaux was sufficient to set the alarm bells ringing. MI5 and the Palace were becoming more than a little concerned at the way Bedaux appeared to have integrated himself with the Duke and Duchess of Windsor. Bedaux, a man of great energy, had first contacted Wallis while she was in the South of France staying at Lou Viei, the home of Herman Rodgers, an American friend. Bedaux had wasted little time. The first reference to his involvement came on 12 December in the first letter Wallis wrote to the Duke following his arrival at the Schloss Enzesfeld:

Darling,

My heart is full of love for you and the agony of not being able to see you after all you have been through is pathetic. At the moment we have the whole world against us and our love – so we can't afford to move about very much and must simply sit and face the dreary months ahead and I think I will have to stay here. It may be safer than moving and a house is more protection than a hotel from the press and the fanatics.[2]

She goes on to discuss several alternatives where the Duke might stay and mentions: 'A man called Bedaux – Americans – have offered their place to you. It is near Tours. The Rodgers say it is lovely.' At this stage there was no suggestion that this might be used as the venue for the Duke and Duchess's wedding. The subject had not been considered; that would come later. Wallis was suggesting it as somewhere for the Duke to stay until her divorce was absolute.

Several months were to pass but we can assume that Bedaux kept in touch and left the offer of his villa open. The Chateau de Candé, his impressive restored residence near Tours, was eventually chosen by the couple as the venue for their marriage which took place on 3 June. Bedaux also offered the Duke and Duchess his hunting lodge in Hungary for their honeymoon and the couple spent the last three weeks there before moving to the Hotel Meurice. It was reported by those maintaining a watch on the Duke that Charles Bedaux had visited them while they were in Hungary. It had become obvious that Bedaux was becoming very close but what wasn't known is what Bedaux hoped to gain in return for all this display of generosity.

Bedaux was a naturalised American who had returned to Europe to represent a group of American companies with interests in France and Germany who were anxious to protect their sizeable investments in the event of war breaking out between the two countries. It seems strange that Bedaux's real intentions have not been more closely scrutinised. Many previous writers have suggested that Bedaux's desire to ingratiate himself with the Duke was simply to improve his personal standing with members of the Third Reich. While it is true that Bedaux was certainly anxious to co-operate with Hitler and his ministers, this was not his primary intention in getting the Duke of Windsor involved in his affairs. Whatever his motive, his task was simplified by the failure of the various Government departments to co-ordinate their activities. In a classic case of the right hand not knowing what the left was doing, the Government agencies concerned assumed that someone must have checked on Bedaux; nobody had. Everyone, including the Palace, decided that he must have been checked and found satisfactory. By the time it was realised what a dangerous man he was, it was too late. Ironically, it was George VI who handed Bedaux his greatest opportunity to ingratiate himself with the

Duke. The Duke assumed that he would need his brother's permission for the venue of his marriage, as he anticipated that even if the King and Queen would not attend then several other members of the family would, and therefore the place chosen would require the King's formal blessing. He was to be disappointed – none of the family put in an appearance. The Duke and Duchess favoured a villa called 'La Cröe' in Antibes but the cautious King, remembering the displeasure felt within the family over the couple's ill-advised trip in 1935, decided that anything that took place on the French Riviera would create an unfavourable impression. He believed the area presented an unfortunate image, regarded by many as a playground of the idle rich where the endless rounds of parties and reckless living smacked of decadence. Consequently the King refused to give 'La Cröe' his blessing and in doing so he played directly into the hands of the devious Bedaux who had placed the Chateau de Candé at the Windsors' disposal. The couple, who had never seen it, accepted. Bedaux was delighted, knowing that the reaction this would have in Berlin would increase his standing at a time when he was anxious to ingratiate himself with the Nazi regime; they had confiscated a number of his businesses and he was trying to negotiate their return.

Charles Bedaux was a fascinating character whose part in this story provides the first link between what was happening in Europe and what eventually took place in the United States. Born in France, Bedaux emigrated to the United States in 1907 after serving in the French Foreign Legion. In 1917 he became an American citizen. When he first arrived he found work on the construction of the tunnels being built in the clay under New York, during which time he developed the 'Bedaux System', which was an early form of work study. It consisted of dividing every hour into 60 'Bedaux Units' which hardly seems very original. The system involved timing each individual operation and allocating a number of these units to each task. Workers who carried out the work in less than the allotted time were rewarded, any who failed were penalised. Bedaux managed to scrape together enough money to set himself up in business and was retained by some of the largest companies in America who were anxious to introduce his methods into their factories. These included IG, ITT, Standard Oil, General Motors, Ford and Stirling Products. His revolutionary methods, regarded by the labour unions as a means by which employers could force down wages, were to result in frequent strikes. Despite his unpopularity he was successful and amassed a huge personal fortune. He owned properties in Scotland and

North Africa, an estate in North Carolina as well as several magnificent houses in Europe.

While Bedaux was employed to protect the interests of his American clients, he was also working for himself. Totally devoted to self-interest, he was eventually to be highly regarded by the German High Command and the Vichy Government of France. The extent of his influence with the Third Reich placed him in a unique position to cultivate the friendship of the Duke of Windsor and act as a go-between.

Bedaux's life is a fascinating one. It has been well documented by others and does not need to be explored here, but his part in whatever was planned that day at the Hotel Meurice is not immediately clear. We shall see he remained in Europe and seems to have continued with his operations on his own behalf and that of his American clients. The real clue to what was discussed lies with Errol Flynn. To discover the outcome of that meeting it is necessary to follow his movements over the next few years.

Chapter Ten

The Visit to Meet Hitler

THERE ARE SEVERAL curious aspects of the meeting at the Hotel Meurice that need to be examined; it would be no exaggeration to suggest that it proved a turning point in the relationship between the former King and the Third Reich. The fact that it took place at all demonstrates that the Nazis, instead of abandoning the Duke as it appeared they had, were back in contact and adopting a more high-level approach. This was the point when events took on a new and sinister turn. The meeting was of vital importance and cannot be explained away as several previous commentators have done.

Up to that point the Nazis had made all their contacts with the Duke through emissaries – de Ropp and Saxe-Coburg-Gotha seem to have confined themselves to simply persuading him to maintain his pro-German stance and to use his influence to make sure that the British Government remained kindly disposed to Hitler and the Fascist Government of Germany. Now all that changed.

There is no evidence of any contact between the Nazis and the Duke in the days immediately before the Abdication or during the time that he spent alone in Austria. This would appear reasonable: it would come as no surprise to discover that the Nazis had written him off, concluding that the Duke was no longer in a position of influence. While in propaganda terms his support might still have had more value, in view of his changed circumstances they realised that anything he said would gradually have less and less authority. The Nazis would have kept abreast of developments. They well knew the situation that had developed between him, his family and the British Government, who were all trying to dissociate themselves from the former King, and would have correctly assumed that the British were anxious to wash their hands of him. They would therefore have decided that his value to Germany was likely to prove fairly marginal.

Against this background what possible explanation can there

be for the visit to his hotel by two of the most powerful men in the Nazi leadership? Why had the Duke suddenly become the object of attention of two high-ranking Nazis who had obviously decided that what they needed to discuss was so important that they were prepared to travel to Paris expressly for the purpose? It might be that the two Nazis simply wanted to appraise themselves of the situation in Britain, to get the benefit of the Duke's opinion about many of the views held by leading figures in Britain, and preferred to have them at first hand rather than to allow members of the diplomatic service to meet with the Duke and relay the information to Berlin.

There had never been any contact at this level before, but there was a perfectly reasonable explanation. While he remained King, the Duke could not have met them without the permission of the Prime Minister who, not unnaturally, would have wanted to be advised of the purpose of the visit and would in all probability, assuming he was willing to allow it to take place at all, have insisted that the Foreign Secretary be present during any discussions. Ribbentrop had been in contact with the former King – he was known to have visited the 'Fort' frequently – but he was not trusted with anything important and was treated as little more than a messenger for Hitler. Now with a dramatic change in the Duke's circumstances it was reasonable that any contact between the Duke and the Nazis could be carried out on a more direct basis – the need to rely on low-key emissaries was over.

However, there is a flaw in this explanation: the Duke had already agreed to visit Germany, where he would inevitably have met a number of leading Nazis including Hess. Had there been any wish to discuss the situation in England, or to be updated, Hess or Bormann would not have had long to wait. Within two weeks the Duke would be in Berlin where there would be ample opportunity to raise any topic. It seems inconceivable that Hess or Bormann would travel to Paris and risk drawing attention to themselves to discuss something they could so easily have raised in the comfort of their own drawing-room or over the port after dinner.

The fact that it was Hess, the deputy Führer, who in 1938 was still highly regarded by Hitler and other members of the party, together with Martin Bormann who attended the Paris meeting makes it highly significant. Bormann was also powerful in the party – history would have to wait until after the war for his true role to be understood. Up until the time of Hitler's death Bormann was simply regarded as an efficient, hard-working and devoted secretary to the Führer, but when his true role was established it became clear that he had been a great deal more. Many writers and historians who have studied the role of the Nazi leaders now all agree that Bormann was the driving force behind Hitler, a clever calculating man who had an almost Machiavellian control over his leader, to whom he remained loyal until the end. It was Bormann and the equally supportive Goebbels who remained faithful and stayed to supervise the funeral pyre on which their leader's body was dispatched to the flames rather than allow it to be paraded through the streets in triumph by an advancing Russian Army. Bormann had previously served a term in prison for complicity in a political murder: he was regarded with understandable trepidation by all the other members of the party. Although his rise to power made him a very influential figure, throughout his life he preferred to remain in the background, content to manipulate those who craved the limelight. He, more than anyone, was privy to everything that was going on in the mind of his leader. The very fact that the two most powerful men in the party travelled to Paris indicates that some important development was being discussed and that it would have had the Führer's full support.

The presence of Bedaux and Flynn only serves to add to the mystery, but the very fact that they were there at all provides a sure indication that they had some part in whatever was being planned. Later it will be seen that their presence was crucial and would eventually provide the lead to what was afoot. The fact that Bedaux was there might be explained away: he had established himself as the contact man and had demonstrated to the Nazis that he could manipulate the Duke, a situation he had assiduously worked to achieve. However, there is no evidence that he had previously had any contact at this level. Flynn's presence on the other hand is not so easy to explain away.

To understand what was going on it is first necessary to dispel the explanation that has previously been advanced for this meeting. Several writers have suggested that the purpose of this unusual gathering was in some way connected with the proposed visit of the Duke and Duchess to Germany and their subsequent meeting with Hitler. This can be ruled out; the arrangements for that visit which was allegedly for the purpose of studying housing conditions in Germany had already been made. In any event the making of such arrangements were not sufficiently important to warrant bringing these two high-ranking Nazis to Paris. All the arrangements for the Berlin visit had been made some weeks before. The job of escorting the Duke and Duchess had been given to the infamous Dr Ley, the Nazi Minister of Labour. The suggestion that led to the visit had come from the devious Bedaux during the time that the Duke and Duchess were still on honeymoon. Bedaux had gone to Germany to discuss the return of his businesses that had been commandeered by the Nazis and is known to have initially broached the subject of a visit with Dr Hjalmar Schachts, the Nazi financial genius. As a result of their various negotiations, Schachts authorised the businesses previously confiscated to be returned on two conditions. One was that Bedaux's operations would in the future come under the control of Dr Robert Ley's Labour Front and the other was that Bedaux should contribute $50,000 to the National Socialist Party, a thinly concealed bribe. Bedaux and Dr Ley subsequently agreed that a visit by the Duke and Duchess to Germany would be a huge propaganda coup and Dr Ley not only gave it his support but suggested that the Duke and Duchess meet Adolf Hitler. Some time in early June Bedaux travelled to Austria where the Duke and Duchess were honeymooning at Schloss Wasserleonburg and was able to persuade the Duke to agree to take part in the visit. Following this he again contacted Dr Ley who proceeded to make all the arrangements for the trip. The Duke was later to recall this in his memoirs:

> My recollection is that Bedaux was enthusiastic about the splendid things that I would find in Germany. However, he had gone no further than hint to German friends that I would welcome an opportunity to see for myself how well the country was doing under National Socialism. He talked mostly about Dr Schachts's grasp of monetary theory, a subject that fascinated Bedaux. I remember his explaining to me a scheme for having the Bedaux work unit adopted as an international unit of value, as an alternative to gold. It was all over my head. He did advance a new thought, though, during his talk. It was that if our tour ever came off, I should broaden it to take in different segments of German industry as well as the latest housing developments . . . I saw nothing wrong in having a look at the new factories, but was wholly ignorant of the politics and economics of labour. I did know something about housing.[1]

This tends to indicate that the Duke was ambivalent about the visit and what it might achieve or why it had been arranged. This cannot have been the case previously. When Prince of Wales, the Duke had expressed a desire to meet Hitler but had abandoned the idea on the orders of George V. The Duke's memoirs are not a very reliable source: written many years later, they deliberately tried to sanitise and gloss over the period of his contact with Nazi

Germany. There remains no question that it was the prospect of meeting Hitler that was the attraction. Whatever the Duke thought, Bedaux was in no doubt. He was already following a clear strategy. His aim had always been to ingratiate himself with the Duke and demonstrate that he could manipulate him to go along with any of his intrigues. The purpose was fairly transparent: he was sending out a clear sign that anyone who wanted to involve the Duke in anything needed to include Bedaux in those plans. This went a lot further than wanting to ingratiate himself with the Nazis. It was equally important that he should impress his various powerful clients in America as that held out the promise of potential profit. The Nazis welcomed the proposed visit to Germany. It was a good opportunity to demonstrate to anyone in Britain who was less than enthusiastic about the Nazi cause that the former King was not only prepared to meet them but anxious to demonstrate his enthusiasm for the improved social conditions that were a result of the rising prosperity which accompanied Fascism.

It is fairly easy to establish that the arrangements for the Duke's visit to Germany following Bedaux's suggestion were all made well before the Duke and Duchess returned from their honeymoon. This confirms that the meeting at the Hotel Meurice was totally unconnected with the visit to Germany and another reason must be found. Unfortunately, we have very little to go on. We can only deduce what was discussed from those scraps of evidence in Hess's report to Hitler and from the subsequent actions of those who attended. What are we to make of the remark that 'there is no need to lose a single German life in invading Britain. The Duke and his clever wife will deliver the goods'? What goods? What did Hess imagine that the Duke and Duchess were in a position to deliver? Homeless, living in a hotel in a foreign country, at odds with the Royal Family, forced out by a hostile Government and with most of their former friends now trying to distance themselves, anything they were in a position to deliver was, on the face of it, limited.

However, this meeting must not be dismissed. To have reported its outcome in such glowing terms to his leader meant that Hess believed it had been a success. The only explanation that can be placed on his enthusiastic remarks is that Hess confidently expected that the couple's circumstances were about to change dramatically. Hess's reported comments to Hitler refer specifically to the invasion of Britain, and the only way the Duke and Duchess could influence anything that would result in an unopposed landing was to persuade the British people not to resist such a move. To do this they would have to return: the idea that they could influence events from France could not have been seen as a serious option. Any attempt would have only further inflamed the King and angered the Government of Britain, and the probable outcome would have been a backlash against the Duke which would have reduced his already limited support to zero.

The only explanation that fits the facts is that Hess was anticipating a time when the Duke would regain his position of influence and be able to use it in Germany's favour.

At this point in the investigation we have the advantage of hindsight. We know that on many occasions the Nazis wanted to assist the Duke of Windsor to regain the British throne; there are innumerable references to this suggestion. The existence of a formal agreement has long been suspected but never been discovered. The nearest that exists is a memorandum sent on 3 May 1941 by J. Edgar Hoover to President Roosevelt's secretary, Major General P. Watson, which read:

> Information has been received at this Bureau from a source that is socially prominent and known to be in touch with some of the people involved, but for whom we cannot vouch, to the effect that Joseph P. Kennedy, the former Ambassador to England, and Ben Smith, the Wall Street operator, for some time in the past had a meeting with Goering in Vichy France and that thereafter Kennedy and Smith had donated a considerable amount of money to the German cause. They are both described as anti-British and pro-German.
>
> This same source of information advised that it is reported that the Duke of Windsor entered into an agreement to the effect that if Germany was victorious in the war, Herman Goering through his control of the army would overthrow Hitler and would therefore install the Duke of Windsor as King of England. This information concerning the Windsors is said to have originated from Allen McIntosh, a personal friend of the Duke of Windsor who made the arrangements for the entertainment of the Windsors when they were in Miami recently.[2]

That the Duke was prepared to discuss his return to England with Goering is not particularly important. It has long been suspected that he probably discussed it with several Nazi leaders. Equally it should come as no surprise that Goering was prepared to plot against Hitler – he realised that many of his leader's decisions were leading Germany towards eventual defeat. Goering was well aware that by launching the attack on Russia before dealing with the British Hitler had made a colossal mistake. From that point onwards he began to look for ways to usurp him. The J. Edgar Hoover memorandum only confirmed that he had met with the Duke and given him an assurance that if Goering took over he proposed to follow the policy started by Hess and Bormann in 1937.

We know that both Hess and Bormann were fervent advocates of Hitler's policy, which all the Nazi leaders slavishly supported until it became obvious in the summer of 1940 that it was never going to be successful, namely that Britain and Germany should form an alliance and join in a pact to defeat Communism. This remained the central plank of Nazi foreign policy until late 1940 when, with great reluctance, it was finally abandoned due mainly to the appointment of Churchill as Prime Minister. Hitler realised that the British under their new leader were not going to do anything but fight to the death.

It is difficult to suggest any interpretation other than a return to England by the Duke which could have resulted from the meeting at the Hotel Meurice that day in early September. Considering how the Duke and Duchess were feeling totally abandoned, it seems that Hess and Bormann had picked a propitious time to suggest a scheme to the Duke and there seems little doubt that they found him more than receptive to such an idea. The couple were very bitter about everything. In their current frame of mind it would not have been that difficult, particularly in the light of his previous admiration and support for Fascism, for the Duke to allow himself to be seduced by such an outrageous plan.

If we return to *The Windsor Story* we read in the chapter entitled 'An Embittered Honeymoon' how things had not gone well for the couple. The Duke had finally accepted that his family would have done anything to prevent his return and the Duchess had come to believe that the family would never accept her. The Duchess is reported to have said: 'The Duke and I had a long talk about how best to cope with the situation. Our decision was to make a life for ourselves as if his family didn't exist.'

These simple sentences sum up how they both felt, and add up to a realisation that their life had become a total disaster. The depression that had become more acute during the honeymoon had finally destroyed any dream they had of being welcomed back to Britain. 'The love affair of the century' was dead – they had run out of options, the future looked bleak. Then, when they were at their lowest ebb, along came Hess and Bormann with a plan to reverse everything that had happened and allow the Duke to rewrite history. There is little wonder he welcomed them to his suite. The timing was perfect, the Duke must have thought it was divine intervention to discover a way to regain his throne with his wife at his side and the most powerful military machine in the world at his back. Nothing could stop him.

To accept that this was what was discussed at the Hotel Meurice, we must discover whether there is any additional evidence. As has been seen, this can only come from the actions of the people who attended this incredible meeting. Apart from the Duke, whose role was obviously going to be passive, forced to play a waiting game, who would make the next move? The two senior Nazi figures, while they were deeply involved, were hardly planning this to be an operation the Germans intended to carry out, otherwise why should they have allowed Bedaux and, more importantly, Flynn to have sat in on what was clearly intended to be a highly secret meeting.

Hitler was unquestionably the mastermind behind the scheme being advanced by his two most trusted lieutenants. He would continue to try and convince the world that all he wanted was peace and that he had no intention of coming into conflict with anyone, while all the time continuing to build up his forces for war. His public stance between 1937 and September 1939 when he marched into Poland is well known. To discover what was planned we must turn our attention to Bedaux and Flynn. Bedaux does not seem to have done anything out of character. Following the meeting he made a short trip to America, the purpose of which will be explored later, and on his return he continued to work with the Nazis in Europe. During the next two years, he was to become active in ingratiating himself with the Vichy opposition in France working to undermine the resistance of the elected Government of Premier Deladier, ready for the day when the Nazis would invade. There is no record of any further meetings with his friend Flynn in the months that followed, so it can safely be assumed that for the time being his part was over. Having set up the initial meeting he devoted his energies to his various other enterprises, leaving the finer details of the plot to his partner, the man who was to become the driving force, Errol Flynn.

Following the meeting Flynn returned to America and did not leave there until he had completed the shooting of *The Adventures of Robin Hood*. The suggestion that Flynn was the central player in the conspiracy is supported when we examine how it was that he came to be in Paris during 1937. Flynn was staying at the Hotel Plaza Athenée in a suite that had been provided by Warner Brothers following the company's move to extricate him from Spain. Using their considerable political influence, they arranged for their Spanish agent to get Flynn out, send him to Paris and remain there until arrangements were made to send him back to Hollywood and start his next picture. This explains why Hess and Bormann couldn't wait until the Duke travelled to Germany to discuss the plot. Time was of the essence if Flynn was to be involved, for days later he was destined to return to Hollywood. This alone indicates that Flynn and his contacts were vital to the success of the scheme – why else would his travel arrangements dictate the agenda?

Whatever was planned nothing seems to have occurred during the remainder of 1937. While it is inevitable that Hess was gathering information to enable the plan to be put into operation, nothing dramatic occurred. This was not surprising, nor was it strange that details of the plot did not come to light during the examination of the Nazi records after the war. Such was the intense secrecy of the operation that details were known only to the Duke, Hitler and the four who attended the meeting.

There was a very good reason for this. The Nazis were aware of the high risk strategy of what they were contemplating and while they probably realised that time was not crucial, they needed to move more with caution than with speed; the risks were tremendous. We know from captured German records that war, when it came, arrived sooner than Hitler anticipated. Several reliable sources have established that Hitler had predicted (and would have preferred) that he could have waited until late 1942 or early 1943 before he found himself at war with France. During the next two years Hitler would play the 'cat and mouse' game as only he knew how. Even as late as the beginning of September 1938 he was drawn to remark, 'Heaven has fallen on me', on learning that Chamberlain was coming to see him.[3] To have the Prime Minister of the greatest empire in the world coming on his hands and knees to seek peace was a great boost to his ego. However, we now know that events overtook him and he was forced to bring his plans forward.

It can only be speculation as to what Hitler had in mind when he embarked on the task of replacing the King with the Duke of Windsor. It has always been known that he wanted to effect an alliance, but had he managed to return the Duke he would have destabilised the British Government and that would have led to civil war, or the new King would have been able to persuade a new Government not to oppose Hitler but negotiate an alliance. Whatever the outcome it would have given Britain more important things to think about and turned their attention away from what was happening in Europe. Whatever happened, the Nazis would have wanted to ensure they were seen not to have anything to do with it, which explains the involvement of Errol Flynn. Flynn was riding on something of a high. Due to the success of his films he was not only able to greatly increase his salary, but was also able to arrange to have more time off between films. What nobody had yet realised was that he was using his not inconsiderable talent to work on behalf of the Nazis. The very fact that Flynn was in Paris was as a result of his part in the Spanish Civil War. What he did in Spain is still something of a mystery and even over the years little has been discovered, but there is no doubt that he was mixed up in something on behalf of the Nazis when it was revealed that he had been in contact with Gestapo personnel working in Spain. This period of his life need not concern us. The truth, if it could be discovered, would probably provide a fascinating study in itself. However, what is relevant is what Flynn subsequently did following being seen by British intelligence in the company of the Duke of Windsor. Flynn was not there to meet Hess or Bormann – he had met them days before in Berlin, he had accompanied them when they travelled to Paris. No, whatever was going on, the Duke and Flynn were central to something. All the evidence points to some sort of plot being hatched.

To give serious consideration to the existence of a plot in 1937 to put the Duke of Windsor back on the British throne it is necessary to establish how it was to be done. The idea that Hess should consider returning the Duke to the British throne and that it would provide the key to success of a policy that was close to the heart is not fanciful. Of all the German leaders he fervently believed that world peace was dependent on the defeat of Communism. Hess was the architect of 'Operation Barbarrosa', the plan to invade Russia. It was a part of the dream that he and Hitler had shared and discussed back in 1924; it was their ultimate aim. Not only does it form the central theme of *Mein Kampf* but a study of this incredible book also reveals that both Hitler and Hess were alive to the danger and folly of attempting to fight on two fronts and what problems the German Army would face if it embarked on a Russian campaign before they dealt with the British. Hitler had gone so far as to vow that this was something he would never allow to happen. Hess was even more determined.

However, keeping Britain out of the war was simply the first step; with the Duke's backing following his return they both hoped to elicit British support for the defeat of Communism, but even failing that, they wished to keep Britain out of the war until they had dealt with Russia. Additionally, they knew that it was highly unlikely that France would go to war without Britain and there was the added advantage that America was almost certain to remain neutral. The meeting at the Hotel Meurice must have left Hess confident that the first step had been taken in a plan to neutralise any danger posed by Britain.

The advantages offered by such a plot would have solved almost every problem that faced German foreign policy. The prize on offer was immense. Had the plot conceived at the Hotel Meurice been successful the future of the world would have unquestionably changed. With no doubt about its attractions, Flynn had been tasked with the job of bringing it about. What did he do next?

Chapter Eleven

Flynn Makes Plans

SEVERAL DAYS AFTER the meeting, Flynn together with his wife, Lili Damita, with whom he had previously become estranged but was now temporarily reconciled, returned to America to continue with their respective film careers. Plans were well advanced to begin filming what was to prove his greatest role. *The Adventures of Robin Hood*, a lavish, spectacular production that would rightly ensure Flynn's place in the history of the silver screen. Filming began at the end of September with Flynn playing the title role. If the events that occurred at the Hotel Meurice are to be believed then the irony of the situation must have appealed to his well-developed sense of mischief. As with so many of Warner Brothers productions of the period, the film's plot paid scant attention to historical accuracy, and with what he had discussed in Paris still fresh in his mind Flynn must have regarded his new film as having a rather familiar ring about it. *The Adventures of Robin Hood* was loosely based on the legend of the English outlaw and recounts how the evil Prince John, the King's brother, was attempting to steal the throne of England from the rightful King Richard I. The wicked John was foiled and defeated by Robin Hood. The Crown of England was preserved for King Richard 'The Lionheart' who had gone abroad to fight in the Crusades having turned his back on his country and its people. This legendary story and several instances that form part of the dialogue must have caused Flynn great amusement. During the banqueting scene, shortly after the film opens, there is an exchange between Flynn and Olivia de Havilland, who played Maid Marion, when she interrupts Robin, who is being highly critical of the wicked John:

> *Maid Marion*: Sir, you speak treason.
> *Robin (with wicked grin)*: Fluently.

Whether this was in the original script or was suggested by Flynn has never been revealed, but it is the kind of remark he would have enjoyed making. His real, off-screen treason, had it become known, would have certainly found him arrested, made to face trial and probably hung as a traitor. Fortunately for him, the true extent of his duplicity was not discovered until after his death in 1951.

The Adventures of Robin Hood was completed on 27 January 1938 and Flynn began to devote himself to his real-life role in the affairs of two modern Kings of England in whose life he had been cast to play a part. Kept busy in America he had to wait until May before he could return to Europe and put the next part of the scheme in place.

Errol Flynn was a highly complex character who led a complicated and, to use a well-worn cliché, 'a larger than life' existence, but his lifestyle more than that of anyone else deserved this description. His entire life, both private and professional, was a restless search for excitement. As an actor he often proved difficult to handle and drove all who tried to work with him to despair. Ironically, it was Michael Curtiz, the Hungarian producer hated by Flynn, and whose feelings towards Flynn were little short of outright contempt, who was responsible for making Flynn's best films, those for which he will always be remembered. During his time as a film actor Flynn earned vast sums of money, yet he was always in financial trouble. His problem was that he never really grew up; apart from a dark side to his character that led him to get involved in espionage, his behaviour resembled that of an adolescent who had failed to mature and seemed unable to avoid the trouble that followed him wherever he went. Throughout his turbulent life he never showed any responsibility or remorse for his often disgusting behaviour. He had a passion for practical jokes, and a very cruel streak, particularly in his attitude towards animals. Flynn was completely amoral, his entire life was driven by the demands of his tremendous ego which became manifest in his 'to hell with everyone' attitude. Before, and on a number of occasions after he became involved in films, his quest for adventure led him into drug-running, gun and gold smuggling, work as a gold prospector, slave trader and eventually involvement in international crime. A study of his life leaves one with a feeling that he was incapable of any compassion for any living thing, which owes its origins to his rather unhappy childhood. All through his life Flynn could not shake off this feeling. Believing he was not loved made him self-centred and led him to think that if he was to exist he needed to fight the world.

There are strong indications that when he became absorbed in his life as a film star he gradually lost the ability to distinguish between reality and the make-believe world in which he found himself. To support this, a passage taken from his autobiography is particularly revealing:

> Beyond these instincts for public life I had political feelings. I am even emotional about them. I was going to be Sir Galahad and clear up every part of the world. There is the touch of the revolutionist about me. It was nothing more than a pipe dream, but idealistically I was on sound ground.[1]

It is perhaps inevitable that this person who spent a great deal of his working life assuming and getting inside the persona of exciting and famous people, and who genuinely believed that he had been a pirate in an earlier reincarnation, should suffer from these delusions. To have become confused about his real identity is perhaps understandable in the rarefied air of the life he led. His confusion was not helped by long periods when his mind was affected by the effects of drug abuse, venereal disease and sickness brought on by depression. In the end he totally lost touch with who he really was.

Flynn was to prove not only a good liar but a master at disguising the truth. His autobiography *My Wicked, Wicked Ways* is now regarded as a work of almost pure fiction. Flynn not only managed to tell the story he wanted people to believe, he also managed to persuade Earl Conrad, the writer with whom he collaborated, to believe it too. Conrad later wrote a book about the time they spent together while working on the autobiography. It is entitled *Errol Flynn: A Memoir*, written and published after Flynn's death. In it Earl Conrad tells us:

> No one else I ever met contained the essence of enigma in human form as did the celebrated actor-cavorter.
>
> Flynn, who wore a squarely shaped question mark on the handkerchief pocket of his suitcoat for over half a lifetime, was as much a puzzle to himself as to those who tried to understand him. He wore that question mark because he was hailed by the uncertainty of existence – somewhat crucified by it, as if he was desiring above all things to know the living unknown.

Later in *Errol Flynn: A Memoir* Earl Conrad confesses: 'Even when I finished working on his autobiography, *My Wicked, Wicked*

Ways, I privately knew that I only partially understood him.'

Whoever Flynn believed he was, he was a dreamer and a compulsive liar who almost certainly came to believe his own fabrications. For example, he was fond of telling people that he was born and raised in Ireland, that he was a descendant of a noble Irish family, the Flynn O'Flynns, and had once swum the Irish Channel. He frequently also boasted that he had won an Olympic gold medal boxing for Australia. None of this contains a shred of truth: there is no evidence that he ever set foot in Ireland, he certainly wasn't born there. While it is true that his father was descended from a poor immigrant family that originally hailed from Ireland and settled in Australia, his fame as an Irishman came from a totally different quarter. This originated with an instruction from Jack Warner, head of Warner Brothers, who gave him his first break in films. He told Flynn to tell everyone he was Irish, the publicity department at Warner Brothers did the rest. Flynn himself confirms this in his autobiography, describing his first few days in Hollywood: 'I confronted this strange look of incredulity in one person after another in Hollywood, when I saw that they all wanted to believe I was an Irish lad grown up in Ireland and come straight from Ireland.' Another anecdote that Flynn records in his autobiography, which also turned out to be incorrect, is that he insisted on the same line being written into all the Western films he appeared in to explain his accent:

Cowboy: Where you from, partner?

Flynn: I happen to come from Ireland, but I am as American as you are.

The first sign of Flynn's involvement in international politics came when he and a companion, described in his autobiography as 'a Dr Koets', went to Spain during the Civil War on the pretext of covering events for *Cosmopolitan* and *Liberty* magazines owned by William Randolph Hearst, himself a Fascist supporter. Dr Koets was travelling as Flynn's 'photographer', but in reality he was a mythical figure dreamed up by Flynn to use in his autobiography. The truth about his companion is as curious as that of Flynn himself: Koets was really a cover name for a well-known and dangerous Nazi agent called Dr Herman Erben. In *My Wicked, Wicked Ways* Flynn ignores the trouble that the two men had in getting to Spain. At the time of his visit to Europe Flynn held a British passport, but he had a deep and enduring hatred of the British learned at his grandmothers' knee. She had filled his mind with tales of supposed or actual atrocities carried out by the British in Ireland in the days before she had left for Australia, and which probably grew with the telling. It has also been suggested that his mother Marella (who was a descendant of Fletcher Christian of the *Mutiny on the Bounty* fame) was particularly anti-semitic and this attitude Flynn acquired from her. There is no record of when Flynn and Erben first met, but it was natural that both men were to become close friends and that Erben was to persuade Flynn to channel his desire to get involved in international intrigues to work for the Nazis.

The reason Flynn found himself in Europe in the summer of 1937 is interesting and worth recording as it explains many of the things that were going on and, in particular, it demonstrates the type of recruit that the Nazis had selected to carry out their devious work.

In his autobiography *My Wicked, Wicked Ways* Flynn records that he received a telegram from his friend Dr Koets which read: 'Arriving Hollywood Monday noon with 1200 monkeys. Koets.' Flynn alleges he was overjoyed to learn of Koets's arrival. He showed the telegram to his friend John Decker who was staying with him. He asked: 'What the hell is he doing with twelve hundred monkeys?' To which Flynn replied: 'Who knows? Who gives a damn! He's coming!' Flynn recounts how he told Koets that he was having trouble with Warner Brothers, not an unusual situation, and went on to reveal some of the problems he was having with his then wife Lili Damita. Telling Koets that he wanted to get away from her and the 'film factory', he asked his friend to help. 'We can go anywhere you like,' the mythical Koets was supposed to have replied. 'But there is a hell of a good war going on in Spain – civil one, the best kind for scientists like ourselves. What do you say?' Flynn then goes on to describe a series of escapades that he and Koets were to get up to, involving a drunken spree during which he purchased a lion which proved something of a problem when they took it in a taxi to Chicago. The lion became so much trouble that they handed its lead to a hotel receptionist who was unaware of what was on the other end and promptly vanished. Flynn also records with amusement that he caught gonorrhoea during this time, something of a regular event, which he somewhat delicately refers to as 'The Pearl of Great Price' and ends this bogus series of escapades by describing how the two men caught the boat for Europe and went to Spain.

However, American State Department records paint a different picture. Like most of Flynn's autobiography the account of how the two men made their way to Spain was completely untrue. The man referred to as 'Dr Koets' didn't exist, or if he did

120

he has never been discovered. What is certain is that he was not the man who left America with Flynn. The American State Department files clearly establish that it was Dr Herman Erben who had imported a consignment of monkeys when he arrived from Africa. Erben was well known to the authorities as a Nazi agent. American intelligence had long been taking an interest in him following a report of the interest of the American Consular Service who had opened a file on him after it was discovered that he had been involved in the murder of the Austrian Chancellor Engelbert Dollfuss on 25 July 1934. This particular crime occurred when a party of Hitler's Gestapo burst into the Chancellery and an SS man by the name of Oskar Planetta shot the Chancellor in the throat. Those present, including Dr Erben, stood around and watched the poor man suffer a painful and lingering death.

American intelligence, well aware of Flynn and Erben's friendship, had previously visited Flynn in an effort to warn him off. They told him about an incredible incident that had occurred some time before. Dr Erben had been employed by the McCormick Lines (where he had signed on a vessel called the *West Malwah* as the ship's doctor) and while it was passing through the Panama Canal Erben was spotted taking photographs of gun mountings on several British and American ships. The captain kept a close watch on Erben who did not bother to hide what he was doing or his personal feelings. At the New Year's Eve party on board he wiped his dirty hands on the American flag hanging in the saloon and when asked what he was doing, gave the game away by shouting that he was only an American because it suited him and when war broke out he would enlist in the German forces and anyone who dared to criticise Hitler in his presence would have Erben's teeth in his throat or be smashed to pulp. It would appear that Erben was drunk because he went on to boast that he had assisted in the murder of Dollfuss in Vienna. This was followed days later when he screamed insults at the crew of the *Southern Cross* which had brought President Roosevelt to a peace conference in Buenos Aires and shouted 'Heil Hitler' to the crew of a German freighter. Later on the same voyage he went on the rampage one stormy night off Rio de Janeiro, roaming the decks with a loaded revolver threatening to shoot people. When the vessel docked on 6 January at Rio, the Brazilian authorities took statements from the passengers and crew. Erben, his cover blown, was deported to New Orleans, where before he left he stole the *West Malwah's* drugs and surgical instruments. Flynn listened to this story without any apparent interest, but immediately the State Department men had gone he contacted Erben and told him to come to Hollywood.

Flynn himself had no problem getting to Spain; he sailed on the Queen Mary on 24 February 1937 and as the holder of a British passport was afforded every courtesy as befitted the big star he was. Dr Erben, on the other hand, was having nothing but trouble. He was having obstacles placed in his way by everybody. The State Department refused to give him permission to enter Spain and despite Flynn's assistance and influence with a number of people, including Randolph Churchill, the Spanish authorities would not allow him a visa. However, due to the shortage of doctors the Spanish authorities suddenly announced that they were prepared to allow in anyone with medical skills. Dr Erben was a surgeon and was eventually given a pass allowing him to enter.

Some years later, in an astonishing confession to A.J. Nicholas of the US State Department's Passport Division on 25 April 1938, Erben explained that the purpose of the mission was to obtain photographs, names and addresses of all the German soldiers who were fighting for the Loyalists against Franco and his supporter Hitler in the Spanish Civil War. These particulars were taken to Berlin and delivered into the hands of the Gestapo. The families of those disloyal to Hitler were punished, either by sending them to a concentration camp or by murder.

Before he left Flynn is known to have told several people that he was taking $1,500,000 from Loyalist and pro-Communist sympathisers in Hollywood to the Loyalists in Spain and was going to hand the money over to the Government in Valencia. Promising people one and a half million dollars seems to have been a habit with Flynn – he was to do the same thing a year and a half later. On both occasions he arrived empty-handed. When he had been in Spain for a few months, Warner Brothers, anxious to protect their investment and under pressure from the State Department, who were still worried about his association with Erben, instructed their Spanish representative to get Flynn out of Spain. They installed him in a suite at the Hotel Plaza Athenée in Paris while arrangements were made to ship him home. A day or so later Flynn was amused and astonished to read the headlines in the French newspapers: 'Errol Flynn Est Mort'. His reaction was typical, he would sit in the hotel foyer taking great pleasure from watching people's expressions when they lowered their newspapers and saw him sitting there with a silly grin on his face. Several days later he left for Berlin, then returned to Paris to begin a new and exciting phase of his life.

Chapter Twelve

Enter the IRA

IF WE ACCEPT that Flynn had been given the task of master-minding the plan to replace the existing King with the Duke of Windsor we need to discover how this plan was to be achieved. As has already been established, it was a highly dangerous strategy for the Nazis, particularly in the late Thirties when, had it been discovered, it would almost certainly have precipitated the start of the Second World War at a time when the Third Reich was in no position to resist. While the build-up for war was gaining momentum the German nation was far from ready; had war broken out at that time there is no question that the German Army would have been defeated. The authority for this comes from no less a person than Hitler himself, who is on record as saying little more than a year earlier: 'We had no army worth mentioning, at the time it would not even have had a fighting strength to maintain itself against the Poles.' It is well known that Hitler always expected that war would break out several years later; he had warned his generals that he anticipated his attack on France and the Low Countries would be mounted in 1942. However, had a plan to overthrow the existing King and interfere with the government of Britain been discovered, it would have brought such a sense of outrage that the country would have immediately been thrown on to a war footing despite Britain being equally unprepared. Any move against Hitler would almost certainly have had the support of France, who was Britain's military ally at the time and who would have been obliged to honour her treaty obligations, as would Poland. Hitler would have found himself threatened on two fronts, a situation to which he was alive and something he was determined to avoid. Time would prove him totally justified: this was the very situation that would eventually prove to be his downfall. The risks of any move against George VI were enormous, but Hitler had clearly decided that the prize was worth the risk. He was nothing if not a gambler.

123

There is one other aspect that needs to be considered. In 1937, in a political sense, Hitler was secure. His following among the general populace was almost total, but his aims and ambitions were deeply distrusted by the army generals who still remembered the previous conflict and were less than anxious to find themselves at war again. Had the plot been discovered, the most immediate problems Hitler would have faced would have been internal and there is little doubt that the army would have overthrown him.

By giving the job to Bedaux and Flynn the Nazis proved very astute. They could allow these two to carry out whatever plan was adopted and, having studied it, given it their approval and provided any covert assistance it might require, they could watch it develop with little risk of their involvement being discovered. Had anything gone wrong, they could join in the general abhorrence and could successfully protest their innocence in any part of it. Had news of the scheme leaked out, it is certain that Flynn and Bedaux would have been eliminated by Nazi agents to ensure their silence.

When the meeting at the Hotel Meurice had given the task to Flynn, it would have been obvious that it would be necessary to provide a cover organisation to carry the blame had the scheme been discovered or, more importantly, if it was successful. The success of the scheme was totally dependent on avoiding the outrage that would have followed the assassination of the British monarch had it been traced to Germany and implicated the Nazis.

Events were to play directly into Flynn's hands. By the middle of 1938 when he returned to Europe to put his scheme in place there had been an important development. There was an organisation, one that fitted the bill, ready made and already very active. The IRA. The Irish Republican Army was beginning a high-profile bombing campaign in Britain. Flush with funds from America, believed to be well over a million pounds, the Army Council in Dublin was busy making plans that Flynn would have had no difficulty in discovering from his contacts in America. The plan being worked out in Dublin was a simple one, to attack the British and bring the Government to the negotiating table. The IRA had a new Chief of Staff. Sean Russell was determined and completely sold on the idea of violence as a political weapon; he was also the man responsible for the influx of funds after his successful trip to America in 1936 and 1938 when he was the IRA quartermaster. He had been appointed the new Chief of Staff in the election of February 1938 and had immediately set about throwing aside the lethargy of the previous years, declaring in a fighting speech that he intended 'to bomb Britain', which one unfortunate newspaper reporter took to mean that the IRA had acquired an airforce, which curiously enough Russell took up and alleged, in a speech some time afterwards, was what they had done. The campaign was to cause great destruction in Britain: cinemas, theatres and banks were targeted. One night in London's Piccadilly, the Midland, Westminster and Lloyds banks were bombed and the whole area shaken so badly that the front of the Midland Bank fell into the street. Madame Tussaud's was hit by a balloon bomb that exploded in the Chamber of Horrors: Henry VIII's head was blown off but the Red Riding Hood tableau was saved when the bomb in Grandma's bed failed to explode.

All through its long existence the IRA had been a traditional enemy of the British Government, regarding it as a legitimate target for acts of terrorism. The IRA had a long memory and held the British responsible for most of the troubles in Ireland. In particular it was mindful of the many atrocities carried out against the people of Ireland. The dreadful stories of the behaviour of the so-called 'Black and Tans' will long live as proof of British brutality. Many of the stories have grown with the telling but there was genuine bitterness of the treatment that preceded the orchestrated sell-out of the Irish nation with the surrender of 1923 when Lloyd George and Churchill forced Michael Collins to accept partition and the creation of a separate state in the north as the price of peace, thereby making sure the IRA still had a cause to fight, one that would encourage Irish people throughout the world to rally behind the cause of Irish unity. Such was the fear that the IRA created by its bombing campaign of 1938 and 1939 that on 24 July 1939 Sir Samual Hoare, the Foreign Secretary, introduced the Prevention of Violence Act to Parliament to control Irish immigration and extend the right of deportation and the detention of suspects. It was pointed out that there had been 127 IRA outrages since January. Flynn must have seen the existence of the IRA as a heaven-sent vehicle as a cover for his operations. He began to make his plans.

If he wanted to create a situation where the people of Britain would consider allowing the Duke of Windsor to return and take a role where he could influence events in the Nazis' favour there was only one real possibility that had any chance of success. That was to assassinate the King. Had the King been murdered and the blame attributed to the IRA some time during the bombing campaign of 1938 or 1939, there would have been a clamour in Britain to recall the Duke of Windsor. The problems that had surrounded his marriage to the Duchess would have been conveniently forgotten. With Britain suddenly advertising a vacancy for a Sovereign, he would have been seen as the best and only candidate: it was, after all, the job for which he had been trained. From that point onwards Hitler would have been home and dry; with his personal puppet on the throne, he could gradually infiltrate the Government and influence events until he had built up enough support for his dream, Anglo-German unity. Eventually Hitler would be in a position to undermine any opposition in the way that had proved so fatally effective in Germany, Austria, and eventually France and everywhere his evil tentacles spread. The peaceful invasion of England, when it came, would be a foregone conclusion. He would claim as he had done in the case of Austria that he had 'been invited in'. Hess's prophecy would have come true: '. . . the Duke and his clever wife would deliver the goods . . . not a drop of German blood need be spilled to invade Britain.' The idea, like most brilliant ideas, was both simple and clever.

Assassination, a favourite method of the Nazis to bring about political reform, was the only real solution. Any attempt to re-introduce the Duke of Windsor by any other means would have met with fierce opposition and given rise to a split in public opinion heavily weighted in favour of the Government of the day. The Duke had lost a great deal of his former support in Britain – most people had simply forgotten him. Now that the country had settled down under its new King and Queen it was not in the mood for another change. Civil war was not an option, and would inevitably have failed. Any support that the Duke might have mustered at the time of his abdication was now fragmented. Mosley's attempt to establish the British Fascist Party was running out of steam, the movement was finding it difficult to spread out of the East End and the attitude towards Fascism was beginning to harden. The war in Spain, the invasion of Abyssinia and the disturbing rumours already beginning to filter out from the continent were already beginning to worry the ordinary man in the street. However, faced with having to find another King there seems little doubt that most sections of public opinion would have advocated the return of the Duke of Windsor. Churchill in particular could have been relied upon to voice his support and call for his return and faced with the dilemma, there is little doubt that the British people, together with the Empire, would have gone along with the idea.

It will almost certainly never be revealed where the idea to kill George VI came from, but Hess was clearly in favour of putting the

Duke back on the British throne and would have been instrumental in drawing up the plan. There were plenty of people close to the operation who would not have been the least bit appalled at the prospect. Neither Flynn nor his companion with whom he had recently returned from Spain were strangers to murder, Erben in particular, it seems, was proud of his involvement in Dolfuss's assassination and being a fanatical Nazi would, if he knew what Flynn was planning, welcome a chance to take part. Murdering the King of England on behalf of his hero Hitler would have held a strange attraction for this violent and often unstable man.

The Nazi leadership would not have hesitated. Having decided to murder the King of England it was now simply a matter of deciding where and when. If we ignore the morality of what was being suggested, it clearly offered a simple and effective solution.

It is not known whether it was Flynn's decision to use the IRA as a cover. British intelligence were always convinced that he was in contact with the Republican Army, but no evidence has ever been produced of his connection. However, they were so obvious a choice that the idea could have come from anyone. We can assume that the question of killing the King while he was in England must have been studied. At first sight it was the obvious place, and plans to carry it out must have been made. However, by September 1937 it was widely known (having been reported in the British, Canadian and American press) that the King and Queen were to visit North America and Canada in the summer of 1939 – the first visit there by a reigning British monarch. Suddenly the idea of the murder being carried out in the USA became an attractive option. There were several advantages: it was a country with a reputation for violence on the other side of the world where the Germans wanted to exert an influence and were building up support. To attempt the murder of the King while he was there had one serious drawback: they could no longer use the IRA as a cover and needed some other organisation to be made responsible. However, there were many advantages in considering America. Both Flynn and Bedaux had considerable contacts there and could be relied upon to find some way of covering up for what was planned. The fact that it was going to be done there had an overriding attraction for the Nazis – the murder would inevitably cause a rift in Anglo-American relations that at the time were not particularly good anyway and would help persuade America that it had no place in getting involved in the affairs of Europe. It was then that Flynn, who was nothing if not resourceful – he had saved his own skin on too many occasions to allow a change of plans to divert him – was inspired. Having found a good idea he was loath to abandon it, and he produced what can only be described as a master stroke.

It is not widely known that Flynn returned to Europe in May 1938. It was not until the FBI files were declassified in 1985 that it was established he came to attend a special meeting in Lisbon that remained a secret for 47 years. These files record that not only did he go to Portugal in the May of 1938, but also that his movements were again observed and recorded by MI6 who reported his arrival to London. The news of his presence in Portugal was not judged to be particularly important, being dismissed as a short holiday, and consequently it did not attract the attention it might have done. This resulted in a totally incorrect conclusion being drawn. Seen in connection with the other information that has come to light, his visit was an event of the highest significance.

To recognise the importance, and to form the connection with the meeting Flynn previously had with the Duke of Windsor, Rudolf Hess and Martin Bormann would, at the time, have required the intelligence services, still unaware of the purpose of the Paris meeting, to follow a rather tortuous route. The FBI files reveal that Flynn's reason for going to Lisbon was for the specific purpose of meeting Sean Russell. Nobody attempted to make the connection with the previous meeting. Why should they? All the intelligence agencies had convinced themselves that Flynn was involved with fund-raising for the IRA; the fact that he was meeting its new leader was not seen as particularly important. This meant that the wrong conclusions were drawn. Due to a failure to co-ordinate the reports it received of Flynn's movements in Paris, with the reports from those watching him in Lisbon, the two incidents remained separate. The truth is that Flynn was never involved with the IRA, he had never met Russell previously, and had no former dealings with the IRA. MI6 could not have been more wrong.

The release of the FBI material means there is no longer any mystery about why Russell agreed to meet Flynn in Portugal. The reason was rather mundane, it was simply about money. Finding the funds to allow it to carry on with its atrocities is an on-going function of any terrorist organisation. Russell found himself in receipt of a tantalising offer he could hardly resist. Then, as now, the IRA was constantly in need of funds. Initially, Flynn probably used an intermediary in the United States known to Russell to contact him and give the necessary assurances, but the lure of the prize that Flynn was offering would have been sufficient to draw Russell to Lisbon. Flynn sent word to Russell that if he would

INSTRUMENT OF ABDICATION

I, Edward the Eighth, of Great Britain, Ireland, and the British Dominions beyond the Seas, King, Emperor of India, do hereby declare My irrevocable determination to renounce the Throne for Myself and for My descendants, and My desire that effect should be given to this Instrument of Abdication immediately.

In token whereof I have hereunto set My hand this tenth day of December, nineteen hundred and thirty six, in the presence of the witnesses whose signatures are subscribed.

SIGNED AT
PORT BELVEDERE
IN THE PRESENCE
OF

Edward RI

Albert

Henry

George

Above: Edward VIII tells the world of his decision to abdicate. (Popperfoto)

Left: The Instrument of Abdication.

The Duke and Duchess on their honeymoon in Paris. (Popperfoto)

The Duke and Duchess leaving Berchtesgaden. (Popperfoto)

DEPARTMENT OF STATE
WASHINGTON

May 31, 1939.

My dear Mr. Hoover:

I hasten to acknowledge the receipt of your letter of May 29, 1939 giving information concerning Sean Russell and Joe McGarrity and their possible activities in connection with the visit of the King and Queen of England. This matter has been receiving constant attention and I understand that the two men have now been located. Your cooperation in this case is appreciated and I shall thank you to send me any other information regarding Russell and McGarrity which may reach you.

Sincerely yours,

G.S. Messersmith
Assistant Secretary

John Edgar Hoover, Esquire,
    Director, Federal Bureau of Investigation,
        Department of Justice,
            RECORDED & INDEXED
            Washington.

Left: This letter from the State Department shows that interest was being taken in Sean Russell prior to the visit of the King and Queen in June 1939.

Right: The *Daily Express* of 7 June 1939 carries the story of the fears of an IRA plot against the King and Queen. (*Daily Express*)

Above: The Duke inspects French lines, 4 November 1939. (Topham)

Right: Hitler enters Paris in triumph, 1940. (Popperfoto)

JBO:ael   December 30, 1940

MEMORANDUM FOR THE IMMIGRATION AND NATURALIZATION SERVICE

                    Re: SEAN RUSSELL, alias, JOHN RUSSELL;
                         IMMIGRATION AND NATURALIZATION

                    In confirmation of a telephone call with
          Mr. A. R. Mackey, of your Department, on December 28,
          1940, relative to the whereabouts of Sean Russell,
          I wish to set forth the following information:

                    The most recent information reflected
          in our files concerning Sean Russell, reveals
          he was in San Francisco, California, the
          latter part of August, 1940, and was stay-
          ing with the Right Reverend Richard Collins.
          However, this information has not been con-
          firmed. There are also various reports of
          Russell having returned to both Ireland and
          Germany, and of his subsequent return to
          this country under a fictitious name.
          There has been no verification of these
          latter reports.

                              Very truly yours,

                              John Edgar Hoover
                                   Director

This letter from J Edgar Hoover shows that six months after Russell's death
nobody knew where he was.

20/2/41

AN GARDA SIOCHANA.

éire

OIFIG AN CHOIMISINEARA,

BAILE ATHA CLIATH.

to this communication
addressed to
Commissioner,
Garda Siochana,
Dublin.

ring number quoted :—

/846/40.

matters should be made
subject of separate com-
...

```
CRIME BRANCH
   SECTION 3

   19 FEB 1941

  DESPATCHED
 Gárda Síochána
```

An Rúnaidhe,
Roinn Dlíghidh agus Cirt.

      I am directed by the Coimisinéir to
state that information received indicates that
I.R.A. in Northern Ireland have been warned
through Sean Russell, who is stated to be in
Germany, that the Germans will invade this
country by air with parachutists, gliders, etc.,
between 14th. and 17th. March, 1941.

P. Canoll Árd-Cheannphort.

    a.s. Leas - Choimisinéara.

Letter from the Irish intelligence files warning of a German invasion.

Above: U-65 leaving Wilhelmshaven with Ryan and Russell on board on 8 August 1940.
(Horst Bredow, U-Boot-Archiv)

Left: Statue of Sean Russell in Fairview Park, Dublin. (Gwynne Thomas)

come, he would meet him and hand over one and a half million dollars collected from the anti-Nazi League in Los Angeles as a donation to the IRA funds. This was a tempting offer and had been cleverly designed to appeal to Russell. Many early sources confirm that Russell was anti-Nazi, but due to his later involvement this fact tends to be overlooked. If he had suspected he was being drawn into anything that involved the Nazis he might not have been quite so keen, although previously, in his role as the IRA's quartermaster, he had visited Berlin and Russia to seek financial assistance. This seems to indicate that he was never too bothered about the source of funds as long as they were available. With a prize of that magnitude on offer he wasn't likely to hesitate.

If Russell thought it was too good to be true, it was. This was presumably the same $1,500,000 that Flynn had talked about taking to Spain: the outcome was the same. True to form, again he arrived empty-handed, but employing the boyish charm for which he was famous, he managed to gain Russell's confidence. The two men appear to have got on extremely well. This is not surprising. Russell had a reputation for impressing those with whom he came in contact, and this would be borne out later during his time in Germany when he is known to have made a big impression with his Abwehr contacts. Flynn was clearly impressed; it is believed that the reason he called his only son Sean stemmed from the respect he had for the IRA leader. Explaining why the $1,500,000 had failed to materialise must have taxed even Flynn's eloquence, but his powers of persuasion were sufficient to convince Russell that Flynn's fame and contacts in America were such that raising that kind of money would present little problem. That part of the story had at least a ring of truth about it.

Looking back over the events in Lisbon it isn't difficult to see how Russell was drawn into a dangerous plot that he knew nothing about. He was obviously impressed and not a little overawed by Flynn who was, after all, a big star at the time and a hero to his many fans around the world. Hitler was said to regard Flynn as his favourite film star and was known to watch all his films at his home in Berchtesgarten. Russell, we are told, was a simple man who had no time for politics; being known as a man of action, he would have been putty in the hands of a rogue like Flynn who had spent his entire life conning people. It would have been easy for him to persuade Russell to agree to visit a country where he already had many friends and supporters from two previous trips and which had proved to be the traditional source of the IRA's funds and support.

Chapter Thirteen

The Chief of Staff

FOLLOWING THEIR MEETING Russell returned to Dublin and Flynn, having achieved his purpose, went back to Hollywood and continued to make films for Warner Brothers. 1938 was to prove a busy year for Flynn; he was forced to work harder than ever before. He was kept busy making a variety of films as diverse as *Four is a Crowd*, a whacky comedy, a domestic drama called *The Sisters* and, finally, something a bit more to his taste, *Dawn Patrol*, a story about flying set in World War One in which he starred with David Niven. There was a reason behind this gruelling schedule. Flynn was in financial trouble, this time greater than usual. While holidaying in the Bahamas in early February, he had fallen in love with an 80-foot-long, 22-foot-beam sailing boat which from the moment he saw he knew he must have. The boat's owner, John Alden, was asking $12,500 for her and despite the fact that he was in debt everywhere Flynn managed to scrape together the money, most of it as advances from the studio against his future films. Flynn re-named the yacht the *Sirocco* after one he had previously owned, and he was obliged to make several films in quick succession to reduce his borrowings and pay the thousand dollars a week running costs of his latest 'mistress'. Having managed to slip away to meet Russell he was forced back to continue to work hard, but now that things were falling into place there was little more that could be done until the following year.

During this period he was under constant surveillance by the FBI who were keeping the studio informed, warning them that he was spending a great deal of time in the company of known Nazis. Foremost of these was Fritz Wiedemann, the German Consul General in San Francisco, with whom he was frequently seen. The FBI also informed Warner Brothers that Flynn was having an intense love affair with a singer called Gertrude Anderson, who was a Swedish national. Her name was on the American Government's list of known Nazis and she was believed to have contacts at the highest level in Berlin. Meanwhile, Warner Brothers

130

were making strenuous efforts to keep Flynn's activities quiet and away from the press. Flynn was a 'hot property', they were more than anxious to protect their investment and were less concerned about what Flynn was up to in his private life. As long as he continued to roll up on the set for work, they remained content.

By 1938 the FBI suspected that in addition to his contacts with known Nazis he was also spying for and actively working for Berlin.[1] Such was the suspicion surrounding him that the *Sirocco* was banned from all ports on the West Coast except Wilmington where she was based. Even so, this was not enough to prevent Flynn using her for running gold and guns from Mexico; the latter he is known to have smuggled ashore at Wilmington and sold. The gold he kept, although he was perfectly aware that it was illegal for private citizens to hold stocks of this precious metal.

Meanwhile, Sean Russell seems to have slipped back into Ireland in much the same way as he must have slipped out. No evidence has ever been uncovered to show that anyone in the IRA or the Irish authorities had been aware of his trip to Portugal.

If we continue with the premise that Flynn chose Russell because he was the Chief of Staff and was known to have collected money in America for his cause, then it was an inspired choice. Russell was one of the most controversial men to have ever headed the IRA. Regarded by many to have a genius for terrorism, he was an intensely practical man, as might be expected from his former life as a cabinet-maker. He had no real interest in politics and little time for the organisational routine that marked many of the former IRA leaders. He had, in fact, stood for election as Chief of Staff in 1937 and received a great deal of support, but he was opposed by Sean McBride who had been seconded to the Army Council and was currently holding the office until a permanent leader could be elected. McBride, a Dublin barrister, accused Russell of failing to keep proper records and of being unable to account for a great deal of the funds he had collected as quartermaster, including money to purchase a motor car. McBride was able to make a case and Russell was court-martialled, found guilty and dismissed, though nobody seriously believed that he had taken anything.[2] Known to be totally committed to the cause, he was regarded as scrupulously honest, a fact that was borne out when in February 1938 Russell was elected Chief of Staff despite not being a member of the movement, or being allowed to attend any of the election meetings. There is further evidence that nobody really suspected Russell – the normal sentence of an IRA court-martial was a bullet in the back of the head, certainly not expulsion.

So what do we really know about Russell? One description, taken from an article that appeared in the *Sunday Express* of 20 July 1939, written by C.A. Lyon, gives us a picture that seems typical:

> About five feet ten inches in height, grey eyes in a face that is very hard set and has a jutting chin. Above the fanatical face sprouts fluffy upstanding red hair, the hair has descended his temples. Broad shouldered and stocky, respectably dressed. Much oratory has not made him a good orator; he gets excited and bellows.

In a Garda file in Dublin the author discovered a curious footnote that 'his red sports car was a common sight in Dublin and he was fond of taking children for picnics in it' – which presumably was the car that was the subject of the court-martial. Another description can be found in Charles Higham's *American Swastika*:

> ... vigorous, stocky and muscular ... distinguished by a wild brush of rapidly greying hair that stood up from his head like the mane of a lion. His sharp, shrewd, enquiring eyes stared out of a nest of wrinkles ... high forehead, aquiline nose. Square jaw indicating formidable combination of intelligence and will. Broad shoulders, craftsman's hands inspire confidence in his followers ... general manner and schoolmasterly charm hides his true nature, which is vengeful and severe and Jesuitical. His hatred of the British is harsh and unyielding.

Born in 1893, Russell had been a member of the IRA since leaving school. He joined the Irish Volunteers in 1914 and was interned as a member of Sinn Fein after the 1916 rising. His name appears in the records of those who took part in the so-called Easter Rising, though there he was referred to as 'John Russell'. This is curious; only on one other occasion was he known to have used that name before – as will be seen that will prove significant, being the excuse for his 1939 arrest in Detroit. Following his release he was appointed the IRA's Director of Munitions from 1919 to 1921 and remained active in the movement following the surrender of 1923. He is known to have visited both Russia and America to try and secure arms and finance in his role as Quartermaster General following his appointment in April 1936. He was elected Chief of Staff in January 1938 when Frank Ryan, the former Chief of Staff, left for Spain to fight in the Civil War. Russell was to hold the post until his bizarre death.

There is in a now declassified FBI file in Washington a reference to a letter Russell wrote while he was in San Francisco during August of 1939 to an Anne O'Farrelly who was, at the time, interned in Mountjoy Prison in Dublin. The file entry refers to her as his former mistress. Apart from this no other reference to his private life seems to have survived.

Russell's period as leader of the IRA, often referred to as 'The Years of Disaster', was not marked by any spectacular progress; in fact it was to prove the most barren period in the organisation's history. Russell has been credited with masterminding the bombing campaign of 1938 and 1939 in the Irish Republic and on the British mainland, but this proved largely ineffective and, in the final analysis, counter-productive. The IRA degenerated into a dispirited rabble with little in the way of policy other than to oppose the established Government. Beset with factions operating independently of each other, they confined themselves to robbing banks and the odd street fight. The prospect of war in Europe gave the Irish Government under Eamon de Valera, who became fed up with all these disruptive tactics, an excuse to move against them. The result was that the Irish administration provided itself with formidable powers to deal with the troublesome organisation. Using the threat of being drawn into war and the desire to remain neutral, they grasped an opportunity to pass legislation that proved swingeing. On 14 June 1939, the Dail passed the Offences Against the State Act, which for the first time declared the IRA an unlawful organisation. Under the provisions of the Act marches and public demonstrations were banned, but it contained other measures that were to have more devastating effect. The Act gave the State power to arrest and imprison without trial members of what had now become an illegal organisation. These powers were strengthened and made even more effective with the passing of the Emergency Powers Act which allowed for internment until the cessation of hostilities in Europe. This was done ostensibly to protect the State against all foreign nationals, but its main effect was to deal a serious blow to the IRA. Most of its known members either fled the country or were rounded up. Some 400 were interned either in Portlaoighise Prison or at the internment camp at the Curragh. According to IRA sources this figure was to increase to 2,500 before they were all released at the end of 1945.

The fact that Russell went to America in April 1939 is well known. When questioned he always maintained that he went to raise funds and lecture about Irish unity to anyone who would listen. However, back in Ireland, it was generally accepted that he had slipped out of the country to avoid arrest and internment. Irish intelligence was expecting him to return secretly and remained constantly on the alert. Department G4 of the An Garda Siochana, which dealt with surveillance of members of the IRA, regarded the possibility of his return as inevitable: they were kept busy following up reports that Russell had been seen in various parts of Ireland well into 1941, long after he was dead. It might be significant, but it seems that all these alleged sightings occurred in bars in several different parts of the country.

Russell's visit to America has never been satisfactorily explained. Several prominent writers who have studied and written the history of the IRA have accepted the view taken in Ireland at the time at face value and have not tried to establish any other reason. In the light of what happened this is perhaps understandable. The reason Russell went to America has always puzzled those who have studied the part he played in the IRA's history. Even those who were close to him were equally baffled. Jim O'Donovan, whom Russell appointed as the IRA's liaison officer with German intelligence, and who was regarded by them as their most reliable contact in Ireland, when questioned on this very point after the war by Otto Stephan, the German author of *Geheimaufrag Irland*, translated and published as *Spies in Ireland*, trotted out the usual well-worn explanation: 'It was in order to organise further financial help for the IRA.'

When pressed as to whether it was normal for the Chief of Staff of the Army to leave his troops in the middle of a campaign and cross the Atlantic, O'Donovan hesitated and then advanced the theory that Russell may have been a victim of an IRA intrigue, suggesting that those plotting against him wished to replace him as Chief of Staff and may have persuaded him that he was the only one who could successfully carry out the fund-raising mission. This explanation seems equally unlikely. While he was not universally popular with all factions within the IRA, no evidence of a plot to unseat him has ever come to light. When he went to America he was warmly welcomed by Clan-na-Gael, the sister movement which was in touch with, and has always had a great deal of influence over, the IRA in Dublin. This suggestion is further dispelled by the fact that no one attempted to usurp Russell's position while he was absent. All we can deduce from Jim O'Donovan's remarks is that the IRA were as much in the dark about Russell's movements as everyone else. They believed, as did most people in Ireland, that Russell had fled to avoid internment but it now seems that what Russell always maintained, that he had gone to America to raise funds, was the truth. The only curious thing that remains was Russell's trip to Portugal and why he did not confide in anyone in Ireland about this visit. Several eminent writers who have written about the history of the IRA and have included details of his short but important contribution to the movement's struggle have failed to mention this. Most of these writers have had personal contact with Russell's contemporary IRA colleagues and the failure for the mission's existence to have been mentioned before the FBI files revealed it leads us to suspect Russell kept it highly secret. It is reasonable to assume that Flynn warned Russell to keep this visit a secret from those members of the IRA in Ireland, or that Russell was so sceptical about receiving such a huge amount of money that he anticipated coming back empty-handed and preferred to wait until his return before announcing it as a triumph.

Chapter Fourteen

Russell in America

SEAN RUSSELL ARRIVED in America some time towards the end of April 1939. There was nothing unusual about his visit; he had been given a 30-day visa by the State Department after they had received assurances from James Orr Denby, the American Chargé d'Affaires in Dublin. Russell was to create a problem that would cause him trouble later: for some reason that has never been explained both his passport and visa were made out in the name of 'John Russell'; the only other recorded instance of when he called himself 'John' was back in 1919. However, the State Department were well aware of who he was and where he had come from, although they appear to have been a bit confused about his political affiliation. A State Department memorandum prepared at the time describes him as having 'pronounced Communist views' and interprets the purpose of his visit as 'to contact Communist organisations'.

While Russell moved about America he was accompanied by his old friend Joseph McGarrity whom he had first met when McGarrity visited Dublin in 1926. He was going to look after Russell and arrange his movements and speaking engagements as he had on the two previous occasions when Russell had visited America. McGarrity, an American publisher, was the head of Clan-na-Gael, the Republican organisation founded in New York in 1867 which had spread until it had branches in most American cities. Clan-na-Gael drew its support almost exclusively from the large expatriate Irish community who had emigrated and settled in the United States but who still retained a nostalgia for their homeland, and in particular gave support to the Republican movement back in Ireland. Clan-na-Gael has traditionally been very supportive of the IRA and proved to be the principal source of funds and weapons for many years, enabling the IRA to continue its terrorist operations. However, Clan-na-Gael has always sought to underplay its role in the fuelling of violence. Throughout its long history it has proved a springboard for ambitious Irish-American politicians who have used it as a power base from which to launch their careers. Clan-na-Gael has always sought to encourage support for Irish unity by trying to marshal the American public behind the Republican cause rather than allowing itself to be regarded simply as an organisation for the funding of terrorism.

When Russell began his tour of America he made no attempt to hide his presence. This is not surprising: his visit, aimed at raising funds, would demand a high public profile. It must therefore have come as something of a shock to find himself the centre of intense media speculation that quickly spread, even across the Atlantic. When he arrived he would have imagined that his visit would be similar to that of his two previous ones when on neither occasion had his presence given rise to any trouble or controversy. This time, however, things were to prove very different. Following his arrival Russell headed for Los Angeles; there was a sound reason for this – the whole impetus for his visit was at the suggestion from Errol Flynn who had agreed to assist Russell in raising funds, holding out the promise of being able to raise large sums from his connections. This must have seemed plausible. There were many former Irish who had found work in the film industry: foremost among these was John Ford, the well-known director who had filmed in Ireland and who is known to have supported the IRA. There is no record of whether Russell met Flynn or visited Hollywood; it is likely not. It seems that events overtook him. The first record that has survived of what Russell was doing came on 18 May when he gave an interview to the *San Francisco News*. In an article published the following day they quoted him as saying: 'We declared war on Great Britain last January 12th.' The article went on to explain how the IRA had formally declared war on Britain when they handed in a declaration signed by members of the Army Council to Lord Halifax, the then Foreign Secretary. Russell's statement was not strictly accurate – it was actually the 16th – because the declaration of the 12th gave four days for compliance and was followed by another declaration on the 16th which confirmed that a state of war existed. The ultimatum was not taken seriously and was dismissed by the British Government as a publicity stunt. The IRA's response was to mount several bomb attacks that left two people dead and 15 people badly wounded.

That Russell was openly boasting about the IRA's activities to the press demonstrates that he was making no secret of his whereabouts or that he was campaigning on behalf of the IRA. He seems to have embarked on a similar programme to that previously, lecturing branches of Clan-na-Gael, speaking on local radio and giving interviews to the press in an effort to win support and attract funds. He must therefore have been as shocked as anyone to read the story that appeared in newspapers all across America. This report taken from the *Los Angeles News* of 28 May is typical:

> Photographic and photostatic evidence purporting to link Californian Nazis with the so-called agents of the IRA in a plot to assassinate the King and Queen have been sent to Scotland Yard, police revealed today.
>
> Police said the evidence submitted to them said the programme was as follows:
> (1) Assassination of the visiting British Royalty.
> (2) Launching of a destructive campaign of sabotage attacking British shipping on Pacific coast.
> (3) Propaganda campaign to foment ill feeling between the British and American peoples.

This press report, carried by most of the regional newspapers across the States, does not reveal where this information came from, apart from 'the police', and while making a connection between the Californian Nazis and the IRA it didn't name Russell or mention that the Chief of Staff of the IRA was in the country. This in itself is curious. At first glance it seems little more than press speculation and ignores a curious incident that took place in Los Angeles around the 18th. John H. Lechner, of the American Legion's Public Relations Committee, called all the city editors to a press conference where he introduced a Dr Alfred Dinsley, a supposed cancer specialist, although nobody seemed to have known very much about him. An astonished gathering of press men listened as Dr Dinsley announced that he was a 'British Secret Service agent' who worked for a section called F10. He proceeded to give an account of Russell's movements and went on to explain that Russell had come to America with the sole purpose of murdering the King and Queen.

The British Consul in Los Angeles acted quickly. He denied that a section called F10 existed and stated that even if it did, Dr Dinsley would have rendered himself liable to criminal charges under the British Official Secrets Act by revealing its existence. There has been a suggestion that this incredible incident was deliberately engineered by Russell and McGarrity to divert any attention they might later attract. If this were the case it is hard to see what advantage could accrue from such a move. Russell and

McGarrity could move without hindrance, they had no need to draw attention to themselves. With a perfectly genuine cover story for their activities, why should they have sought deliberately to embroil themselves in what was a somewhat dubious enterprise and raise the question of an assassination attempt on the King and Queen? Whoever the mysterious Dr Dinsley was, he seems to have disappeared without trace and his allegations were not taken seriously by the American authorities nor did the British Consul appear to become suspicious of Russell's intentions. Finally the press seem to have dismissed the story as a hoax.

There was no reason why anyone should have been particularly concerned at the allegation of a pro-Nazi/IRA plot in that early summer of 1939; there was little, if any, evidence to connect the two. While it is true that Russell had gone to Germany in 1936 to try to raise funds he came away empty-handed and his visit to Russia met with a similar response. Desperate for money the IRA tried any source that might offer support. It was from America during the same year that he obtained the funds for the 1938 bombing campaign in Britain and in Ireland. Bowyer Bell, writing in his book *Secret Army: The History of the IRA*, considered by many to be the definitive history of the IRA during this period, tells us, when examining the 1938 bombing campaign:

> The Army Council, deep at work in the isolation of Dublin, gave no real thought to a foreign alliance, other than the Clan. While there is some evidence that certain members of the Abwehr were keen to develop links with the IRA there was less enthusiasm among the leaders of either organisation. Certainly there was no formal contact or working relationship in 1938 and certainly not in America.

If the intention of the Dr Dinsley incident was designed simply to divert American intelligence away from Russell's activities, initially it seems to have had the desired effect. Richard B. Hood, the head of the FBI in Los Angeles, sent a telegram to Washington describing the whole incident as a hoax. However, at the same time, another FBI agent, Nathanael Peiper, reported that he had bugged a meeting in San Francisco where Russell was alleged to have discussed a bomb plot with Fritz Wiedemann of the German Embassy. Having considered all the evidence, J. Edgar Hoover came to the conclusion that the whole thing was nothing more than a series of wild rumours and the FBI took no action.

Even before the story first broke in the American press on the

23rd, it seems that both British and American intelligence were beginning to question Russell's presence and wonder if it might have some other, more sinister, reason than simply to collect funds. There is some evidence for this. A letter has been discovered, written by Norman Kendal, an Assistant Commissioner of the Metropolitan Police Special Branch at Scotland Yard. Dated 18 May and sent to the State Department a few days before the American press was making its own connection between the IRA and the pro-Nazi interests in America, it was the first time that Russell seems to have been mentioned in this connection. However, Kendal did not appear to be unduly concerned, he wrote:

> Information has been received that this man is in the United States of America for the dual purpose of raising funds to finance the present campaign of sabotage and to instigate hostile demonstrations by Irish Republican elements there during the visit of Their Majesties the King and Queen.
>
> This information is forwarded as the Commissioner knows it is the desire of the United States authorities that the visit should pass off without any untoward incident, and he would be grateful if, in the event of Sean Russell leaving the United States of America, the name of the ship on which he leaves, port of arrival in Europe, etc., he could be notified.[1]

It seems clear from both the tone and content of this letter that Kendal was more interested in learning what Russell's movements were likely to be when he left America rather than anything he might be planning while he was there.

What is unclear is whether Kendal was aware of the Dinsley revelations when he wrote his letter to the State Department. While it seems unlikely, it was possible. He could have been informed by telegram – the time difference would have allowed this. Whatever was the case he does not seem to have been overly concerned about the threat of an attack on the King and Queen.[2]

However, the press report on the 23rd changed all that; several agencies began to consider the possibility of a plot and the supposed conversation in San Francisco was re-examined. One of the reasons which prompted the allegations to be taken seriously was that Russell was alleged to have mentioned in the bugged conversation in San Francisco that the attack, when it came, would be 'to waylay the Royal couple in Detroit as they crossed over from Windsor [Ontario, Canada] on the train'.

More than anything else it was probably the mention of

Detroit that caused those responsible for the Royal couple's safety to become concerned. Detroit was the centre of the pro-Nazi movement in America and the base for some very powerful people. Most prominent of these was Father Charles Coughlin, without whose incredible life story no account of Nazi intrigues in America would be complete. Father Coughlin, born in Ontario, Canada, in 1891 to Irish-American parents, was ordained in 1916 and had become the incumbent of a Roman Catholic church called 'The Shrine of the Little Flower' in the Royal Oak suburb of Detroit. He was a man of considerable energy who in addition to his pastoral duties managed to combine several functions not normally associated with the work of the Lord. Father Coughlin was the proprietor of a political magazine called *Social Justice*. It was one of a number of methods he used to dispense some of his remarkable political ideology. Coughlin also had a regular programme on CBS radio where he made some incredible pronouncements. It has been estimated that, at its peak, his media empire employed over a hundred people who were kept busy dispatching political material and answering his huge volume of mail. In addition he ran a small but highly successful commercial enterprise called 'The Shrine Super Filling Station' on a site opposite his church, where, in addition to selling fuel and oil products supplied by both Shell and Standard Oil of America, he operated a hot-dog stand and, more curiously, a bookstall selling crucifixes, prayer books and the usual religious items: however, in addition to the bibles, he offered copies of his *Social Justice*, *Mein Kampf*, *The Life of Pope Pius the XI* alongside The *Myth of the Twentieth Century* by Alfred Rosenberg, a book disapproved of by the Vatican because it advanced the doctrine of pagan worship. In addition to this curious collection of publications there were metal swastikas and reproduction Iron Crosses, both First and Second Class, that apparently found a ready sale among his many followers.

Father Coughlin was not only a Fascist but possessed an almost blind devotion to both Hitler and Mussolini and he seems to have been able to advance a reasonable explanation for everything they did. In an article in 1939 in *Social Justice* he wrote: 'The Rome-Berlin Axis is serving Christendom in a particularly important way.' On several occasions he advocated that 'America become a Fascist corporate State in which democracy would be perpetuated'. How he reconciled all this political claptrap with what was going on in Europe and Abyssinia he was never to reveal. His ideas were completely irrational but his admiration for Hitler knew no bounds and he continued to churn out his brand of political propaganda on behalf of Nazi Germany without any real opposition. His radio programmes had a wide audience and the circulation of his *Social Justice* magazine has been estimated as over a million copies a month. Coughlin was a powerful voice and a dangerous man. He was anti-Roosevelt and was active in continuing to preach the message of anti-semitism, trotting out the well-worn Nazi rhetoric that all Jews were Communists and that international Jewry had financed the Russian Revolution. This theory, of course, came directly from *Mein Kampf*; it was something that Hitler believed and frequently used, and was the subject of many of Goebbels's speeches. Father Coughlin's continual attack on the Jews was to bring him into conflict with Archbishop Edward Mooney of Detroit, who demanded that he retract some of his more outrageous remarks about the Jews, but Pope Pius XII came to Coughlin's aid and gave him support. This effectively gave him a free hand; from that point onwards nobody in the American Catholic community dared challenge Coughlin. During the late Thirties he continued to pour out his incredible utterings, most of which were an almost verbatim repeat of the words of that equally fanatical bombast, Dr Goebbels.

It was inevitable that during his stay in America Sean Russell would come into contact with Father Coughlin – they were old friends. They had met in 1934 on the first occasion when Russell had gone to America and were to meet again on his second visit in 1936. The two men had a great deal in common – Russell was a devout Catholic who would have had a certain amount of inherent respect for this disreputable cleric – but the reasons for their friendship went a great deal deeper. We know that Russell was sympathetic to much of what Coughlin stood for, particularly his anti-British stance. Apparently Russell sent Coughlin a telegram expressing his good wishes every St Patrick's Day and also on the anniversary of the British defeat at Boston in the War of Independence of 1775, clearly some private joke, but it demonstrates how they both shared a hatred of the British. This is borne out when we learn that Coughlin was also a supporter of the IRA. All through the Thirties he had sent money to support the cause, and in addition sent political anti-British propaganda material to Dublin for distribution throughout Ireland.

However, it must not be assumed that the link between Russell and Coughlin is evidence that Nazi interests in America were supporting the IRA, or implies that there was any organised Irish support for Fascism. Father Coughlin was acting on his own behalf; the connection between American-Irish interests and

Coughlin's Fascists was much more simple and direct. Coughlin drew his support from the working classes in Detroit, many of whom worked either in the car industry or in the businesses that had sprung up to support it, where many of these workers, former Irish immigrants, had found work. Inevitably there was a great deal of common membership between the Fascist movement and that of Clan-na-Gael, but what was not so generally known was that Coughlin had several very powerful backers. After the war, when the full extent of many American companies' wartime activities were uncovered, it would be revealed that Coughlin was not the fool he might have seemed but the front man for a very powerful pro-Nazi movement in America. His most powerful friend and supporter was one of the richest and most powerful men in the United States, Henry Ford, who employed many, if not all, of Coughlin's supporters in Detroit. Cleverly, Ford managed to maintain his image as a benefactor doing good work for the poor in America while at the same time plotting with the Nazi leaders to rid the world of the Jews and establish world Fascism.

Detroit in the late Thirties was a hotbed of political intrigue and the base for terrorism led by Father Coughlin, whose supporters were known to have attacked several American Army bases. The news that the Chief of Staff of the IRA was travelling to Detroit was enough to start the alarm bells ringing. With the prospect of him joining up with Father Coughlin combined with the rumours that were circulating in the press of a plot to harm the King and Queen, it was little wonder that everyone in the various intelligence agencies suddenly began to sit up and take notice.

Chapter Fifteen

The Press Begin to Take an Interest

THE FIRST INTIMATION that anyone in Britain was to have about what was taking place on the other side of the Atlantic came on 6 June when the *Daily Mirror* carried a headline story from its reporter in Saskatchewan, Canada, who broke the story:

> Threats said to have been made against the King by notorious members of the outlawed Irish Republican organisation have resulted in still stronger guard being placed on the Canadian border. Police now examine occupants of every car from the United States and are searching all luggage.[1]

The following day the same newspaper followed this with a story from its special correspondent in Niagara: 'There has been a round-up of suspects at Hunter, Ontario, gaols are full of men police think are safer behind bars until the great day is over.'

The *Daily Express* that same day carried on its front page a story from its staff reporter, C.V.R. Thompson, from Stratford, Ontario, Tuesday, 7 June. Its headline read:

> KING'S GUARD WIRES ARREST THE IRA CHIEF
>
> The arrest in Detroit yesterday on the eve of the visit of the King and Queen to the USA of Sean Russell, Chief of Staff of the IRA, was made by 'G' men following a request by Chief Constable Conning of Scotland Yard, Special Branch, that he be watched. From his tiny bedroom in the Royal train, Mr Conning has 'shadowed' Russell. By telegrams dropped off at small stations in Canada's wilds he has kept in constant touch with agents in Los Angeles and San Francisco, New York and Washington. Every evening he has had a new report. Early today there was a telegram from Detroit, Russell had arrived by plane. He is now held in Detroit jail.

In another account under the headline CAPTAIN'S POWERS, Thompson reported:

It is possible that Russell may be deported to Eire. If he were put on a British ship the captain could take him into custody if asked to by Scotland Yard.

During a recent Irish Race Conference in Chicago Federal officers privately sounded out some delegates regarding the possibility of demonstrations during the Royal visit. Russell has now been detained pending investigations of charges that he made a false and misleading statement in connection with his passport. It is alleged that he has overstayed a thirty-day visitor's visa.

The *Daily Telegraph*'s own correspondent in Detroit also reported that Russell was arrested when he arrived from Chicago, and mentions that he was accompanied by Joseph McGarrity of Pennsylvania, a member of 'The Sons of Ireland'. The report goes on to reveal that McGarrity was also arrested but released without charge.

It would be reasonable to conclude from reports reaching the London press that the Americans had simply complied with the British request to arrest Russell on what was patently a trumped-up charge, hold him for a few days until the Royal party left the States, then release him and let him carry on with the original purpose of his visit. Anyone who thought that was in for a rude awakening. The *Daily Express* of 8 June had already broken the news. In a short piece on its front page it reported that Russell had been released on the orders of John Zubrick, Chief Immigration Officer of the US Labor Department, and went on to say that Russell was being watched wherever he went. The report confirmed that Russell had been arrested before the King and Queen had arrived at Windsor, Ontario, on the pretext that his visitor's visa had expired.

If Russell had gone to America with any intention of carrying out some secret operation, any chance he might have had now seemed to have been blown; suddenly he found himself thrown into the limelight with more publicity than he could ever have dreamed possible. The British press began to paint a picture of a country that had suddenly woken up to a crisis in its midst. An article in the *Daily Mail* of 8 June 1939 revealed that the US Government had mobilised 13,400 armed troops, had issued a directive that all private aeroplanes were to keep clear of New York and in the event that this was not observed an anti-aircraft battery had been moved into position at Fort Hancock. The *Mail* went on to report that navy minesweepers had been deployed to drag the nine miles of New York Bay that lay between Fort

Hancock, New Jersey, and Manhattan. Reading this report today conjures up a picture of one of the largest cities in the world preparing for some sort of invasion. Another report by the *Mail*'s correspondent in New York the previous day had given additional information about the degree of activity that was suddenly going on. In an article headed US HUNT FOR BOMB HAUNTS, the correspondent described how the New York police had been employed on a massive hunt for bombs and anyone who might be planning to use them. It reported that 27 flying squad detectives in a fleet of police cars had begun a search of suspicious cafés. This was, we were told, in addition to a large-scale search of 15 dance halls where agitators were believed to have stored bombs for terrorist activity. It seems that from its initial inertia over reports of a plot against the Royal couple, every department in America was on full alert. So what was the reason behind all this frantic activity?

The events that occurred in America during May and June of 1939 are somewhat difficult to understand. The panic that the rumours about what Russell might be planning while he was in America seems to have taken everyone by surprise. The simple fact is that nobody on either side of the Atlantic seems to have considered that there would be any particular trouble or danger to the Royal Family during their visit and the confusion that was clearly present seems to have existed to the modern day. When Donald Zec (whose book *The Queen Mother* was serialised by the *Sunday Times* in 1991) was asked by the newspaper to comment on the story in 1993 he said he was not aware of a conspiracy to harm the King and Queen.[2] However, he is also reported to have said: 'Royal advisers wanted the King and Queen to travel across the Atlantic in a British warship because of serious Foreign Office concern that the Germans might stage a mid-Atlantic hijack.' This is an incredible suggestion and, on the face of it, can hardly be taken seriously. In May 1939 Hitler was more than anxious that Britain and Germany remained friendly; he was hardly likely to do anything that would interfere with his plans. His main aim was to keep his future intentions secret. Historians have revealed that the last thing he wanted was to find himself at war with Britain or America; appeasement was still the order of the day. The hijacking of the King and Queen of a seemingly friendly power *en route* to another equally non-belligerent nation would hardly have been conducive to the maintenance of peace and on first examination the suggestion seems utterly ludicrous. However, if it has any origins in truth then it opens up an interesting and previously never before revealed insight into what was going on. That the Foreign

Office under Lord Halifax was prepared to consider that the King and Queen might be in danger from Nazi Germany raises the possibility that there might have been some substance in that belief. Whatever lay behind the suggestion, the information has never been made public. Donald Zec is a highly respected journalist; he is unlikely to have made such a remark unless he believed his source was reliable. However, there is another reference to this incident in the book *Queen and Country* by David Sinclair, which deals with the life of the Queen Mother and suggests a totally different reason:

> Bertie and Elizabeth set off for the tour of Canada and the United States from Southampton on 6 May, aboard the liner *Empress of Australia*. (They had intended to travel in the battleship *Repulse*, but the King had decided that in view of the ominous signs of war the battleship should remain with the fleet.)

This is supported by all the other available evidence which points to the fact that there was no concern shown about the Royal visit until it was under way. The first reports of concern came after the King and Queen had arrived in Canada. Sadly, the papers of Lord Halifax that could possibly shed some light on this are inexplicably closed until the year 2016, which only adds to the confusion about what the British Government knew of what was happening.

The reason for Russell's release is interesting. Among the material contained in the file on Sean Russell declassified by the Irish Government in January 1993 and placed in the Public Archives in Dublin is a collection of reports, letters and random information that various departments of the Irish Garda collected during the period when they were keeping track of Russell.[3] Apart from letters, the file contains a large number of cuttings, mostly from American newspapers, which reported what was happening during Russell's time there. While it is true to say that there are several references which give rise to the assumption that Russell might have been involved in a plot to kill King George VI and Queen Elizabeth during the summer of 1939, it contains little to show that a plot actually existed. All the information is based on the assumption by the American press that the existence of a plot had been discovered. What proved even more disappointing was that all the reports appear to emanate from the same source. The accounts in different newspapers which range from the *Detroit News* in the North to the *San Francisco News* in the West, to the *Chattanooga Times*, the *Tennessee Times* and *Cincinatti Times* in the South, all carried the same story and all versions show a remarkable similarity. This tends to indicate that the story was being syndicated by a press agency and distributed to the various regional newspapers across the States, most of which printed the story without adding anything to the reports. These reports tell that when he was arrested, an aggrieved Russell was alleged to have retorted: 'What did you expect I was going to do? Throw a bomb across the river? – Windsor and Detroit are on opposite sides of the river that forms the border.

Immediately following his arrest the story took on a dramatic twist. The next report reveals how 75 members of the American Congress informed the President that they would not attend the Congressional reception for the King and Queen unless Russell was released without delay. Their anger seems to have emanated from the fact that Russell was being held by the FBI at the request of Scotland Yard until the Royal couple left the country. The reaction of the Congressmen makes it clear that powerful forces were at work. The fact that Russell was the self-confessed leader of an illegal organisation which had led a bloody bombing campaign in his own country and that of nearby Britain, resulting in the deaths of seven innocent people and the injury of almost 200 more, scarcely seemed to matter, that he'd been openly boasting to anyone who cared to listen that his organisation was at war with the British suddenly seemed irrelevant. Russell himself was now of little importance. The argument ranged over who was running America, the administration in Washington or Scotland Yard. The press took up the issue and began to ask questions like: 'was America going to behave like some colonial power, to jump every time the British told them to, or were they going to decide for themselves who they were going to arrest?' It was a masterpiece of juxtaposition, a clever piece of political sleight of hand by an influential group of politicians led by the Congressmen from Pennsylvania, Connecticut and Ohio who, while they were not necessarily pro-IRA, all owed their position to the support of a large Irish vote which they needed to maintain if they were to be re-elected in the coming election. The revolt of such a large body of Congressmen presented F.D. Roosevelt with a serious problem. A boycott of his Washington reception, intended to be the highlight of the Royal visit, by so many important politicians was a considerable embarrassment. Russell's only crime was that he had used a false name and his visa was a few days out of date; in the face of such a transparent charge the President had little option but to cave in. Russell was released on bail of $4,000 and told he would have to return to court to face charges in September. The Dublin file contains no sign of any contact between the American Secret Service and Irish intelligence nor any correspondence between the two governments. This only confirms that the Irish Government was unaware of what Russell was doing in America. Knowing he was there they made no request for his extradition despite the fact that he was wanted in Ireland.

Many well-known biographies of the late King and the present Queen Mother have dealt with the Royal visit. None reveal any difficulty. In fact, the visit was regarded as an outstanding success which, when seen against a background of American public opinion at the time, was quite remarkable.

The country the King and Queen had left behind was gradually becoming resigned to the threat of war which now began to seem inevitable. Compulsory National Service had been introduced for the first time in the nation's history following Hitler's repudiation of the Munich Agreement. The belief that Hitler could be trusted was already beginning to be questioned.

The State visit had come about as a result of an invitation by the Canadian Prime Minister, Mackenzie King, while he was in London attending the Coronation. This was later followed by a similar suggestion from the American President that they should include a visit to the United States, the first ever by a reigning monarch to North America. F.D. Roosevelt, in his invitation, wrote in 1938: 'I need not assure you that it would give my wife and me great pleasure to see you, and frankly it would be an excellent thing for Anglo-American relations if you could visit the United States.'

While the President of the United States was enthusiastic in offering the hand of friendship to the British Royals, there were many there who wanted nothing to do with the situation developing in Europe. Many Americans were anxious to avoid being sucked into a war that they saw as having nothing to do with them. One of the more vociferous voices was that of the former American Ambassador in London, Joseph Kennedy, who said in December 1938: 'Keep out of it . . . I feel more strongly than ever that this nation [*America*] should stay out, absolutely out, of whatever happens in Europe.'

It was thought that Kennedy was expressing the view held by the vast majority of Americans. It would be some time before his true role was discovered and it was revealed that he was a fervent pro-Nazi supporter, a close friend of Reich Marshal Goering, with whom he had been dealing for some time.

The general feeling in America in 1939 was totally different from that of several years later. There was a great deal of anti-British feeling, owing its origins to several sources. Many people still thought of Britain as a colonial power and still remembered their recent history that had prompted America to throw off the yoke of colonialism. A great deal of bitterness and hostility was still evident in certain areas. Significantly, there has always been a strong Irish presence in America – the Irish vote in 1939 has been calculated as five million. American politics has always been dominated by those of Irish ancestry; we are reminded of this by R.F. Foster writing in *Modern Ireland 1600–1972*, published in 1988. He tells us:

> In fact, by the twentieth century there was a strong strain of Irish-American politics that was not antipathetic to collective welfare measures; and more radical Irish-American labour organisers sometimes went against Democratic Party caucuses and tried to overthrow them from the inside. They, in turn, aroused the antagonism of the Catholic hierarchy and organisations like the Ancient Order of Hibernians, who played the Irish Nationalist card against them. It is probably correct to say that the Democratic Party represented more relevant issues, to a larger number of Irish-Americans, than organisations like Clan-na-Gael or the AOH. It is a cliché that by 1963 the President of the United States, the Speaker of the House of Representatives, the Majority Leader of the Senate and the Chairman of the National Committee were all Irish-American Catholic Democrats; but a revealing cliché all the same.

Apart from the Irish, who were predominantly anti-British, there was also a large, former immigrant, population who had fled Central Europe in the period following the first World War to escape poverty and hardship. There was a growing admiration for the rise in prosperity apparent in Germany under the Fascists, hence this important group was strongly pro-German. Apart from these powerful factions there remained a widespread feeling of hostility left over from America's intervention in the First World War. American involvement was seen as a turning point in the conflict, but it left the American people with a deep feeling of disappointment over their contribution, they felt it had not been appreciated and had been largely ignored by the French and British.

However, the Royal visit went off without incident and was regarded as a valuable contribution. There is little doubt that the

Queen made a very favourable impact wherever she appeared. The normally isolationist *Washington Post* carried as its headline 'The British re-take Washington' and in an editorial it noted that the welcome was 'not the result of calculated Government dragooning to create the effect of popular enthusiasm but wholly voluntary and sincere'.

The Royal couple arrived back in London on 22 June to an enthusiastic welcome, as well they might – they had done a magnificent job, winning the affection of millions in both Canada and the United States. The visit had laid the foundation for the Anglo-American co-operation that was to prove so vital later.

Following his release Russell resumed his original schedule. He continued to give public lectures and, from everything we learn, he made no attempt to conceal his whereabouts. All rumours and speculation about bomb plots were forgotten and became just yesterday's news.

Chapter Sixteen

Russell Goes Missing

THE SAFE RETURN of the King and Queen meant that any speculation about an assassination plot was forgotten. The British press was not short of material; the developments taking place in Europe were giving the newspapers during the summer of 1939 more than enough to fill their pages. They had no need to devote time and space to what was seen as a non-event. The danger, having been averted, was not likely to resurface.

While the tour was in progress the welcome afforded to the Royals, and the Queen in particular, had given correspondents in America plenty to write about. There were no reported hostile demonstrations by any faction; indeed, such was the clamour of welcome that the demand for tickets to attend the various functions and parades overwhelmed the authorities and outstripped supply. On the face of it, all that Flynn's intrigues to persuade Russell to go to America seem to have achieved was to stir up concern to the point of panic and make sure the Royal couple were given a great deal more protection than had previously been thought necessary, while at the same time increasing the American public's interest in the Royal tour.

It would be easy to fall into the trap of believing, as everyone else seems to have done, that Russell could have gone to America to harm the King and Queen and that all the attention his presence attracted had prevented him achieving that aim. This is almost certainly not true. It all came about because his visit happened to coincide with the Royal tour and Russell found himself caught up in circumstances he neither anticipated nor sought. The suggestion that gave rise to the original concern (that he had been in touch with the pro-Nazi 'Bund' in America) can easily be explained away by his decision to visit Detroit. His subsequent arrest was nothing more than a panic reaction to pressure from the British authorities who have, traditionally, always been a trifle paranoid at the mention of the IRA, though understandably so at this time due to the havoc and disruption that the bomb attacks were currently causing in Britain.

If we accept this version of events, and it seems reasonable, it is supported by the facts and totally consistent with this argument to learn that following his release Russell continued with his lecture tour of America. There was no suggestion that he went into hiding; he is known to have addressed several public meetings in the weeks that followed. The press continued to report his appearance at meetings and rallies; one held in August in Chicago under the auspices of the Irish-American National Alliance was reputedly attended by 10,000 people. There Russell boasted about the fighting ability of the IRA. However, something must have happened during his time in America because his involvement took a different course. Previous accounts taken from newspaper accounts of the time reveal that while Russell had been arrested on 5 June, it was his subsequent failure to appear at a hearing in September that caused the State Department to issue a deportation order when he did not answer to his bail. From this point onwards the entire business takes on an entirely new air of mystery.

It has never been revealed how long Russell intended to remain in America; had his visit been a simple fund-raising and speaking tour, it seems reasonable to assume it would have lasted about six weeks. He would not have wanted to remain away from the IRA in Dublin for too long, and in any case his visa had expired by 7 June. It seems reasonable to conclude that had he not been arrested he would have quietly left the country and returned to Ireland. Equally there is no reason to doubt that had he surrendered to his bail, he would have simply been ordered to leave the country for overstaying the period covered by his visa, the normal sequence of events. There is evidence to suggest that this is exactly what the State Department expected; it has been revealed that Ava Warren of the passport office arranged for the return of Russell's passport unofficially via his lawyer to enable him to leave.

However, when the captured German records were examined after the war, they reveal that Russell did not leave, instead he remained hiding somewhere in America until April 1940 when he went to Berlin, arriving in the German capital on 3 May.[1]

Clearly something happened to cause Russell's change of heart, something to make Russell join forces with the Nazis. This appears to contradict the assertion that Russell was not involved in the assassination plot, but is not necessarily correct. Several other writers have assumed that because he went to Germany following the supposed murder plot he had been working for the Nazis all along, and this was the reason that he went to America. This interpretation does not necessarily follow and disregards Russell's meeting with Flynn. That Russell subsequently went to Germany does not necessarily link him with the plot: everything else is circumstantial and owes more to coincidence than truth.

The popular explanation of why he went to Germany needs to be examined. The usual reason given is an attempt to play down his connection with the Nazis and explain it away by claiming that it was the only way he could obtain a passage back: this is patent rubbish. It seems strange that the explanation advanced as to how Russell came to end up in Nazi Germany has been so readily accepted. Had anyone challenged this assertion then they would have seen quickly that it was false; the idea does not stand up to examination. The suggestion that Russell was trapped in America and could not make his way back to Ireland without German assistance is so much nonsense.

The impression that Ireland was somehow difficult to reach during the latter part of 1939 is simply not true. There was no shortage of shipping travelling between America and Ireland. Shipping records show that several ships a week carried grain from America and it would have been a relatively simple matter for a man with Russell's connections to have been smuggled on board with false identity papers to travel as a member of the crew. That this was a real possibility is confirmed: Russell not only met with Harry Bridges, the President of the West Coast Maritime Union, during his stay, he also had many contacts with the largely Irish-controlled labour unions who could have made his exit simple. But why should he want to leave surreptitiously anyway? Russell had done nothing except overstay his welcome and had not committed any crime.

Food shortages caused by British ships that had previously traded with Ireland having been diverted to carry munitions and food for Britain meant that rationing was introduced in Ireland. The need to provide food and essential raw materials forced Sean Lemass, the Irish Minister of Supplies, to set up the Irish Shipping Company. This Government-owned company bought or leased a dozen or so ships. Many were old, but they were manned with great fortitude by Irish mariners who, sailing as neutrals under the Irish flag, braved the submarine-infested waters of the Atlantic throughout the entire war. It wasn't until 17 August 1940 (later this date will be seen as highly significant) that Germany declared a wide sea area around Britain to include the waters around Ireland as a blockade area, informing neutrals that they sailed there 'at their own risk'. Prior to this the Germans had endeavoured to observe the neutrality of ships of non-belligerent nations and were particularly anxious not to upset the Irish, accepting the Government assurances that goods imported were only for internal consumption and would not be re-exported. It wasn't until 20 February 1941 that De Valera, speaking in the Dail, complained about the effect of the blockade, reporting that eight Irish ships together with several flying the Greek flag had been attacked by German aircraft, which had resulted in the death of 27 seamen and a further seven injured. He told the Dail that the German Government had been made aware of the strong feeling aroused by these acts of aggression.[2]

In opting for neutrality Ireland may have found herself cut off politically, but in practical terms it was quite easy to get there and back again. A passenger ferry ran from Fishguard to Rosslare; the *St Patrick*, owned by the Fishguard and Rosslare Railways and Harbour Company, sailed regularly, including the day dreaded by all seamen, Friday the 13th. On that day in June 1941, when ten miles off Strumble Head making her way to Fishguard to meet the boat train from Paddington, she was hit by four bombs from a German long-range bomber and sank. The service was resumed which, according to official estimates, enabled some 18,500 Irish men and women to emigrate every year, mainly to Britain where 50,000 served as volunteers in the armed forces.

Even if Russell hadn't wanted to risk travelling on a British or Irish vessel, there were plenty of American merchant ships trading with other parts of Europe. The U-boats, only too aware of the effect torpedoing the *Lusitania* had in 1917, were anxious not to repeat the mistake. The myth that he could not leave with German assistance was finally dispelled when it was learned that he left on the American passenger ship, the *George Washington*, sailing as a member of the engine-room crew.

The manner in which he left is interesting and gives a clue to why he was heading for Germany. When he left New York he was smuggled aboard the ship posing as a blind musician who was joining the ship's orchestra. A year later Dr Hermann Erben was also to leave America for the Far East and China with the help of his friend Errol Flynn – he too posed as a blind musician. As has already been said, Flynn was never a man to waste a good idea.

So the explanation of why Russell turned up in Germany can safely be ignored. The story probably owes its origins to the efforts of Nazi intelligence who were anxious to provide a reason for his presence in Germany.

Despite all the speculation in the British and American press, it can be safely concluded that neither Russell nor the IRA were involved in a plot to harm the King and Queen. For a secret organisation, the history of the IRA is very well and meticulously documented by several eminent writers; they have never given the suggestion any real attention. They seem to have accepted the explanation as to why Russell went to America, and have never offered a convincing reason why he went to Germany. Nobody has suggested he went to kill the Royals. These books were written in the late Seventies and the evidence from America did not surface until the late Eighties.

Never since its formation (curiously enough in Canada in 1866) has the IRA regarded the Royal Family as its enemy. Never in its long and often bloody existence has the IRA ever made any attempt on the lives of members of the Royal Family or regarded them as a legitimate target. This has always remained IRA official policy and has been generally observed. However, with the regrouping and the formation of the Provisional IRA in 1969, this policy has not been strictly followed. A somewhat cynical rider has been added that any member of the Royal Family who is a member of the armed forces can be regarded as a legitimate target. This ploy has been exploited by many of the younger and more ruthless members of the organisation to circumvent the rules. It is well known that practically every member of the Royal Family is a colonel-in-chief of some regiment or other, so while the official policy remains, there have been several breaches.

The most publicised of these was the murder carried out by Thomas McMahon of Earl Mountbatten while he was on holiday and without any form of protection at his family home at Mullaghmore in County Sligo. While not strictly a member of the Royal Family, he was very close. His murder and that of members of his family caused widespread disgust. Lord Louis was 79, and his long military career had never brought him into contact with Ireland; indeed, his high-profile involvement with the handing over of much of the former colonial power to national governments should have made him someone the IRA might have respected. Despite the efforts of Bobby Sands, the then Chief of Staff of the Provisional IRA who tried unconvincingly to provide a logical reason for this cowardly attack, it has always been regarded as mistake. The damage it did to the IRA was considerable and was felt for some time, alienating much support. If it was intended to be a publicity stunt it backfired badly.

There have been others. *The Sunday Times* reported in 1993

that Sean O'Callaghan, currently serving a long jail sentence, was responsible for the bomb that was discovered and defused shortly before the Queen visited Sullom Voe, the oil terminal in Scotland, and that he was also responsible for bombs found on several army bases and in a box at a theatre that was intended to be used by the Prince and Princess of Wales. But apart from these incidents, which occurred in more recent times, there has never been any attack on what has always been regarded as a soft target. The various security lapses at Buckingham Palace confirm how easily attacks might have been made. Most leaders of the IRA have been too aware that any attempt on the Royal Family would result in a terrible backlash that would be counter-productive and alienate much sympathy particularly among their American supporters. All through its long struggle the IRA has regarded the British Government as the real target, believing the struggle to be political.

To return to 1939. It is difficult to hypothesise on the effect the assassination would have had if it had been successful. Clearly, once the initial shock and revulsion subsided the immediate effect would have been to cause a serious rift in Anglo-American relations; while this would only have been temporary, public opinion in America would eventually swing behind Britain as a result of the horrors carried out by the Nazis and the realisation of what would happen if Britain, standing alone, failed to halt them. It is reasonable to suppose that this would have still happened, but a temporary setback would have been inevitable. Had it been discovered that the IRA were responsible, the main effect would have been felt in Ireland. The incident would have inevitably provoked widespread hostility throughout the world directed towards the Irish. The majority of decent American-Irish would have dissociated themselves from the outrage, and the long-term lack of American support would have proved disastrous. This support was, and is, even to this day, vital for the organisation to continue.

The reaction in Britain is easier to predict. Public outrage and hostility towards the Irish would have forced many to flee the country for fear of reprisals. There would have been a great deal of anti-Irish feeling which would have led to riots in the centres such as London, Liverpool and Coventry where the Irish immigrants have traditionally gathered. Violence almost certainly would have erupted as the way many would have chosen to express their fury and disgust, and public opinion would have forced the Government to act. Under the Prevention of Violence (Temporary Provisions) Act 1939 that had already gone through Parliament, the police would probably have welcomed this opportunity to expel many suspected of being members of the IRA. The British Government had become concerned by the threat that Ireland represented when it announced that it intended remaining neutral; they were constantly alive to the possibility that it might be invaded by Germany and used as a jumping-off ground for an invasion in the West. An attack on the King and Queen would be seen as a welcome excuse to invade Ireland. As it was, after he came to power Churchill had to be restrained periodically from mounting an offensive against Ireland. He had something of a blank spot when he directed his mind towards the Emerald Isle and the IRA. One of his first actions in September 1939 when he was appointed First Lord of the Admiralty, causing the famous signal 'Winston is back' to be flashed around the fleet, was to send out a memo to all departments: 'If they [*the IRA*] can throw bombs in London, why should they not supply fuel to the U-boats?'[3] The fact that the IRA didn't have enough hand-guns to go round, let alone the vast quantities of U-boat fuel needed and the means of handling it, was something he didn't bother to stop and consider.

The following day, 6 September 1939, he returned to this theme. He wrote to the Director of Naval Intelligence: 'What is the position on the West Coast of Ireland? Are there any signs of succouring U-boats in Irish creeks and inlets? It would seem money well spent to secure a trustworthy body of Irish agents to keep most vigilant watch. Has this been done? Please report.'

Churchill's anger grew from his intense bitterness over the so-called 'Treaty Ports' of Cohb, Berehaven and Lough Swilly, used by the Royal Navy in the First World War, but which the neutral Irish refused to make available during the Second. All naval strategists are agreed that this put the Royal Navy at a considerable disadvantage during the Battle of the Atlantic. It seems that Churchill was deeply suspicious about what was going on in Ireland and remained convinced that U-boats were being refuelled there despite the lack of evidence. In a secret memorandum to the First Sea Lord and Deputy Chief of Naval Staff on 24 September he returned to his fears:

> There seems a great deal of evidence, or at any rate suspicion, that U-boats are succoured from the West of Ireland ports by the malignant section with whom De Valera dare not interfere [*the IRA*]. And we are debarred from using Berehaven, etc. If the U-boat campaign becomes more dangerous we should coerce Southern Ireland both about coast watching and the use of Berehaven.

Coastal Command flew regularly over neutral Ireland and the waters beyond – the Irish didn't complain because there was little they could do about it. Any sign of a U-boat would have been seen and reported, but Churchill was never convinced. Nine months later, when he became Prime Minister, he had to be dissuaded from thoughts of mounting an offensive 'to save Ireland from Nazi invasion'.

There is little doubt that had the IRA assassinated the King they would have brought about their greatest ambition, the reunification of Ireland. But their triumph would have been short-lived. Ireland would almost certainly have been unified under British military control and it is inconceivable that Russell failed to understand this. Even had he gone to America to harm the King and Queen, it is certain that he did not have the backing of anyone in Dublin. The IRA Council would never have given such a plot their blessing, and no evidence of the existence of the plot has ever surfaced in Ireland. Of course, it is conceivable that Russell was acting alone but again this seems highly unlikely, and we can disregard the possibility that Russell went there as a hired assassin employed by Nazi interests who wished the King dead. Organised crime in America in the late Thirties could have provided a home-grown contract killer without much difficulty and, from what is known about Russell, always a 'man of action', there is no evidence that he ever killed anybody despite his dedication to a cause that employed violence to promote its political aims. Finally, had the IRA been involved in this strange business, why would they choose to carry out the attack while the Royals were in America rather than in Britain? In their own country the Royal Family were given almost no protection, whereas the police in America were armed and more than proficient in the use of weapons; it must have been realised that a high level of protection would be provided for a State visit. Surely an attack in some rural location in England would have been preferable to the crowded streets of New York?

If we accept that Russell and the IRA had no motive or wish to harm the Royal couple, or to disrupt the visit, we are left with only the original belief that Russell was tricked by Flynn to go to the States to act as a cover if the scheme was discovered, or was successfully carried out. It was a perfect solution: a serious rift would have opened up between Britain and America, and Britain would extract her vengeance on the Irish. Hitler and his cronies could afford to stand back and distance themselves from the ensuing trouble their scheme had caused. It was an effective and neat solution. However, the plot seems to have been a victim of its own ingenuity: the probable reason that no attempt on the life of the King was made came from the attention that the press unwittingly directed towards Russell. Instead of quietly carrying on with his mission as he was supposed to do, through no fault of his own he hit the headlines and as a result the amount of protection provided for the Royal couple while they were in America foiled any chance the Nazis might have had. The exposure of Russell by the enigmatic Dr Dinsley had ruined a plan to remove the existing monarchy of England, with a perfect cover provided by Flynn in place to divert the blame from the real perpetrators and make the way clear for the Duke of Windsor to be invited to return.

If we believe that Russell was not involved, are we to conclude that no plot existed? And how can we explain Russell's return to Germany? Clearly it was not for the reason that has been given. Russell had no particular association with Germany or support for the aims of Fascism prior going to America. However, it seems that this might not have been the case when he eventually left.

Chapter Seventeen

The Nazis in America

BEFORE WE DISMISS as rumour and speculation the events that occurred during the time that the King and Queen were in America as largely the work of the American press and conclude that Russell was not involved, it is worth pausing to decide whether or not there was a plot and who might have been behind it.

It is not difficult to see why there had been no serious concern about Russell's presence until it was discovered that he had arrived in Detroit, when the whole affair began to assume a totally different aspect. There were a number of pro-Nazi factions in the United States but the most powerful was centred in Detroit, the capital of the American car industry. There the Fascist movement was well organised, adequately financed and vociferous. Several pro-Nazi organisations were a source of trouble and had caused problems for the American administration for some years, so it was inevitable that the moment Russell made contact with Father Coughlin the FBI began to take the whole thing seriously. While there was very little hard evidence to suggest that Russell had any contacts with other pro-Nazi interests, there was the original report about his bugged discussion with Fritz Wiedemann in San Francisco where it was alleged he talked about a supposed bomb threat. Sadly, the actual transcript of that conversation has never been discovered. Later, during May, the very suggestion that the IRA was involved in a bomb plot was enough to make American intelligence turn their attention to other organisations with Irish connections.

It is not difficult to see why the incident caused such concern. Under Russell's leadership the IRA had renewed its bombing campaign in Ireland and the British mainland with great effect. Their capacity to inflict terror was beyond doubt and amply demonstrated in attacks in London and Sheffield which had occurred within days to signify the anger at Russell's arrest. Nobody on either side of the Atlantic doubted their ability to deliver an attack both quickly and ruthlessly. A suggestion that

161

they had moved their operations to America would have been regarded as a worrying development. The Russell incident increased the FBI's interest, and one of the effects of this close surveillance was the closing down of Clan-na-Gael's operations in 1939 until the war was over. In 1946 the organisation was allowed to resume its former activities.

All the various law enforcement agencies in America were taking a great interest in the Fascist connections of prominent businessmen. Now, with the prospect of an Irish dimension to this problem (something they had previously never considered), it became very worrying. There were a large number of Americans who claimed Irish descent – it was estimated as close on five million in 1939 – and if they could be persuaded to join the other known anti-Government elements this marked a serious development.

There were many prominent people opposed to Roosevelt; his thinly disguised support for the British would, they believed, draw America into a war that most Americans did not want nor consider any of their business. At the same time the Nazis went to tremendous lengths to influence American politics and foster anti-British feelings in the hope that this would keep America out of the war.

The pro-Fascist movement in Detroit was heavily supported by Henry Ford who controlled over half the American motor industry. Once voted the third greatest man in history after Napoleon and Jesus Christ in a poll carried out by a popular newspaper, it was Ford who had revolutionised the manufacture of the motor car, making it affordable to the masses. This brought a great prosperity to America and gave Ford a huge personal fortune. A man of simple tastes, Ford enjoyed a puritanical lifestyle and demanded the same of his employees; he was also a great admirer of Hitler and believed in the same things. As early as 1919 Ford had developed a hatred of the Jews and spoke out regularly against them. Much of his writing in various periodicals expanded on the theme that the Jews were responsible for most of the troubles in the world. Ford's book, *The International Jew*, published in 1927, contained much of the hatred that Hitler was later to espouse. Ford believed and frequently voiced the opinion that 'international financiers were behind all wars', which was a common theme of Hitler who was convinced that it was Jewish money that had fuelled the Russian Revolution. The fact that the two men had a mutual admiration is well known. Ford was singled out for praise in *Mein Kampf* and there was a large photograph of him in Hitler's office. At Hitler's trial in 1924 it was testified by

Erhard Auer that it was Ford who had provided Hitler with the money to finance his political aspirations.

That Ford was a fervent Fascist who wanted and worked towards a German victory is now no secret. When the war was over it was learned that Ford's companies in France and Switzerland had been repairing and providing vehicles for the Wehrmacht while at the same time turning out vehicles in America for the US Army. This was to continue throughout the entire war, contributing vast millions to the Ford coffers at the expense of the lives of servicemen of both sides. It has also been revealed that Ford France had set up a factory in North Africa to build trucks and armoured cars for use by Rommel's Afrika Corps during the desert campaign with the enthusiastic approval of Henry Ford and his son Edsel, who by that time was running the company.

When Henry Ford laid the blame for war on international financiers, he could well have included the world's truck and car manufacturers, for he was not the only one to profit from both sides. The owners of several other large automobile companies were similarly involved with the Nazis. Irénée du Pont, the head of the du Pont family who controlled General Motors, was equally committed to the Nazi cause and was responsible for providing finance for the Fascist rise to power in Germany. General Motors poured $30,000,000 into German companies preparing the munitions of war between 1932 and 1939, using the feeble excuse that they could not get the money out. Most of this money came from building armoured cars and trucks for the German Army through their subsidiary Opel. Several companies were involved in similar contact with the Nazis in the build-up for war. Prominent among these were General Motors, Ford, Standard Oil, ITT, IG and Stirling Products, all companies that had employed Charles Bedaux to represent their interests in Europe.

In 1934 Irénée du Pont, who was totally opposed to Roosevelt, is known to have been mixed up in a coup d'état to overthrow the President. Together with members of the Morgan's Bank, du Pont and his group of backers made $30,000,000 available to a group of terrorists and began to look for someone to act as a sort of Führer who would take orders from his Fascist backers and turn America into a Fascist state. They picked on one of the most popular soldiers in America, General Smedley Butler, the legendary commander of the Marine Corps. Butler was horrified to learn of what was being proposed. Being a loyal American he refused to have anything to do with the treasonable suggestion. However, being shrewd, he waited until he learned all the details about the plot before reporting it to the President.

Roosevelt was faced with a dilemma. To have arrested the directors of two of the largest companies in America at a time when the country was coming out of a terrible recession could have precipitated another Wall Street crash. So he refused to take any action, instead he allowed details to be leaked to the press.

The press eagerly picked up the story which was front page news for a while, but eventually the perpetrators, who were represented by a well-known attorney, Gerald McGuire, were able to dismiss the attempted coup as a preposterous idea. Gradually, by skilful argument, they persuaded the press it was nothing more than an unfounded rumour; Butler had made the whole thing up. However, a committee set up to examine the evidence reported, though its findings were not made public, that 'certain persons made an attempt to establish a fascist organisation in this country' and revealed that the plan was real enough. They disclosed that over a million people had been guaranteed to join and that the arms and munitions necessary were to be provided by Remington, which was a du Pont subsidiary.

The conspiracy was backed by several industrialists with German interests and sympathies who included William S. Knudsen, President of General Motors, and Baron von Schroder. Due to their powerful positions in American industry, Roosevelt was powerless to bring them down, but having thwarted them they remained a thorn in his side, continuing to get involved in Nazi-backed schemes to promote Fascism and preach anti-semitism. It is also worth repeating that during this period Bedaux was employed by all the companies who were conspiring against the President. The fact that these and many other powerful business interests in America had embraced Fascism and endeavoured to use their power and wealth to bring about a change of leadership in the United States would have been in favour of any scheme to put a known Fascist sympathiser, the Duke of Windsor, back on the throne of England. Any such plan would have been more than welcome and would be expected to attract considerable backing. The suggestion that the Nazis were prepared to murder the Sovereign of another country should come as no surprise: this was a method they had employed previously, and there was no reason why they should not do so again.

There is irrefutable evidence that later the same year a plot was discovered to murder Roosevelt and again there was no doubt that Father Coughlin was involved; he was a supporter of Major

General George Van Horn Moseley as President. Moseley was supported by the Christian Front and was associated with George E. Deatheridge, who was the leader of the Fascist movement, the 'Knights of the White Camilla', which was financed by Berlin. In 1940 J. Edgar Hoover became aware of a plot to rally 300,000 Irish-American members of the police to seize the White House and install Moseley as President. Several plots were discovered that can all be traced back to anti-semitic Fascist organisations that were plotting against the American administration.

It is therefore reasonable to assume that any of the several organisations dedicated to advance the cause of Fascism who were active in America with the support of big business could have been persuaded to carry out the supposed assassination, either using their own assassin or using one that the Nazis could have sent over. The whole thing seemingly came unstuck because of the curious press conference where the mysterious Dr Dinsley appeared, set the story running and promptly vanished. It is interesting to speculate on who Dr Dinsley was and for what organisation he was working. His intervention, although dismissed as a hoax at the time, was the trigger that set the alarm bells ringing and which forced the American authorities on to the alert, and from that point onwards the chance of carrying out the supposed assassination was greatly diminished. Whoever he was and whoever was behind his appearance remains a mystery; the probable explanation is that he was exactly who he said he was, an agent working for British intelligence. Having learned of Russell's arrival and although unaware of why he had come, they decided to start a rumour that could result in his arrest and deportation. The fact that they were only partly successful and Russell was released must have come as a disappointment, but having got the matter into the newspapers they had done enough to ensure Russell's movements were monitored and the security provided for the King and Queen increased.

Logically, this should have been the end of this particular story. The evidence that a plot to kill the King and Queen was believed to have existed is irrefutable. Material available in the State Department Archives in Washington and the Public Archives in Dublin proves it. There is also a limited amount of information in the Public Records Office at Kew, and the reports published in the newspapers of the time which are held in the British Library Newspaper Library. While it is relatively easy to establish what happened during the Royal visit, that is not the end of this particular story, but merely the first and admittedly failed attempt to bring the Hess strategy involving Russell to fruition.

Had Russell returned to Ireland there would be grounds for dismissing the whole story as simply speculation. However, the even greater mystery remains. Why did Russell not return to Ireland? Something must have happened to force him to become a fugitive and not leave legitimately. Failing to surrender to his bail and allow himself to be deported was, on the face of it, a stupid move for a man who intended to remain active within the IRA. It rendered it impossible for him ever to have entered the United States legally again. This would have been serious for the Chief of Staff – the main IRA support and funds always came from the United States and being unable to visit and lecture would have been a real disadvantage.

There is no difficulty in establishing that he left the country in April 1940 and went to Germany by way of Italy, which at the time was a neutral country. Following his trail from that point onwards is relatively straightforward and not open to doubt: his movements were carefully recorded by the Nazis and can be traced through the captured papers, particularly those entries that appear in the Abwehr War Diary. No reference to his time in America can be found, neither does the recorded history of the IRA contain any reference. The files of the FBI and Irish intelligence reveal their efforts to discover where he was; the declassified information is evidence that all the various intelligence agencies were making strenuous efforts to find him and that these were to continue until the Nazi records finally revealed his fate. If British intelligence is holding any information that might shed any light on Russell that has not been released, they are presumably still waiting for hell to freeze over before parting with it, knowing that the revelation could lead to the uncovering of events that include the Duke of Windsor's war efforts. Being unable to establish what Russell was up to is very frustrating, especially knowing that during this time he must have undergone a transformation to the Nazi cause, but being unable to prove it.

We can safely assume that Russell was in touch with several Fascist elements who were themselves in close touch with Nazi interests and who were all either Nazi-financed or being funded by powerful American interests who wanted to exploit the situation in Europe and turn America into another Fascist state on the lines of that being peddled by Hitler. He was also known to have met Fritz Wiedemann, who was under almost constant FBI surveillance, aware as they were that he was frequently observed in the company of Flynn. But the reason probably lies in a different direction. Russell came under the influence of one Oskar Karl Pfaus, who has been credited with developing the most potentially dangerous sabotage campaign in the United States. Pfaus is described by Ladislas Farago in his book *The Game of Foxes*:

> The closest a devout Nazi would come to being a Renaissance man, an anachronistic intellectual adventurer with an inquisitive soul. His vast talents for mischief-making were destined never to be properly rewarded. But he gave his best to the cause. Pfaus had come to America in the Twenties in a flood of disillusioned, frustrated Germans of the World War I generation. A hobo, a forester, a prospector, a cowboy and a newspaper columnist at various times, he was nominated for the Nobel Peace Prize by an admirer carried away by Pfaus's missionary zeal in expounding a pseudo-religious movement of 'Global Brotherhood'. He also served in the United States Army and was a cop in Chicago where he learned the tricks of undercover work on assignments against the Capone-Arcado mob.

Eventually he became editor of the German language paper *Weckruf und Beobachter* (*Roll-call and Observer*) and he came to the attention of German intelligence. Dr Tannhauser, the German Consular General in Chicago, suggested he return to Germany where he arrived on 2 December 1938 and began his training with the Abwehr under Lieutenant-Commander Walter Schneidewind who worked for Division II, controlled by Lieutenant-Colonel Lahousen, which was responsible for contacts with discontented minority groups in other countries, preparation of sabotage activities and other special tasks. Pfaus went to Ireland to try and establish contact. He landed at Harwich on 2 February 1939 and made his way to Dublin via Holyhead. His first attempts had something of a shaky start: he met General Eoin O'Duffy, leader of the Irish Fascists or 'blueshirts' who were opposed to, and had fought, the IRA since the Peace Treaty of 1921. However, after some time, he did meet with the IRA and while he did not meet Russell, he is known to have met with his close supporters. Pfaus spent the rest of his time trying to develop links between the IRA and the Nazis, but had only indifferent results. He must have had some success as the *Daily Telegraph* of 12 May reported:

> The police in Dublin are investigating reports of the dissemination of German propaganda among former members of the IRA in County Donegal. Importance is attached to this matter, in view of

suggestions that IRA activities in Great Britain are receiving assistance from Germany. A former IRA officer in East Donegal stated
that he had received a letter addressed to him under his rank and
title in the old IRA organisation and bore signs of having been
opened before it was delivered to him. The contents, mainly anti-
semitic, are stated to have been issued from Hamburg. They
comprise a letter signed by Dr Goebbels, Propaganda Minister,
leaflets, statistics and a small bound book dealing with Germany's
position in relation to churches and world Jewry. It is presumed that
the Germans have obtained a list of former IRA members and wish
to recruit them for their purposes through propaganda material.

Enno Stephan reveals in *Spies in Ireland* that Russell did eventually
meet Pfaus and asked him to accompany him to America, but that
he declined as he alleged there was no prospect of setting up a
successful underground there. However, we learn from Ladislas
Farago that 'a lively Irish underground was active in New York
and Boston and that Sean Russell, the former Chief of Staff of the
IRA, was living in exile in New York'.[1]

Lahousen arranged for an apparently respectable 48-year-old
Austrian businessman called Karl Franz Rekowski, who lived in
America, to meet Russell, and it seems certain that it was he who
persuaded Russell to work on behalf of the Nazis. Under the code
name of 'Richard I', Rekowski was provided with a large sum of
money – $200,000 – and was known to have told Berlin that
'Irishmen are expensive', but later it was discovered that he was
forced to invent a number of apparently successful acts of
terrorism in an effort to keep the supply of funds coming. What
now seems clear is that much of this money was finding its way
into IRA coffers, and Russell's conversion to the Nazi cause was
somehow a result of this. To discover what part Russell intended to
play it is necessary to follow him to Berlin. The mystery of who
suggested he went must remain a secret, but we can be sure that
from the moment he arrived, whatever was planned, his role was
going to be vital; he was involved in a very special mission.

Russell's movements had come almost full circle. The reason
he found himself in the United States had begun in Paris; his visit
engineered by Errol Flynn working with Charles Bedaux, who was
working on behalf of powerful American concerns with massive
interests in Europe.

There is another strong reason that has been advanced as to
why Russell should want to assist the Nazi movement to
overthrow the British. American pressure was building up on De

Valera to enter the war on the side of Britain. While Russell was hiding in America David Grey was appointed US Minister to Ireland and almost from the moment he arrived he began to apply pressure on De Valera to join the British struggle. The *Taoiseach* described Grey as 'an impossible man' and being a relative of Roosevelt he was suspected of trying to force Ireland into war to enable American naval ships to have a base in Ireland. Had Ireland joined in the war – and it was the only Commonwealth country not to do so – it would have had serious political implications for the Republican movement in Ireland. This, as far as Russell was concerned, could have been the end for the IRA. An uneasy truce had always existed between the two Governments but the gulf between them was widening and Ireland was becoming less dependent on Britain. The prospect of a renewal of co-operation, while widely acceptable to the British, was something few in Ireland wanted. Both Governments would have liked nothing better than to smash the troublesome organisation, but they have always drawn back from real co-operation to achieve it. The Irish Government of the late Thirties, having fought for and secured a break from Westminster, had formed themselves into the Fianna Fail party and wanted to forget their former Sinn Fein antecedents. Their refusal to enter the war was based more on the wish not to renew political links with Britain than any real objection to finding itself at war with Germany. The Irish were not so foolish as to believe that, if Britain fell, they could remain immune to the attention of Hitler. As far as Germany was concerned Ireland was a bigger economic prize than Britain: Ireland was a net food exporter and while it was short of grain to feed its people, its meat and dairy products would have been widely welcomed in Germany.

Chapter Eighteen

The Conflict in Europe Begins

MEANWHILE HITLER'S MARCH into Poland changed every-thing. No longer could he explain away his military excursions by saying that they were aimed at the recovery of those territories that Germany had been forced to relinquish in 1919. The invasion of Czechoslovakia had finally exposed his duplicity; his constant reassurances that he had no territorial demands were now seen as a hollow sham. While everyone had been aware for some time that he wanted to resolve the question of the Danzig corridor, his strike against the Poles and the ferocity with which it was delivered took the entire world by surprise. Even the German generals regarded this audacious move with a certain amount of trepidation, unsure of how the rest of Europe would react. Hitler had gambled again, but this time he had miscalculated. This time his nerve had failed him: he had allowed himself to be driven into action, permitting himself to be panicked into believing that the Russians, who had already invaded Finland, were planning to turn their attention on Poland. A Soviet occupation of Poland would have deprived him of much of the material he needed to carry out his war in the East and would have seriously jeopardised his plans. So, in the way that had served him so well, he made another pre-emptive strike, gambling that the British and French Governments, with no stomach for a fight, would do nothing except deliver diplomatic protests and refer the invasion to the League of Nations where it would fail to find any support for positive action. For the first time Hitler's instincts let him down. He totally misread the signs; Russia had no intention of moving against Poland and while Britain and France were still anxious to pursue their policy of appeasement and adopt a conciliatory posture, both were bound by treaty considerations to support Poland in the event of attack. So, with reluctance, on 3 September 1939 they issued their ultimatum: unless Germany immediately withdrew from Poland a state of war would exist.

The news of the German move seems to have taken the Duke of Windsor by surprise and galvanised him into action. The effect was dramatic; suddenly he saw this as his opportunity to return to Britain and re-establish himself with his family. Wasting no time, he instructed Walter Monckton to open negotiations with the Palace while he made arrangements to leave La Croë and return. Expecting to be welcomed now that his country was at war, he saw a golden opportunity to present himself and to take his place at the head of his former army. He imagined this would prove popular and that he could recapture the charisma that he once enjoyed as the dashing officer sharing the danger with his troops, an image that had served him well on the previous occasion when the nation found itself at war.

The reaction his defection had on Hitler, and more particularly on Hess, can only be imagined; to have lost the man so central to their plan must have come as a terrible blow, for it seems certain that the Duke had not bothered to discuss his intentions with them, but acted impetuously. However, this was no sudden attack of patriotism; instead he expected to grasp the opportunity to resurrect his previous intention to discover a position of power in Britain where he could influence events. This is clearly demonstrated when we learn that before he left La Croë there was an exchange of telegrams with Hitler. Even though the Führer must have had several other things on his mind, he found time to reply:

> Berlin, 31 August 1939
> I thank you for your telegram of August 27. You may rest assured that my attitude towards Britain and my desire to avoid another war between our two peoples remains unchanged. It depends on Britain, however, whether my wishes for the future development of German-British relations can be realised.
> Adolf Hitler.[1]

This seems a rather cold and threatening response but it is not difficult to see the intention behind the message, Hitler was simply confirming what everyone was to come to know – he did not want nor did he expect the British to react by declaring war. Three days later the two countries were at war and the Duke was making plans to return.

However, in common with his friend Hitler, the Duke miscalculated. Nothing but humiliation awaited him in England. The last thing the King or the rest of the family wanted was to embrace what they had come to regard as an errant troublemaker and have him assume any place in public life. The Royal Family were at something of a loss to decide how to deal with the situation and reluctantly the King was persuaded to offer two positions in which the Duke might serve. The Royal Family did nothing to encourage his return but, believing the Duke would be satisfied, Walter Monckton flew in a small aircraft to Antibes to ask the Duke which he preferred. The Duke proved less than enthusiastic about either post. Refusing the offer of a return flight, he and the Duchess decided to motor back and resolve the issue.

The Palace ignored their return; they even refused to send a car to meet them. It was left to the faithful Churchill to hastily arrange some sort of homecoming. In his role as First Lord of the Admiralty he gave orders to Lord Louis Mountbatten, who was 'working up' the recently delivered destroyer HMS *Kelly* at Portsmouth, to sail and collect his cousin the Duke, together with the Duchess, and return with them to Portsmouth. Churchill sent his son Randolph to travel on HMS *Kelly* to welcome the Duke and Duchess and gave his son a letter to hand to the Duke. He wrote: 'Welcome home! Your Royal Highness knows how much I have looked forward to this day.'

There was a moment of light relief during the journey over. Randolph changed into the uniform of his regiment, the 4th Hussars, but was embarrassed on meeting the Duke to hear him say: 'Randolph, your spurs are not only inside out but upside down! Haven't you ever been on a horse?'

Winston Churchill, acutely embarrassed at the apparent disinterest of the Royal Family, felt obliged to lay on some sort of a welcome at Portsmouth. He arranged for a naval guard of honour and a Royal Marine band to play as the ship docked, which, coincidentally, was at the same berth from which the Duke had left on the night following his abdication. As the Duke and Duchess disembarked, and as if to prove something of an omen for what was to come, the band played the shortened version of the National Anthem, the first six bars reserved for members of the family other than the Sovereign. The Duke, who had gone very quiet, suddenly snapped as they were driven away: 'The short version by God!'

The couple, who had left the South of France on the 8th, three days before, and travelled to Cherbourg to meet the *Kelly*, had discovered that no arrangements had been made for their accommodation. Consequently, on arriving in Southampton, they were obliged to drive to the home of 'Fruity' Metcalfe in Surrey and stay there. The following morning the Duke presented himself at Buckingham Palace to meet the King. From the moment he arrived he was left in no doubt of the feelings the family still harboured. If the Duke had been serious about effecting a reconciliation he could not have approached his task in a more foolish fashion. He began by pleading for the use of the title he so badly wanted for Wallis and, with an amazing lack of sensitivity, going on to suggest that if she were so honoured it would enable her to attend to certain Royal public duties, thus relieving the King and Queen of some of their work load. The prospect of 'Her Royal Highness the Duchess of Windsor' loose in London society was probably viewed with about as much enthusiasm as the prospect of German troops marching up Whitehall. This stupid suggestion set the tone for what was to follow. The King was clearly worried about what his unpredictable brother might get up to next. George VI was still smarting over a speech his brother had made a few months previously. Although the British press had failed to report it, the incident had caused acute embarrassment. The speech, made in May, a few days before the King and Queen had left for America, was delivered in Verdun, the scene of some of the worst fighting and heaviest British losses during the First World War. Broadcast from a hotel in the town, the BBC refused to transmit it, thus preventing the British people from listening. The refusal was thought to be as a result of Government pressure, but this was strongly denied. However, the speech was relayed to America and the rest of the world where it was heard by an audience estimated at 90 million. In it the Duke said:

> I speak simply as a soldier of the last war whose most earnest prayer it is that such a cruel and destructive madness shall never again overtake mankind. For two and a half years I have deliberately kept out of public affairs, and I still propose to do so. I speak for no one but myself, without the previous knowledge of any government.[2]

He went on to explain that during his travels his study of human nature had left him with a profound conviction that there was no land where the people wanted war. 'International understanding does not always spring spontaneously by itself. There are times when it has to be deliberately sought and negotiated and political tension is apt to weaken that spirit of mutual concession in which conflicting claims can be best adjusted.' In a voice full of emotion he denounced 'poisonous propaganda' and said he personally deplored, for example, the use of such terms as encirclement and aggression. They could only arouse just those dangerous sentiments that it should be the aim of all to subdue.

It is in the larger interests that peace should be pursued. Somehow I feel that my words tonight will find a sincere echo in all who hear them. It is not for me to put forward concrete proposals – that must be left to those who have the power to guide the nations towards closer understanding. God grant that they may accomplish that great task before it is too late.

Many people have tried to understand what the Duke hoped to achieve by this extraordinary broadcast. There were those who cynically regarded its timing as deliberately chosen to coincide with the American visit by his brother, believing it to have been an attempt to nullify the propaganda effect of the visit. Others, particularly in London, believed they saw Hitler's hand in it. This was a very conciliatory speech which seems to have been aimed at trying to draw attention away from the Duke's reported contacts with the Nazis while still making a case for dialogue and reconciliation between the two countries. More importantly, he was making a veiled reference to his own position, stressing his inability to act while making it clear that he remained available to take on the delicate task of reconciliation if it were suddenly offered to him. If we accept that he anticipated learning of his brother's death within the next two weeks then the purpose of his address is crystal clear. The Duke was telling the world he was available to act and prevent war between the two traditional enemies. There seems little doubt he was paving the way to be invited back as Sovereign, telling the world he would produce a plan that would avert the coming disaster.

While it is unlikely that those advising the King could possibly have been aware of the motive behind the speech, this amongst several other reasons is why nobody wanted the Duke back in British public life. George VI was being advised from a variety of sources, but there was one in particular, a powerful voice to whom the King listened and which he trusted, that was Sir Robert Vansittart, the head of the Secret Service who was concerned at the many reports that he was receiving about the Duke and those with whom he was associating in France. Vansittart advised that the Duke should not be given anything important to do or be allowed anywhere near sensitive information.

Following his discussions with the Palace, Walter Monckton was told that there were two jobs that had been suggested for the Duke. One was the deputy regional commissioner for Wales, the other a liaison officer with the British Military Mission based in

Paris. However, the Duke's attitude and the prospect of Wallis wandering around the various military establishments in Britain made the King think again and he decided that if his brother was to serve anywhere, the further away the better. The meeting which proved a disaster and culminated abruptly ended with the King telling the Duke that he would let him know what had been decided. The Duke left the palace in a furious rage. He spent the next few days waiting to be told what he was to be offered. To pass the time he and Wallis visited Fort Belvedere which they were saddened to find in a state of neglect, the gardens all overgrown. It was the last time they were ever to see it together.

Eventually the Duke was told that his future role had been decided, but not by the King (who refused to contact him). Instead he received a summons from the War Office where he was informed that he had been assigned the rank of Major-General to the British Military Mission at Vincennes. Despite his protests he was given stark choice, it was France or nothing. The position in Britain had been withdrawn and the reason was not difficult to see: the Royal Family did not want the Duchess in Britain. This was another humiliation. As Prince of Wales he held the rank of Field Marshal. In desperation the Duke approached the Welsh Guards, the regiment where he had been colonel-in-chief, to try to persuade them to allow him to serve with them, only to be rejected following pressure from the Palace.

Bitterly disappointed, he and the Duchess returned to France and for the first time since they were married were parted. The Duchess found a suite for herself in a small hotel in Paris and the Duke, accompanied by 'Fruity' Metcalfe, went about his military duties. The role of Metcalfe remains a strange one. He had been a long-time friend and confidant of the Prince of Wales and had remained faithful during the period that followed the Abdication, but there is evidence that he was about to distance himself from the Duke, hoping to serve his country in a more active role. However, it has been alleged that he was contacted on the direct orders of the King and instructed that he was to remain at the Duke's side, act as his ADC and report what was going on to the Palace. If this is true it tends to suggest that 'Fruity' was employed by the King to spy on his brother – which explains many of the things that were to happen later.

It is clear that during the time he spent in London the Duke was humiliated and was finally persuaded that his family and country wanted nothing more to do with him. This was something he had anticipated. Before he returned, he wrote to his mother in the hope that she would help pave the way for a reconciliation, but he received only a painful rebuff. She, in keeping with the rest of the family, made it clear that she was never going to forgive him and the others seem to have taken their cue from her. It is worth noting that during their stay in England in 1939 no one in the family ever met the Duchess; any hope the Duke had of introducing her at court was doomed from the onset. Everyone behaved as if she did not exist, but behind the scenes her presence was the cause of many of the harsh decisions that were taken concerning the Duke. The Duchess was probably not surprised, the Duke seems to have anticipated the welcome they might receive, saying as the *Kelly* slid into Portsmouth: 'I don't know how this will work out. War should bring families together, even a Royal Family. But I don't know.'[3] Behind the family wrangling there was a great deal of suspicion about his motives and the part he could have usefully played, but humiliating him and allowing him to return to France on the clear understanding that he would never be allowed to play a useful part in public life was a grave mistake. It reinforced his previous understanding that the only way he would ever return was with German support. To have denied him this last chance of a reconciliation was a tactical blunder of the greatest magnitude by the British.

In the run-up to the war a great deal of hostility and suspicion existed between the British and French. This was present at all levels despite the two nations being allies and driven to war in common cause. There are many examples of co-operation between officers on the ground but the lack of trust at the higher levels would never be totally overcome. An example of this lack of trust was that during the early days of the conflict there was little, if any, attempt to share information. As a consequence the French were never given access to any intelligence that the British had gathered about the Duke and his activities – which meant that they were a great deal more trusting towards him than they might otherwise have been. The British Command in France had been warned to be careful about what the Duke was allowed to see, but no such warnings were passed to the French.

The decision to send the Duke to France was taken at a meeting between the King, the War Minister Hore-Belisha and the Chief of the General Staff, General Sir Edmund Ironside, and was clearly a solution that was intended to serve the interests of the Royal Family by removing a threat to the King's authority. It would be interesting to learn how Ironside viewed the prospect of the Duke being driven back into the arms of the Nazis, for it was later discovered that he too was sympathetic to the Fascist regime in Germany. Even at the time of the meeting, the Chief of the General Staff was under scrutiny for his contact with Fascist sympathisers, and it was later discovered that he was responsible for the leaking of a highly confidential Cabinet document which British intelligence tracked through Belgium to Berlin. Secret agent Malcolm Muggeridge compiled the report which Vansittart used to force the general to resign. The whole incident was hushed up and was not allowed to become public, but the outcome was not without friction. It has since been revealed that while the King wanted Ironside to be honoured in his retirement, Churchill wanted him dismissed. He was overruled and eventually Ironside was created the first Baron Ironside. Strangely, Hore-Belisha was soon to be replaced – he too was out of favour with the military establishment and this was aggravated by the fact that the King did not like him. When certain of the generals opposed Hore-Belisha as War Minister they found a great deal of Royal support. The reason behind this is not difficult to find; Hore-Belisha had supported the Duke at the time of the Abdication which meant that, in keeping with Churchill, he was disliked by the King and Queen. There is no suggestion that in deciding the Duke's fate those involved were in collusion with the Nazis – certainly Hore-Belisha was a fervent anti-Nazi whose support of Churchill was total, his loyalty never questioned. But Hitler's interests could not have been better served had he been there to arrange things for himself. Placing the Duke in the French camp would provide valuable intelligence which was to find its way to Berlin.

When he reported for duty one of the first tasks to which the Duke of Windsor applied himself was a study of the Maginot Line, the defensive structures on the French border into which the French had poured vast amounts of money. It was an interconnected line of fortifications, built following the First World War, which they were confident would form an impregnable barrier against German invasion of their soil for centuries. This vast line of fortifications and the similar, but less extensive, defensive construction built by Germany remains proof that the generals on either side had learned little from the First World War. Both the Maginot and Siegfried lines were just an elaborate extension of the concept of trench warfare, deep concrete bunkers where troops could hold out for over a year without danger or the need to be supplied. The generals of both sides had failed to realise that war had changed. Standing still would never again be a defence against a fast-moving, highly mechanised army.

The French army was led by General Gamelin, who had his headquarters in the Chateau de Vincennes outside Paris, and the British forces were commanded by Major-General Sir Roland Howard-Vyse, a popular and efficient officer who had his headquarters about five miles away at Nogent-sur-Marne. Gamelin was not highly regarded. He still thought of war in terms of trench warfare and had a disturbingly low regard for military security. It is known that he once left a file marked 'Secret' in a public room at the Hyde Park Hotel in London where it was discovered by an Italian waiter. Military historians have concluded that he was 'the best general the Germans had'.[4]

The Duke joined Gamelin's staff. Being a major-general on the British Mission meant he was welcomed by the French who had a special affection for Royalty, presumably as they did not possess any of their own. For this reason the Duke was permitted to visit and examine the Maginot Line which the French had previously refused to allow any other member of the British forces to see inside. They were very secretive about what they regarded as an impregnable fortress, but one that the Duke quickly realised was nothing short of useless and which offered no protection to a possible attack through Northern France, Luxembourg and Belgium where such fortifications were almost non-existent. This refusal of the French to allow their so-called 'allies' to inspect their preparations would have quickly exposed the defects in this form of defence which would ultimately determine the battle for France. But they were adamant. Even after the *Illustrated London News* had published details and photographs of the fortifications obtained from a German magazine, the French still refused to allow the British to examine the defences. It has been suggested that the Duke was placed in General Gamelin's headquarters to spy on the French on behalf of the British. This may have some origin in truth, but if that were the case it displays a remarkable attitude on the part of the British towards the ally with whom they were preparing a common offensive. For the War Office to have been aware that the Duke was being allowed to visit the French front line and inspect their preparations while issuing instructions to Howard-Vyse that the Duke was not to visit the British front line seems incredible. The reason is clear. The British had a shrewd idea where the information he gained would be passed but that they were prepared to risk details of the French defences to be compromised in that way seems ludicrous.

There are several reports of how the Duke and Duchess frequently dined in Paris in the company of their old friend Charles

Bedaux, who was generally left to pick up the bill for the lavish entertaining the Windsors extended to their friends.[5] Bedaux was presumably well satisfied – the Duke and Duchess were known to be highly indiscreet. There remains no doubt that the Duke was passing on a great deal of information he was gathering about the British and French preparations for the attack that was to come. The fact that Bedaux continued to host these dinner parties is conclusive evidence that he was being used as the conduit by which secret and sensitive military information was passed to Germany. What seems so remarkable is that the British, who were aware of Bedaux's meetings with the Duke and Duchess, simply reported these incidents and nothing further was done. The Duke made no attempt to conceal his relationship with Bedaux; many of these meetings were held in fashionable restaurants under the watchful eyes of British intelligence.

Bedaux, who was totally committed to self-advancement and who had first served as a German agent during the First World War, was one of their most effective spies during the Second World War; he would not have wasted his considerable talents attending on the Duke unless he was obtaining vital information to pass to his Nazi masters. Several people have sought to suggest that the Duke was naïve and unaware of the value of the information he was providing for Bedaux or that he was passing it to Germany, but was simply being indiscreet over the dinner table. This is very hard to believe: the Duke was in no doubt whom Bedaux was working for and to suggest he did not appreciate that the information he was passing on would be of considerable advantage to German army intelligence requires either a considerable stretch of imagination, or to imply that he was completely stupid; which is certainly not true.

There seems no doubt that in studying and reporting on the Maginot Line the Duke did his work well; his report was very thorough, so much so that it provides an interesting anecdote. Later in the war, the American General Patten wanted to know if the guns on the Maginot Line could be turned and used to fire in the opposite direction and thus fire on an advancing Allied army. The only intelligence that the War Office was able to provide was the Duke's report which confirmed that this was not possible.

There is no question that during this period the Duke was very active. His continual presence caused a great deal of disquiet in several quarters, particularly among those who were aware of his close connections with the enemy. The War Office refusal to allow him into sensitive areas caused friction with brother officers who were suspicious of his motives. However, what now appears ludicrous is that he was allowed to visit the French front line at a time when he was barred from visiting the British.

The Duke soon discovered the weakness in the French position; it was commonly recognised among the British Command that if the attack came through the Ardennes France was virtually defenceless. The Duke prepared two reports for the British Staff, both highly critical of the French defensive positions. To have produced these (which are still classified) meant he had obtained access to all the combined British and French battle dispositions including that known as Plan B, which was the plan to send the British Expeditionary Force north in the event of an attack through Belgium. The British had pointed out this danger to the French who refused to consider it, even after they were reminded that the Germans had poured through the Ardennes in 1914 with five divisions. The French retaliated by pointing out that the attack, when it came, would be with tanks and they were firmly convinced that the German armour could not operate in the forest conditions. They did not have to wait long to find out – on 5 May 1940 the XIX Panzers of General Guderian thrust through exactly where the Duke had predicted.

Despite the plan to move the British army north, the end was already in sight as the German army swept south. Bedaux, who had been passing the information on, had provided the German generals with the information about what the enemy was thinking.

On 10 May the German armour swept into the Low Countries. Days later, as predicted, the French line was broken and the German army crossed the Meuse and headed for Paris. Having taken the Duchess to Biarritz the Duke returned to Paris, but finding himself with less and less to do, he frequently spent his days playing golf. Then, suddenly without warning, he announced that he was giving up his post and was going to join the Duchess. Major-General Howard-Vyse was probably relieved – it was known that he had found it difficult to carry out his orders to keep the Duke away from the front and make sure that he learned as little as possible of the army's future plans.

Aware that the fall of Paris was not far off, the Duke collected the Duchess from Biarritz and travelled to Antibes and from then on appeared set on taking no further part in the war. What can be learned from this incredible behaviour? The idea that a major-general, a serving army officer on the General Staff, could simply abandon his post and decide to have nothing more to do with a war in which his country was desperately fighting must be without precedent. Had it been any other officer, he would have faced a charge of desertion in the face of the enemy, a capital crime and one for which several hundred British soldiers had been executed by firing squad during the First World War. Desertion in battle has always been regarded as the ultimate crime by military men. However, in this case nobody seems to have cared. The British headquarters staff were probably glad to see the back of him, and in London the news that the Duke had become bored with the war and had apparently gone to sit in the sun seemed to have raised little comment. Which is all very strange. Even allowing for the confusion that existed just prior to the fall of France, it seems inexplicable that it was not suggested that he be charged in the way that any other officer might.

It is not difficult to see the Duke's motives behind his move. He realised that his usefulness to the German advance was over, and had he remained at his post he would have been ordered to withdraw. Believing that the fall of France was imminent, he knew if he remained at his post he would be ordered back to England where he ran a very real risk that his involvement with Bedaux had been reported and he would be branded a traitor. By making his way to the South of France he was not fleeing the German advance as has often been suggested, but putting himself out of the reach of the British. By this time he did not care what the British would do – the writing was on the wall, the British army was already being forced back, the rout had begun. Like almost everyone else at the time, the Duke expected the fall of France to be followed by a British request for peace. Instead of returning as part of a beaten army he expected the day was not far off when he would return backed by the might of the most powerful government in Europe. His Nazi friends had reassured him that his return to England would not be long delayed when Hitler negotiated a truce and removed the existing Government. Edward VIII's revenge on the family who had humiliated him was not far away: the Duke of Windsor's moment of destiny was about to arrive.

Despite the unsuccessful plot in America, Hess had not abandoned his plan to restore the Duke to power. If the problems faced by a hostile invasion and ultimate defeat of Britain were to be avoided, the Duke remained the best hope. But even if Germany were forced to invade, the Nazis would still require someone to head a Government kindly disposed to Fascism. The strategy that Hess had been entrusted by Hitler to carry out was still the best alternative, and if a war on two fronts was to be averted the time was approaching when it would be put into operation.

181

Chapter Nineteen

The Final Moves

IT IS POPULARLY BELIEVED that Adolf Hitler only ever visited the coast of Europe on one occasion. Whether this is true or simply legend has been impossible to discover, but one thing is certain: the nearest he ever came to the English coast was on 26 July 1940.

As his armoured Mercedes drew up on the promenade in front of what was just a row of burnt-out buildings, he looked over the deserted beaches of Dunkirk, now covered in a tangled mass of wrecked vehicles and equipment abandoned by a fleeing army. It was a scene of carnage, set against a backdrop of the half-submerged remains of several ships destroyed in the brave attempt to snatch the weary British and some of the French army to safety, the site of an operation so magnificently improvised that it was to turn a terrible defeat into something of a triumph and etch the name of this small coastal town on history. The *New York Times* of 1 June 1940 announced:

> So long as the English tongue survives, the word Dunkirk will be spoken with reverence. In that harbour – such a hell as never blazed on earth before – at the end of a lost battle the rags and blemishes that had hidden the soul of democracy fell away. There beaten but unconquered, in shining splendour, she faced the enemy, this shining thing in the souls of free men which Hitler cannot command. It is the great tradition of Democracy. It is the future. It is victory . . .

Admirable stuff, written from the safety of an office basking in the heat of midsummer New York, but on the other side of the deceptively narrow strip of water now the focus of Hitler's gaze, the British had little reason for self-congratulation.

Standing, staring over the calm expanse of sea spread out before him, his eyes were drawn across the blue-grey water that disappeared into a sea mist from which rose the outline of the famous white cliffs. Hitler might well have been imagining that same stretch of sea covered with invasion barges of the type the Wehrmacht were already assembling further along the coast. On 16 June, on signing Directive No 16 in his capacity as Chancellor of the German Reich and Supreme Commander of its Armed Forces, he wrote: 'As England, in spite of the hopelessness of her military position, has so far shown herself unwilling to any compromise, I have decided to begin to prepare for, and if necessary carry out, an invasion of England . . .' Initially codenamed 'Operation Lion', which he personally amended to 'Sealion' as a reminder to those involved of where the dangers in this operation would lie, Hitler instructed his generals to be ready to sail by the middle of September.

It is not recorded whether Hitler smiled. It would not be surprising if he did, for years later the world would learn that he never had any intention of allowing the operation to be mounted. The whole thing was an elaborate ruse to force the enemy across the water to come to its senses and join France in throwing down what few arms it still possessed before the might of the German military machine.

Peter Schenk, writing in his book *Landung in England*, now available in English as *Invasion of England 1940*, a comprehensive account of the planning and preparations for 'Operation Sealion', confirms that Hitler frequently persuaded his military commanders to devote their energies to planning operations that he had no intention of allowing to proceed. 'Operation Sealion' proved a classic example of this. On that day in June he believed that the necessity for the invasion would have disappeared long before September. By then he confidently expected to be in London, leading a triumphant procession down the Mall towards Buckingham Palace at the head of his all-conquering troops. Already he was privately boasting: 'I will drink champagne in Windsor Castle before Christmas.'

Hitler, we are told, was not impressed by what he saw at Dunkirk.[1] The grim evidence of his victory failed to give him any satisfaction, instead he was apparently saddened by the sight of death and destruction. This was perhaps not surprising, for he had a creative side to his character, something often overlooked, and he possessed an artist's love of beauty and sense of order. The Europe he dreamed of creating, 'The Thousand Year Reich', would be full of magnificent buildings. It has been revealed that the reason he spared Paris, a city he hated because of its associations with the Treaty of Versailles and which he once threatened to raze to the ground, was that having seen it, he changed his mind. Admiring its beauty, he saw it instead as a challenge, arrogantly boasting that he would outdo its grandeur and make Berlin the most beautiful city in the world. Albert Speer, his architect, was given the task of designing the new city with an avenue wider and longer than the Champs-Elysees, a railway station of four levels, a plaza 3,000 metres long and 1,000 metres wide lined with the captured weapons of war, and his Arch of Triumph would dwarf the Arc de Triomphe by being more than twice its height. It has recently been suggested that Hitler also planned to dismantle Nelson's Column following the defeat of Britain and erect it in Berlin. What is generally not known is that most of Speer's designs were the work of Hitler himself who produced the original highly detailed sketches that Speer developed. Hitler's dreams of architectural beauty remain the supreme irony: his efforts to create a memorial to his passing would be responsible for the destruction of more elegant buildings, more magnificent churches and cathedrals, even entire medieval cities, than those destroyed by all the other vandals who have ever lived.

His visit to Dunkirk came about almost by accident. He and two companions, his former sergeant in the First World War, Max Asmann, and an old friend, Ernst Schmidt, had arranged a nostalgic visit to the battlefields of the First World War, Messines and Fromelles, Ypres and Langemarck, where as a corporal he fought and suffered the horrors of trench warfare, only to endure the humiliation of ending up on the losing side. Someone had suggested that he make a detour to visit the location of the final battle for France and see the battle-scarred town and the site of the defeat of the French and British at the hands of his victorious army.

France had fallen swiftly. In little more than a month his troops had swept through France and the Low Countries with relative ease. The revenge that Hitler vowed to extract for the indignities forced on the German people by the Treaty of Versailles had been satisfied. His forces had humiliated their former enemy. France sued for peace, by 10 June the Government had fled Paris, and a new Government headed by Petain concluded the armistice on the 17th. The victorious German army marched into Paris and in a final act of vengeance army engineers dragged out the old railway carriage where Germany's fate had been sealed in 1918 and transported it to a short length of railway line in the forest near Compiegne to be the scene of the French humiliation. The episode was witnessed by William L. Shirer, author of *The Rise and Fall of the Third Reich*, who was an American war correspondent. Quoting from his diary he recalls:

Hitler, followed by the others, walks slowly over to it, steps up, and reads the inscription engraved (in French) in great letters: HERE ON THE ELEVENTH OF NOVEMBER 1918 SUCCUMBED THE CRIMINAL PRIDE OF THE GERMAN EMPIRE – VANQUISHED BY THE FREE PEOPLE WHICH IT TRIED TO ENSLAVE.

    Hitler reads it and Goering reads it. They all read it, standing there in the June sun and in silence. I look for an expression in Hitler's face. I am but fifty yards from him and see him through my glasses as though he were directly in front of me. I have seen that face many times at the great moments of his life. But today! It is afire with scorn, anger, hate, revenge, triumph.

Shirer goes on to recall that the French delegation, who had been given no warning where they were being taken, were badly shaken. They were forced to accept a set of conditions that amounted to total submission and were described by the French as 'hard and merciless'. Hitler left the negotiations in the hands of others. Three days later, on his order, the carriage was blown up.

    Hitler, we are told, continued to stare across the Channel, but it can only be conjecture what was going through his mind. He could not have failed to have thought about those events long in the planning but now close to fruition. Within days he expected to have delivered the prize he had dreamed about for two decades.

    Anxious to be away, he lingered for only a moment and allowed himself one last look at the land on the horizon, those white cliffs, so tantalisingly close and yet so frighteningly far if he were forced to invade England, and then he turned, confident that within days the British would follow the French and seek an armistice.

    As he walked away amid the scenes of carnage it would have been difficult not to marvel at everything that had happened with such breathtaking speed since his army struck west with such dramatic results. Since he'd given the order on 9 May, 135 German divisions began to move, crossing into Luxembourg at 5.30 a.m. the following day, so full of confidence they drove with their vehicles' headlights blazing.

    Thirty-nine days later it was all over – France had surrendered. What was left of the British and French armies had been snatched off the beaches and were back in England, without most of their equipment, but with the growing realisation that a crisis faced the world. Germany under Hitler's leadership had achieved in two weeks what it had failed to do in four years less than a quarter of a century before.

Everything had gone a great deal better than anyone in the German High Command could have expected. Suddenly, instead of Hitler urging the leaders of the armed forces to be bold, they had begun to pressurise him. They saw the old enemy wounded, forced to retreat in confusion and now lying virtually defenceless: one good hard blow was all it would take. The demand to invade was becoming difficult to curtail. The German generals were confused at their leader's apparent reluctance, believing Hitler was uncharacteristically beset with doubts for now he urged caution and tried to tell the generals that it would be a difficult and dangerous campaign. Hitler was playing for time; reluctantly he authorised 'Operation Sealion' to keep the generals quiet.

When the German army had gone on the offensive there had been no thought of mounting an amphibious invasion of England, but the German strategists had quickly come to realise that no better opportunity would ever present itself than that offered by a weak and practically defenceless Britain.

Hitler was wise to caution against haste, despite having told his military planners on 2 July to prepare plans for an invasion 'if necessary' by the middle of September. His proviso is of considerable interest. It shows he either expected that by the middle of September British resistance would have collapsed or that he would have a totally different strategy.

The German military were fooling themselves. 'Operation Sealion' was not a serious option. Nobody knew how to mount an amphibious invasion, the technology was not available. Even later in 1944, the massive and well-equipped Allied landings on the coast of France were considered by those in charge as more than risky with the weather an all-important factor. To have attempted it with the limited know-how and resources available to Germany in 1940 would have been to invite Hitler's first military disaster. To find evidence of German lack of preparedness we need look no further than the actions of Major I.G. Teske, the First General Staff Officer of the 12th Infantry Division who on 12 August wrote to his regimental commanders: 'Due to the lack of useful precedents, the following report of 55 BC is submitted.' Included was a translation of Caesar's *De Bello Gallico* which described the crossing of Roman troops from Boulogne to Britain. Julius Caesar and William the Conqueror, who followed him in 1066, are the only two commanders ever to have carried out a successful invasion of England. Both shared the same advantage – the British did not attempt to engage the invading force at sea. Hitler could not hope for similar good fortune.

There is little doubt that those officers and engineers entrusted with producing an amphibious technology virtually from scratch were highly motivated. They worked with typical Teutonic thoroughness and developed a variety of ingenious craft and strategies but had they been called upon to demonstrate them in action they would have discovered that 'Operation Sealion' would be a failure. This was established in 1973 when the Royal Military Academy at Sandhurst conducted joint British-German war-games to try and evaluate the probable outcome. They came to the conclusion that the British navy would have cut off the German supply lines in three days.

But as he walked away, Hitler was far from worried. In a matter of days he expected Rudolf Hess to complete his plan that would enable him to enter London and fulfil all his dreams of a unified and powerful Europe. Only a handful throughout the world knew of his secret plan; the final moves were in place and already the man who was central to the operation was being briefed in Portugal. The figure who would make it possible was putting the final touches to his plans in Berlin. August 1940 would prove the time when all the careful planning by Hess and Bormann would come together; the prize was within his grasp. Even though the German military were anxious to invade, Hitler realised that not only was it likely to prove a disaster, but it also would not be necessary. Even had the might of the German army landed on the beaches of Britain, the battle would have been short-lived, but it would be a hollow victory. As a result Germany would end up occupying a country that was unable to feed itself – its supply of food from America and the Empire would dry up – and it would be left to Germany, which was already suffering food shortages, to either feed the civilian population or allow mass starvation. To control a discontented people would need a vast army of occupation and that was the last thing Hitler planned or needed. One reason why he sought an alliance with Britain from the beginning was to avoid this very problem. Hitler's dream was to rule Britain with a puppet Government and to employ the British army to assist him in the fight against Russia. This was the ultimate prize and is the reason behind his decision not to have allowed the slaughter of the British army at Dunkirk. What other reason could he have had for holding back his army to allow the British to evacuate and fight another day? While it was not known at the time, as Churchill's 'finest hour' speech about the deliverance at Dunkirk confirms, there has always been a great deal of speculation about Hitler's refusal to allow the Panzers under Generals Von Brauchitsch and

Halder to pursue the retreating army and destroy it. However, most historians now accept that the reason that Hitler refused to inflict the final blow that would have destroyed the BEF was that he harboured plans to re-arm and employ the British army to protect his western flank following his hoped-for alliance with the British Government. It is a matter of record that he was still sending entreaties to London to join him as late as 19 July. These were formally rejected by Lord Halifax. It is also known that he intended to make another appeal in a major speech at a rally in Munich in the early part of August but deleted the offer following Churchill's defiant 'fight them on the beaches, we will never surrender' speech.

The British army is sworn to fight for King and Country. Never in its glorious history has it failed in its duty. With a new King and a sympathetic Government Hitler was convinced it would again.

There is no need to look far for evidence that this was what was in Hitler's mind. It was not until the beginning of September that he finally allowed Goering to implement his campaign of bombing to demonstrate his arrogant boast that he could bomb the British into submission in a matter of days. It was not until September that he gave permission for the German navy to massively increase the building programme for new U-boats – previously he had vacillated and refused Doenitz approval. The reason is clear: with the strategy he was following and with the fall of England the need for U-boats would disappear – the Russian campaign would be won on land not at sea.

On that day in July Hitler was beginning to feel frustrated. Despite having achieved one of his long-term and most cherished ambitions with the defeat of the French, he had hoped that with his triumphant campaign and show of military power, the French surrender would have signalled a similar approach from the British. But although a month had passed, there was little sign of any moves in London to sue for an accommodation. Hitler had realised that with Churchill as Prime Minister there was little chance that they would accept Germany's offers of peace, but with the hopelessness of the position staring them in the face he anticipated that those who had opposed the war would now be given a chance to change the Government's mind. Hitler remained steadfast in his aims that had long formed part of his thinking, but his army, and particularly the generals, were straining at the leash to destroy their traditional enemy. Hitler needed more time. He needed to allow the plot he was hatching to develop and avoid the necessity for further military action. He was well aware of the military arguments, he had only to look at the beaches and the surrounding countryside to see the state of the British army. Everywhere was littered with military equipment in ruin, some destroyed in the fierce rearguard action, but most destroyed by the retreating troops to render it useless to the enemy.

Looking across the deceptively calm surface of the Channel it was not difficult for him to imagine a demoralised and poorly equipped army in no state to defend the country. They could offer no more than token resistance. It was a tempting target, but for once in his life the impetuous Hitler restrained his natural desire to act. The reason is now clear: he was confident that the secret operation that would be launched within days could still give him the result he wanted and bring the proud but hopelessly placed British to heel. With a last lingering look at the white cliffs he gave a contented smile and moved away.

Chapter Twenty

The Fall of France

AS HITLER TRAVELLED towards his date with destiny in the forest at Compiegne he was ignorant of the fact that the man he expected to prove his greatest ally in the peaceful conquest of Britain was struggling to make his way to Madrid.

Following the desertion of his post on the British Staff outside Paris to join the Duchess at La Croë (the house they leased on the French Riviera), the Duke had spent his time in the midsummer heat enjoying a carefree life among the palm trees, relaxing alongside the blue waters of the Cote d'Azur and spending his days either playing golf or pottering about in the garden. The evenings were spent in the way he and the Duchess enjoyed best, hosting a never-ending round of glittering parties. Much of the former glamour had gone however. While the Duke did not appear to have any worries, he could not have failed to be conscious of the uneasy, all-pervasive air of gloom that had settled over his friends and neighbours. Many of the British ex-patriates had left; those still hanging on, reluctant to leave their magnificent houses, were already packed for flight. Everyone knew that the Italian army was massing on the border near Menton preparing for invasion , ready to help themselves to some of the spoils of war before their German allies acquired everything. The expected blow came on 11 June when Mussolini threw in his hand with Hitler and joined the Axis, declaring war on Britain and France.

Much of what was to take place over the next few weeks could be explained if it were possible to understand what was in the Duke's mind prior to his move to La Croë. Having correctly anticipated the failure of the French to withstand the German onslaught and the inability of the British to hold the main thrust from the north, he knew the fall of France was a foregone conclusion. Almost certainly before he deserted his position near Paris he had become convinced that defeat was inevitable and that he had undoubtedly played a part, but even if he had not helped by passing secret information to the German military via Bedaux there seemed little doubt about the eventual outcome. This being so, the fact that he appears to have made no plans for his future is revealing. Previous writers have suggested that the necessity to flee to Spain was to avoid being captured by the advancing German army. This cannot be true, for if it were, he chose a most curious way to achieve freedom. Deliberately placing himself as far away from the Channel ports as it was possible to get in France is hardly the best way to have made his way to England.

During those frantic days that surrounded the fall of France and the hectic evacuation from Dunkirk nobody seems to have given much thought as to where the Duke was or where he might go, but this does not explain why, if he anticipated he would have to return to England, he chose to go to Antibes, far away from England and a place from where his return would be difficult if not impossible after the fall of France.

That he chose to go there is totally consistent with the idea that he was waiting until the Germans received a response to the peace terms Hitler had offered the British. Something dramatic must have occurred during those bewildering days in mid-June when the whole of Western Europe seemed to be on the move to persuade the Duke that he was no longer safe in Antibes. There was no reason why he should have had any fears about his safety from the German army – he had plenty of friends in high places. Hitler, Hess and Bormann would have been more than happy to allow him to remain as an internee where he was and, from what transpired later, it seems that was what they had intended. The only explanation for the Duke's change of heart and hurried departure was the invasion by the Italians and the sudden realisation that he might fall into their hands. This he knew would clearly create a difficult situation for him and the Nazis. Mussolini would not have been a party to the Nazi plan and the Duke's capture by the Italian army would have created a difficult diplomatic situation. It was unlikely that they would respond to British diplomatic pressure and repatriate their important prisoner-of-war, while if the Germans asked for his release this would have raised the existence of the plot to return him to England being discovered. There was only one alternative: hurriedly the Duke decided to make a run for it and seek sanctuary in neutral Spain whose Government was known to be friendly to the Nazis.

As a consequence the Duke hastily contacted the British Legation who had themselves fled Paris and were working from a hotel in Bordeaux. Rather stupidly, he demanded a destroyer be sent to Antibes to evacuate him and his party. Not surprisingly this

was refused. This display of high-handed arrogance was simply a
ploy to demonstrate to anyone in England how desperate he was to
return. This totally contradicts the fact that in a matter of days he
would be refusing to return to England despite transport being
made available by the RAF. The Duke would have realised that this
outrageous request was not likely to be taken seriously for not only
had six valuable destroyers been lost at Dunkirk, but battleships of
any sort were desperately needed to protect the Atlantic convoys
that were being attacked almost at will. More importantly, with
Italy now in the war, to have sent any ship into the Mediterranean,
where the formidable Italian navy had already cut off the route to
the Suez Canal and was enjoying mastery of the sea, would have
been a reckless enterprise. In spite of the telephone system being in
turmoil, the Duke eventually managed to get through to Harry
Mack, the First Secretary at the beleaguered British Legation at
Bordeaux, who had far too much to do without bothering about
the travel arrangements of a troublesome ex-King who had deliberately made himself a problem. However, Mack did his best.
Helpfully he told the Duke that the members of the British Consul
at Menton had been told to burn all the papers and make their way
to the Franco-Spanish border at Peripignan and cross over into
neutral Spain, suggesting that the Duke's party joined the convoy
as it passed La Croë.

So on 19 June the Duke, together with the Duchess, Major
Phillips, the Duke's ADC who had hitch-hiked down from Paris to
assist, the Duchess's maid and a couple called Woods, neighbours
and friends of the Duke and Duchess, all set off in a convoy of cars
along roads crowded with refugees.

Several biographies of the Duke have dealt with the
difficulties he experienced, how at the Spanish border he was
refused entry, how he sent a stream of telegrams to London to get
assistance. Eventually he obtained a visa from the French Consul in
Nice. There seems no reason why the Spanish should have refused
him entry but he was held up at Peripignan for the best part of a
week. The Spanish would have been in no doubt as to who he was
– he was travelling with a party of British diplomats who do not
seem to have had any difficulty; Spain was a Fascist country and he
was a known Fascist supporter with many Spanish friends. The
only explanation seems to be that initially in all the confusion, with
hordes of people trying to cross the border, those in charge were
reluctant to allow him to cross until they received instructions
from the Spanish Foreign Office. Meanwhile the Duke obtained a
visa from the French, and the Spanish could no longer refuse him

entry. Following the crossing of the border he went to Barcelona where, after a few days to get over what must have been a difficult journey, he travelled by train to Madrid, arriving on 23 June.

One mystery remains about events at the Spanish border. Why was he not arrested? The Duke was a serving officer of a nation at war; in trying to enter a neutral country it would have been normal for him to be arrested and interned under the terms of the Geneva Convention. That no such action was taken against him suggests that pressure was applied by the British who wanted him free to leave the country. Unquestionably his arrest would have created a diplomatic incident, but had he been arrested he would almost certainly have been repatriated.

The fact that the Duke and Duchess had arrived in Madrid came as something of a surprise to the Nazis who believed they were lying in the sun of the South of France. The sudden realisation that the man who was at the centre of their intrigues was about to slip away from their sphere of influence, and could end up somewhere where they would find it difficult to keep in contact, was something they had not envisaged.

Exactly where they had expected him to go when France capitulated has never been clear; they probably thought that he would decide to stay where he was. The Côte d'Azur never technically came under German occupation, but remained under the control of the Vichy Government where he and the Duchess would have been made more than welcome to see out the war. The Duke had many friends in the Vichy Government and could have remained in comfortable isolation until the Nazis were ready to place him back on the English throne. His sudden departure seems to have caught them on the hop.

Paradoxically, the news that the Duke had arrived in Madrid caused something of a headache for both the German and British Governments. The British were naturally expecting the Duke to request assistance to return, when the problem of what to give him to do would have to be addressed. The Nazis on the other hand were beginning to suspect that the Duke was weakening in his resolve to include himself in their plans and realised that it was time to do something. It was vital that he was kept available.

The events that surround the Duke while he was in Spain have long been debated. Several excellent books have been devoted to this incident alone and their authors have tried to discover what lay behind what happened in those nine vital days before the matter was finally settled when the Duke left Europe for the Bahamas. The principal source of information has come from captured German records released in London and Washington in July 1957. These were the now well-known 'Documents on German Foreign Policy Series D Volume X' which are freely available, the originals in Bonn, with copies available in London and Washington. This series of records are themselves subject to controversy as, on their release, the British Government issued this statement:

> The Duke was subjected to heavy pressure from many quarters to stay in Europe, where the Germans hoped that he would exert his influence against the policy of His Majesty's Government. His Royal Highness never wavered in his loyalty to the British cause or in his determination to take up his official post as Governor of the Bahamas on the date agreed. The German records are necessarily a much tainted source. The only firm evidence which they could provide is of what the Germans were trying to do in this matter, and of how they completely failed to do it.

This statement by the British Government comes as no surprise. It was to be the first of many occasions when the Government tried to suppress the truth and draw attention away from the part played by the Duke and Duchess and their dealings with the Nazis. That the Government should seek to cast doubts on the German records was a clever ploy and was perfectly timed to find popular acceptance. By 1957 the true extent of the horrors carried out by the Nazis had become well known; the terrible atrocities that would be called the 'Holocaust', the inhuman destruction of six million people, mainly Jews, was fresh in the minds of most people. The depths of cruelty and depravity to which the Nazis had been prepared to sink made them less than human in many people's eyes. To have added the falsifying of records, somewhat subtly, telling the world they were so evil that they could not be relied upon to tell the truth, even to each other, was not a difficult step for most people to take. It was a clever move, so typical of the way in which almost every aspect of the Duke of Windsor's activities between 1935 and his death have been manipulated, excused or suppressed by the hand of some official working in secret. When it comes to the massaging of official records, the Nazis were in the kindergarten class compared to the forces controlled by Whitehall and Buckingham Palace. Why should captured German records be a 'tainted source'? They were written at a time when almost the entire world believed that the Nazis were invincible and were poised to control Europe. This statement is incredible: it presupposes that everything contained in the various German letters and telegrams of 1940, instead of being everyday diplomatic traffic, was being prepared for the day when those involved would stand trial for war crimes. The senior Nazis' fascination with fortune-tellers is well known but to have predicted that the Third Reich would fall within five years would have been a remarkable feat. Hitler and his supporters had no doubt in 1940 that the 'Thousand Year Reich' was on course for ultimate victory. These records were simply conveying what was actually happening, and were not expected to be the subject of scrutiny by British and American historians. To cast doubt on recorded fact is an attempt to divert attention from the truth. It was not that the Nazis were preparing a version of world events that would place them in a favourable light, they had no need to distort the truth – only the British Government seems to think they did.

The telegrams and letters that have survived can be taken at face value, but even they only tell part of the story. The distinguished author Michael Block in his book *Operation Willi*, which deals with the events surrounding the Duke in Spain, reveals in his prologue:

> The captured papers . . . also contain twenty-eight other telegrams on the subject which have not hitherto been published . . . With few exceptions, those telegrams, published and unpublished, come from the files of Ernst von Weizacker, the highly intelligent former naval officer who administered the German Foreign Office (Auswartiges Amt) from 1938 to 1943 with the rank of State Secretary. The long efforts of the British Government to suppress them, and the curious circumstances of their eventual (partial) publication . . .

It is from these that Michael Block draws his conclusions about what actually happened.

It is not the intention of this book to re-examine what happened in Spain in any depth, but it is important to understand why the Nazis moved to ensure that the Duke returned to Spain and was kept there until the scheme that was about to be launched in Germany was given some time to produce the effect on England that Hitler desired and which he was prepared to delay any military action to achieve.

The thrust of the argument in this book is the belief that the Nazis wanted to return the Duke to England and to the throne, and has attempted to present an explanation of how they intended to achieve it. To do that it is necessary to examine another mystery, that of 'Operation Dove' which, although well known, has always been regarded as of minor importance and not properly understood. The purpose of the operation would require the Duke being available to ensure that the matter had a successful conclusion. While 'Operation Dove' was taking place, the plan required that the Duke should either remain where he was in Portugal or return to Spain. There would be no advantage in him returning to Vichy France – this would expose him as a Nazi collaborator and risk the existence of the plot being discovered. It was crucial that the Duke's previous involvement with the Nazis should be suppressed so that he would return with the goodwill of the British people. The time for that was fast approaching, but until conditions were right the Duke must be kept isolated. The Germans were beginning to realise what the British already suspected. The Duke was being carefully watched and was clearly having doubts about what he was being called on to do. He had to be persuaded.

Chapter Twenty-one

The Tug of War in Spain and Portugal

WHEN THEY ARRIVED in Madrid, the Duke and Duchess went sightseeing. The Duke, who was reasonably fluent in Spanish, had made a number of friends on his previous visit in 1927 and he was happy to renew their acquaintance. However, one friend was less than pleased – Sir Samuel Hoare, the British Ambassador, who had only been in Spain for a few days, received a telegram that told him the Duke had crossed the border and was making his way to Madrid. Hoare had been close to the Duke for many years, but realised his affection was to be sorely tested. The couple's appearance had given him a problem he could well have done without. This soon became clear when, instead of simply having to arrange for his visitors' return to London, he found himself embroiled in the internal divisions of the Royal Family. This was to become evident when the Duke made it clear that he had no intention of leaving until the question of his and the Duchess's status was established, making it plain that he would not allow either of them to be subjected to the sort of humiliation which had greeted their return in September 1939. Initially the Duke made a series of demands, and while these were subsequently modified, he remained adamant that he intended to have the position clarified.[1]

Meanwhile Hoare arranged accommodation for them at the Ritz Hotel and continued to press the Foreign Secretary and Churchill to obtain a resolution of the Duke's problem by persuading the King to give some sort of recognition that would meet his brother's demands and enable the Duke to leave Spain. Churchill, however, was finding his task difficult. The King and Queen had become afraid that if the Duke were to show up in England his presence could cause something of a crisis, and they believed that his arrival might attract such popularity that there was a real danger his presence might overshadow his hesitant and uncharismatic brother to the extent that the King would find it increasingly difficult to maintain his authority. George VI was supported in this by several of his advisers. One in particular was Sir Alexander Hardinge, who seems to have shifted his allegiance – for many years he had been a loyal supporter of the Duke but he was now a close confidant of the King. Despite the efforts of the loyal Churchill who single-handedly continued to try and advance the Duke's case, such was the advice the King was receiving that it made it difficult for Churchill to gain any formal recognition for the Duke and Duchess, and thus to facilitate his return.

In a fit of desperation and in what must have been the most stressful period of his life, Churchill sent the message that shows his frustration: 'It will be better for your Royal Highness to come to England as arranged, when everything can be considered.'

The Duke was to explain his feelings some years later, in December 1966, writing in the *New York Daily News*:

> [*Winston's*] personal advice to me was not to quibble about terms, but come home and wait patiently while he worked things out. But I could not honour this line. The year before, while we had been in England, the presence of the Duchess at my side had never been acknowledged, even perfunctorily. Before going back, I wanted assurance that simple courtesies would be forthcoming.

Once again it seems the petty divisions among the members of the Royal Family were working to the advantage of the Nazis. The whole tragic story of the former King's willingness to work against the interests of his native country is punctuated with lost opportunities, the failure to settle minor matters that could, so easily, have been accommodated and might conceivably have changed his attitude. On this and several other occasions there is some evidence that the Duke appeared to show some reluctance to becoming involved in the acts of treachery in which he found himself involved, and over which there remains some doubt. Had he been treated with even the modicum of courtesy by his family, he might have drawn back from this final attempt to co-operate with the Nazi plan.

The Duke and Duchess had arrived in Madrid on 23 June and, in an exchange of telegrams between there and London, Hoare desperately tried to get some acknowledgment that would allow them to leave. The British Ambassador was not the only one whose life became disrupted by their arrival.

Ribbentrop received a telegram from Eberhard von Stohrer, the German Ambassador in Madrid, that several sources have described as having an effect that was 'electric'. It read:

The Spanish Foreign Minister requests advice with regard to the Duke and Duchess of Windsor who are to arrive in Madrid today [*the 23rd*], apparently en route to England by way of Lisbon. The Foreign Minister assumes that we might perhaps be interested in detaining the Duke here and possibly establishing contact with him. Please telegraph instructions.[2]

Ribbentrop's reaction on reading the telegram was predictable. He shouted, 'We must get hold of him! Franco must detain him', and asked Stohrer on the following day: 'Is it possible to detain the Duke and Duchess in Spain for a couple of weeks to begin with before they are granted an exit visa?' He added significantly: 'It would be necessary to ensure at all events that it did not appear in any way that the suggestion came from Germany.' There has always been some doubt about whether the Nazis were quite sure what the Duke was up to until this moment, but from now on they would be in no doubt, and when Hitler was told of the telegram he instructed Ribbentrop to arrange for the Duke to be detained in Spain for a few weeks. One of the interesting and revealing aspects of this telegram is that the Foreign Secretary of a neutral country, albeit friendly to Germany, was aware that the Duke had been in constant touch with the Nazis and this adds weight to the contention that the Duke and Duchess were not fleeing the German army when they left La Croë in May.

Meanwhile, word had reached Churchill that the Duke was in contact with several leading Spaniards known to be sympathetic to Nazi Germany. The foremost of these was Juan Beigbeder y Atienza, the Spanish Foreign Minister who, it was believed, had told the Duke he was welcome to remain in Spain: he is reputed to have offered him the use of a castle near Granada (a city of which the Duke was believed to be fond) or a palace near Ronda, high in the beautiful Andalucian mountains. Meanwhile Churchill, who was being kept informed of what was going on, appears to have been openly critical of the Duke for the first time – he threatened the Duke with a court-martial if he failed to return: 'Your Royal Highness has taken military rank, and refusal to obey direct orders of competent military authority would create a serious situation. I most strongly urge immediate compliance with the wishes of your government.' On being shown this telegram, the King commented: 'That should have a very salutary effect.'

It did: two days later the Duke and Duchess left for Portugal where arrangements had been made for them to be picked up by an RAF flying-boat already lying off the coast.

The fact that his old supporter Churchill had turned against him must have come as a devastating blow, as is shown in a letter discovered among the Duke's papers and believed to have been written in the following October:

> I used to have your support until you reached the supreme power of PM since when you seem to have subscribed to the Court's hostile attitude towards me. Due to the negligence of both our military and diplomatic authorities in France I got lost in the shuffle of war and, left to my own devices to avoid capture by the enemy, I duly informed you when I reached a neutral country. You thereupon summoned me back to England, and I felt bound in my own interests to make my compliance with the summons contingent upon a simple and fair request which my brother evidently turned down, you threaten me with what amounts to arrest, thus descending to dictator methods in your treatment of an old friend and former King.[3]

This extract comes from a letter written complaining about his position in the Bahamas and was discovered among the Duke's papers and revealed by Michael Block in his book *The Duke of Windsor's War* which tells us the typewritten draft contains corrections in both the Duke and Duchess's hand – she it was who changed 'gangster methods' to 'dictator methods'. Block warns that while this letter exists, it might never have been sent.

The Duke's anger is understandable but wide of the mark. If any man was given the opportunity to become a 'dictator' it was Churchill, but in spite of his clear-minded understanding and ability to direct the British nation at war he steadfastly refused to act dictatorially and went to great pains to weld together a formidable team to co-ordinate the nation's military forces.

The Duke's decision to go to Lisbon must have come as a huge relief to Sir Samuel Hoare. When the Duke had been in Spain he had been meeting all sorts of people and the Ambassador had lived in constant fear that the Duke might be indiscreet at a time when the future outcome of the war was at such a crucial stage. Churchill had decided that getting the Duke to return would not solve the original problem of what to do with him and in an audience with the King the plan to send him, as Governor, to the Bahamas was born. This suggestion was inspired: it resolved everything. As Churchill was later to confide, 'of all the colonies at that time, it was the least important'. So while Downing Street and the Palace sighed with relief those in Berlin had decided otherwise.

The Duke and Duchess arrived in Lisbon on 3 July and instead of going to the Hotel Palacio at Estoril, where accommodation had been reserved by Sir Walford Selby, the British Ambassador, they went to the home of banker Espirito Santo Silva, known to be a Nazi agent. The reason why the Duke decided to travel to Portugal has never satisfactorily been explained – the explanation advanced by the Duke can be found in Hoare's memoirs, but is less than revealing. The Duke told him that he intended to 'await the reply in Lisbon to the question about his future'.

However, Stohrer reported a conversation that took place between the Duke and Primo de Rivera (Civil Governor of Madrid and friend of the Duke) at which the Duchess was also believed to have been present. The Duke is alleged to have said: 'In Portugal he felt almost a prisoner. He was surrounded by agents, etc. Politically he was more and more distant from the King and the present English Government.' He added that he and his wife 'had less fear of the King who was quite foolish, than of the shrewd Queen who was intriguing skilfully against the Duke and particularly against the Duchess'. Stohrer also revealed to Walter Schellenberg, head of the Gestapo overseas counter-intelligence, that the Duke 'was considering making a public statement and thereby disavowing English policy and breaking with his brother'. This was believed to have been a condition that Ribbentrop had demanded in exchange for the 50 million Swiss francs Hitler had agreed to pay the Duke.

The Duke was clearly playing for time. He had no intention of returning to England for he knew perfectly well his family were unlikely to meet his demands, one of which was that they would recognise his wife. Years later he was to deny that this had been a condition but the question of the Duchess's title had become an obsession and would almost certainly have been a prerequisite. To have given him a position that would befit his former station in life would have meant recognising his wife: this, he was convinced, was something that the family would never accept.

Churchill's threat of a court-martial had shaken him badly; he knew that if it were to be implemented and he were forced to go home he would be in trouble. Already conscious of the intense scrutiny he was under from agents of MI6, he did not need to be told that the possibility of forcible abduction was real. If he were taken back and faced a trial there was a real risk that all his other crimes would be brought out into the open, resulting in humiliation at best, execution as a traitor being a real possibility. By agreeing to go to Portugal he gave the impression that he was co-operating, but this appearance of compliance was short-lived. He began to find all sorts of excuses for not returning; while he continued to vacillate the flying-boats were recalled by the RAF – being 'ships' belonging to a nation at war their stay in neutral territorial waters would have been limited to 48 hours. On 4 July he received Churchill's telegram to inform him of the position in the Bahamas, making it clear it was not an offer open to negotiation, but an instruction.

The Duke faced a dilemma. As has already been said, his reason for going to Spain had been the belief that Hitler would be successful in bringing the British to the point of surrender; certainly when he left La Croë on 19 June it had been a real possibility, but things were changing rapidly.

To understand what was going through his mind it is necessary to consider what was happening in Britain. The answer probably lies in Churchill's determination to fight on. Following the fall of France a British capitulation had seemed inevitable, but now, as every day passed, the British morale was seen to be stiffening. The gloom that had swept the country following Dunkirk was clearing. The famous 'Dunkirk spirit' was born and the British determination which many believe only comes into its own when the odds are heavily weighed against it led the country to prepare to throw everything into a fight for survival. This change of heart can be traced through Churchill's speeches which reflected the mood. When he rose to address the House of Commons on 4 June, a week after Dunkirk, a relieved Churchill was still finding the withdrawal of the army difficult to understand. Telling a packed House that he feared it would be his lot to announce 'the greatest military disaster in our long history', he added that he had feared 'the whole of the BEF would be broken and led to ignominious and starving captivity'. But by 18 June his normally ebullient attitude had returned. His speech made to the House of Commons was very up-beat: 'I am happy to inform the House that our fighter strength is stronger at the present time relevant to the Germans, who have suffered terrible losses, than it has ever been.' He thereby accurately predicted the outcome of the Battle of Britain and ended with the immortal words: 'Hitler knows he will have to break us in this island or lose the war . . . Let us then brace ourselves for our duties, and so bear ourselves that, if the British Empire and its Commonwealth last for a thousand years, men will still say "This was their finest hour".'[4]

The British had begun to shake off their air of defeat and there was also a growing realisation that America would not stand idly by and see Britain defeated. While it was not recognised at the time, the worst moment in the history of the British Isles had passed, the dark days when even Churchill is reputed to have considered the possibility of some sort of accommodation with Nazi Germany were gone. The signs, however small, were there.

Picking the winning side in war is never easy, as a vast army of traitors since the dawn of time could testify. July 1940 became the moment when the Duke was faced with such a choice. He was forced to confront the second difficult decision of his life. Not normally a decisive man, it must have taxed him greatly.

To have remained in mainland Europe would have blown the whole strategy. His future would from that moment on have been inextricably linked to the Nazi war machine. While his former activities were known to members of the War Cabinet, the Royal Family and certain members of the intelligence services, his reputation, as far as the general British public was concerned, was still that of a man who gave up everything for love and was now a displaced person in a neutral country. The sympathy he still enjoyed would have disappeared with the news that he was openly collaborating with the enemy in Spain, a country known to be Fascist, and which, while not a member of the Axis, was still closely aligned to Germany and its evil intentions.

The Duke's only hope of regaining the throne was to maintain his cover. To be invited back after the Germans had achieved either an accommodation or the defeat of Britain was one thing, but to have arrived with the reputation that he had been plotting the country's downfall with the enemy would not have endeared him to anyone. His attempt to gain time and appear undecided is more than understandable.

Meanwhile, the news that the couple had left Spain was relayed to Berlin in a telegram on the night of 2 July. It set in train a series of events that were aimed at keeping the Duke available and making sure he did not renege on the previous agreement to involve himself in Hitler's plans. The telegram of the 2nd was the beginning of a complex and highly secretive operation and there remains no question that it was set in place by no less than Hitler himself. He contacted Ribbentrop in the belief that the close working arrangement he had previously enjoyed with the Duchess could be resurrected to advantage. The German Foreign Secretary was given the job of co-ordinating the operation to make sure that the Windsors returned to Spain and availed themselves of the offer of accommodation that they had been offered.

On 10 July Baron Oswald Hoyningen-Huene, the German

Minister in Lisbon, telegraphed Ribbentrop:

> The appointment of the Duke of Windsor as Governor of the
> Bahamas is for the purpose of keeping him away from England
> since his return would greatly strengthen the position of English
> friends of peace whereupon his arrest at the instigation of his
> enemies could be counted upon. The Duke intends to postpone his
> journey . . . at least until the beginning of August in a hope of a
> change in his favour. He is convinced that had he remained on the
> throne war could have been avoided and describes himself as a firm
> supporter of a peaceful compromise with Germany. The Duke
> believes with certainty that continual heavy bombing will make
> England ready for peace.[5]

While Ribbentrop was probably delighted to receive this
telegram, there was little if anything contained in it he did not
already know. He knew that the British were trying to force the
Duke to leave, but had not learned of his destination. Now that the
Nazis knew that they would have taken some comfort that he was
not going to England but going somewhere where they could reach
him. The last sentence of the telegram is more than revealing. The
idea that the bombing of Britain was suggested by the Duke as a
method by which peace could be achieved is incredible. It clearly
demonstrates on whose side he was. There is no record that he ever
suggested to Churchill that bombing Germany would have a
similar effect.

Back in Berlin the plan to make sure that the British did not
force the Duke to leave was gathering pace. Learning that the Duke
was due to leave Lisbon on or about 1 August, Ribbentrop gave
the instructions to begin an operation to return him to Spain. He
selected a very resourceful officer named Walter Schellenberg who
was ideally suited to the task. But time was running out for the
conspirators. Ribbentrop telegraphed von Stohrer in Madrid on
the 11th:

> We are especially interested in having the Duke of Windsor return
> to Spain at all events . . . from here it would seem best if close
> Spanish friends were to invite him back to stay for a short visit . . .
> we would have to secure the agreement of the Spanish Government
> for the internment of the Duke . . . at any rate at a suitable occasion
> in Spain, the Duke is to be informed that Germany wants peace with
> the British people and the Churchill clique stands in the way of that
> peace, and it would be a good thing if the Duke holds himself in

readiness for further developments . . . especially with a view to assumption of the British throne by the Duke and Duchess.

Several well-known writers have tried to suggest that the intrigues carried out in Spain and Portugal were more an expression of Ribbentrop's fantasies than any serious attempt either to persuade the Duke to co-operate or, in the event of his refusal, to kidnap him and forcibly return him to Spain. This cannot now be seriously believed; not only is it clear that Hitler was maintaining a careful watch on everything that happened but also that Schellenberg was working to his direct order. To look for evidence of a conspiracy between the Duke and the Nazis, it is only necessary to study the telegram he sent to his brother George VI on 23 July in which he urged the King to end the war, telling him to dismiss the Cabinet and replace it with one headed by the elderly but still active Lloyd George, which meant dismissing Churchill, the leader of a democratically elected Government who enjoyed the full support of the people. Whatever the Duke hoped to gain by this incredible suggestion has never been revealed but it could only add to the view that Churchill had, that the Duke had sold his soul to the devil.

As was mentioned earlier, what took place in Spain and Portugal has been the subject of several very comprehensive books, and it is well known that Schellenberg's mission failed and the Duke left Europe on the SS *Excalibur* on 1 August. It was left to von Stohrer to break the news: 'The Ducal couple sailed last night . . . further report about final vain attempt to restrain W from departing follows.'

The assertion that the Duke wanted to remain in Europe is open to some doubt; despite all the telegrams and evidence nothing really conclusive can be discovered, but what is without question is Hitler's desire to have him detained.[6] This is the reason behind many incredible events that are well documented and serve to establish what the Nazis had in mind. The clue to what the Duke was thinking comes from several of the remarks he made at the point of departure for the Bahamas.

When everything about the events of those days in July is examined it is clear that when they first arrived in Madrid the Duke and Duchess were still committed to work with the Nazis towards the day when they would return, but as time went on several things happened that weakened their resolve: the confirmation that the Royal Family would never welcome him back, quickly followed by the realisation that Churchill, the man who had been his staunchest champion, had turned against them, must have been bitterly upsetting. Playing for time, the Duke began to lose confidence in Hitler's ability to force Britain into submission. This made him realise that the outcome that had seemed so certain a month before was suddenly not predictable. The Duke clearly decided to keep his options open and went meekly to what he must have seen was a political backwater on the other side of the world. There he could allow the two great enemies to slog it out and then join the winning side. There is no doubt where his affections lay. Baron von Hoynigen-Huene again is the source in another revealing telegram to Berlin: 'The confidant has just received a telegram from the Duke in Bermuda, asking him to be sent communication as soon as it is necessary for him to act. Should any reply be sent?' There is no record among the captured papers of a response; this can be explained by the fact that by 8 August 'Operation Dove' had collapsed and the role that Hitler had selected for the Duke had gone with it.

Chapter Twenty-two

Hitler's Dream Begins to Collapse

THE DUKE, together with the Duchess, sailed off to face a new life as Governor of the Bahamas, a life he was to find not at all to his liking and where his behaviour would be dogged by further controversy. His wild money-making schemes, the suspicion about the part he played in the mystery that surrounds the murder of Harry Oakes and his involvement with the notorious gangster Meyer Lanskey do not come within the remit of this book but a study of what happened will reveal his true character. Much of what took place in the Bahamas, like that of his time in Europe, is the subject of a great deal of speculation and it comes as no surprise to discover that it too has been played down and suppressed by official sources.

When the Windsors left war-torn Europe they left behind one large unanswered question. Had the moves to keep the Duke in Spain been successful what did Hitler plan to do with him? The argument about whether the Duke was a willing partner or a gullible fool is largely irrelevant unless we discover what role Hitler had in mind for him to play.

There is no doubt that during late June and early July, Hitler came very close to persuading the British that some kind of accommodation was the only way to avoid outright defeat. Halifax had been urging the War Cabinet for some time to seek a similar arrangement 'which would save the country from inevitable disaster'. Sir Samuel Hoare had admitted privately to Beigbeder that 'Great Britain might one day have to come to terms with Germany'[1] and even Churchill had said that he was 'prepared to consider German terms', adding that the aim was 'no longer to crush Germany, but rather to preserve our own integrity and independence and the time might come when we felt we had to put an end to the struggle'.

That the Nazis were pushing hard for some resolution is well known, the fact that they were being supported by the Duke is not. The Duke's telegram to his brother shows that he believed that the

British were ready to collapse. Fortunately for the future of the world the feeling of despondency did not last long – by late July events began to move against Hitler and in favour of the belea-guered British. The Duke seems to have correctly anticipated what was going on in Britain where the nation was taking its lead from Churchill who gradually became more belligerent and outwardly confident that Hitler was not going to attack as the months following Dunkirk slipped by.

If that impression was growing in Britain, it was not matched by a similar feeling in Germany. Hitler began to sense that he was not going to eliminate the British from the war, and by the middle of August he saw the writing on the wall: the British were not going to give in but prove a stubborn and desperate enemy. Helped by a magnificent campaign of propaganda, the British were making it very clear they intended to go down fighting. The German forces on the coast of France were horrified by some of the rumours that were current, such as the suggestion that the British intended to bomb an invading force with mustard gas and had a secret weapon that would set the Channel alight as it neared England. These stories were enough to strike terror in the heart of the bravest invader. Sefton Delmer, an Australian who had lectured in Berlin, made regular broadcasts on the German Service of the BBC to taunt the troops on the other side of the Channel. Delmer, who spoke perfect German, began a series of friendly chats in mid-July aimed at the German soldier to teach him useful phrases in the event of an invasion. 'For your first lesson,' Delmer said cheerfully, 'we will take Kanalüberfahrt . . . the Channel crossing . . . Channel crossing. Now repeat after me: Das Boot sinkt . . . Das Boot sinkt . . . the boat is sink-ing . . . the boat is sink-ing. Das Wasser ist sehr kalt . . . The water is ver-y cold. Now here is a verb that will be most useful. Please repeat after me: Ich brenne . . . I burn . . . Du brennst . . . you burn . . . Wir brennen . . . we burn. And now I suggest you learn another phrase: Der SS-Sturmführer brennt auch ganz schön . . . The SS captain is al-so burn-ing quite nic-ely.'[2]

It has become clear that even when he saw the dream of British capitulation slipping from his grasp Hitler continued to press for the Duke to be returned to Spain to discover what he was planning and why. This requires a close examination of another operation which he is believed to have been personally directing, the timing of which indicates that he would require the Duke to be available to take part.

The cold grey dawn that broke over the deserted sea revealed the black outline of a German U-boat as it rose to the surface and began to roll in the storm-tossed waters a hundred miles from the west coast of Ireland. As the waves, driven by a gale-force wind, crashed over the hull several of the crew of U-65 could be seen dragging a corpse wrapped in the flag of the Imperial German Navy through the hatch and lowering it to the glistening black deck. Huddled against the weather, the men waited impatiently as the U-boat's commander read the burial service before sliding the body over the side and scrambling back through the hatch.[3]

The date was 12 August 1940, still early days in the Battle of the Atlantic where death would become commonplace. The summer of 1940 was just the start of a battle that would intensify and became as hard fought as any of the Second World War. Losses in the cold inhospitable waters of the North Atlantic, a dreadful killing ground for both men and ships, would intensify as the desperate battle of attrition developed. Casualties on both sides would be heavy, losses in the British Merchant Navy would be over a hundred thousand men, while losses in the Royal Navy continued to mount. Death aboard a U-boat would become routine: of the 41,000 men who set out to risk their lives in them, only 26,000 returned.

This seemingly insignificant incident would never have gained its place in history had it not been for the mystery that surrounds the man being buried and the failure to understand what he was doing there. A strange business, this was the end of 'Operation Dove' and with it the end of Hitler's dream. It is a mysterious story that is only partially understood even to this present day.

Apart from the funeral party, one other person witnessed the simple ceremony, a frail man looking a great deal older than his 38 years, a testimony to the harsh treatment he'd received during his recent captivity. Struggling to maintain his balance on the slippery deck, he looked strangely out of place, his lounge suit soaked as he watched his comrade's body disappear into the waves that crashed against the boat's curved sides.

As it disappeared the body signalled more than just another death, or even the failure of U-65 to complete its unusual mission. This was the final act in the bold and daring strategy that Hitler confidently expected to present him with a prize he wanted above all others: the surrender of Britain.

Several years were to pass before the dead man's fate was finally established, to bring to an end the speculation which built up around his disappearance. Various intelligence agencies were actively trying to find out where he was. Even as late as 1943 J. Edgar Hoover, under pressure from the American courts and the

State Department, was insisting that the FBI discover if he was still in America.[4] Irish intelligence, anxious to discover his whereabouts, believed that they had evidence he was alive and living in Berlin. The Irish would have to wait another six months for the first news of his death to filter through. British and American intelligence would have to wait even longer – they would not learn of his death until the war was over.

Five years later, the war over, the man's death no longer a mystery, the incident was brushed aside and almost forgotten. Historians only regarded it worthy of mention because they believed it was simply an attempt by the Nazis to mount an operation in support of the IRA, little more than a Nazi initiative to mobilise what they believed was a sizeable secret army which only required to be supplied with arms and equipment before it would rise up against its traditional enemy, the now isolated and beleaguered British.

So who was this man? Why were his movements the subject of such interest around the world and, finally, what led to his committal, with full military honours, to his watery grave in the Western Atlantic from the deck of a German submarine?

Some days previously, on 8 August, Commander Hans Gerrit von Stockhausen had moved U-65 away from its moorings at Wilhelmshaven and headed towards Norway before setting course for the West Coast of Ireland. The U-boat's mission was shrouded in mystery, its departure remained a highly guarded secret in Germany. It carried two passengers and had orders to return them to their native Ireland. One was Sean Russell, who at the time was Chief of Staff of the IRA. The other was Frank Ryan, the former Chief of Staff who commanded the organisation before he was replaced by Russell in early 1938. What began as a simple operation became dogged with misfortune.

When the voyage was almost complete and the U-boat was less than a hundred miles off the coast of Galway, Russell was taken ill complaining of acute stomach pains. German submarines didn't carry doctors, so a medical orderly, a former medical student, diagnosed that Russell was suffering from constipation and prescribed a strong purgative. Four hours later Russell was dead – he died in Frank Ryan's arms. When U-65 returned to base a top-level enquiry was held, Russell's symptoms were described and two eminent German doctors working independently concluded that he had died from a perforated ulcer.

Russell's chance death must have come as a devastating blow to Hitler and Hess. Ever since the meeting in the Hotel Meurice in

September 1937 Hitler was driven by the idea of returning the Duke of Windsor to the British throne: with the death of Russell his last chance had gone.

The story of Russell and Ryan's fateful journey is reasonably well known, but what is remarkable is the way in which it has been regarded as being of such little significance. Given the codename 'Dove' by the Nazis, it has always been believed that the two men were returning to Ireland with a loosely defined roving commission with no specific objective. Writers who have studied and recorded events of this period and in particular those who have studied the history of the IRA, unaware of the operation's purpose, have failed to give this incident any serious consideration. While it is appreciated that most of the work was published in the Sixties and Seventies, making allowances for the less than complete information available at the time, it is still surprising the almost casual way in which this operation has been regarded.

The first indication of Russell's untimely death in the U-boat came in the summer of 1941, surprisingly not from the various intelligence agencies all anxiously trying to discover his whereabouts but from a letter smuggled out of Germany written by Ryan.[5] This in itself is strange when one considers the Irish Government's unique position. As a neutral country it enjoyed a number of advantages: it maintained continuous diplomatic relations with Nazi Germany which retained a Legation complete with a Plenipotentiary Minister in Dublin throughout the entire war. The Irish enjoyed a similar facility in Berlin and yet it was left to this curious and highly unusual source to inform the Dublin Government of his whereabouts. The Irish intelligence services maintained close co-operation with their American and British counterparts, but surprisingly, learning of Russell's death in the U-boat, they failed to share the information with MI5 or the FBI. The news of Russell's death in a letter written to the Irish Ambassador in Madrid by Frank Ryan provided the answer and should have brought to an end the rumours that continued to circulate on both sides of the Atlantic for several years. Equally strange is the apparent failure of British intelligence (who it is now known had many agents in the German navy, including the U-boat service) to discover news of this mission and its eventual outcome. Most curious of all is why the FBI, who were looking for Russell in America, remained ignorant of his whereabouts until after the war. During the period that followed rumours continued to circulate both in Ireland and America, many deliberately started to encourage speculation and to conceal his true whereabouts suggested that Russell had been murdered by agents of British intelligence.

Recently released Irish intelligence files reveal the extent to which these reports were taken seriously. The suggestion that Russell had been murdered in Gibraltar or aboard an Italian vessel off the coast of Portugal continued and were vigorously investigated, but failed to produce any hard evidence and were not abandoned until news of his death was finally established. This probably accounts for the Irish reluctance to pass the information on; they were not totally convinced that British intelligence did not have a hand in his disappearance.[6]

Prior to 12 August the Abwehr had lost interest in Ireland. German intelligence had long suspected that their failure to land agents there (with two notable exceptions they were all arrested on arrival) was due in no small part to certain factions within the IRA who were happy to betray their so-called allies to the British or Irish intelligence in exchange for financial considerations. The IRA is by nature fiercely patriotic; many of its followers had little enthusiasm for the Nazis although quite prepared to accept Nazi money and arms; they no more welcomed the prospect of German interference in the internal affairs of Ireland than they suffered under the British. Whatever the truth of these stories, Russell's attempt was the only mission to be mounted after the end of July 1940 until much later in the war. An explanation for this can be found in the Abwehr records discovered, almost by chance, in a metal box in the loft of the National Archives in Washington in 1967. Examination of these reveals an entry in the Abwehr War Diary of 18 July: 'Orders of the Chief; No more sabotage missions to be staged via Ireland. In the future, all operations of this kind will be arranged on direct route to England.'

This entry is of particular significance, for not only does it confirm that the German intelligence had lost patience with Ireland, but the fact that the mission went ahead provides evidence that the Abwehr was not responsible. Later chapters will establish the full importance of U-65's mission and explain that the orders for this operation came from a higher authority than Admiral Canaris. Whoever was behind it, it was someone very powerful in the Nazi hierarchy which all adds weight to the contention that instead of being a relatively unimportant mission it was highly significant.

While the death of Russell was to prove devastating for its sponsors, it was not the only setback the voyage suffered. When von Stockhausen reported the death of his passenger he was ordered to take up a position in the North Atlantic and join the hunt for allied shipping. Despite his protestations, Ryan was ordered to remain on board and return to Germany at the end of the patrol. This has previously been explained away by saying that Ryan had not been briefed as to why he and Russell were going to Ireland and while this may be true, it is more likely that the Nazis were afraid he might be captured, his presence discovered and the various intelligence agencies alerted to the existence of this vital operation.

The mission's troubles were far from over, U-boat Archiv has been able to confirm that U-65 sustained damage to one of her hatches as a result of some very heavy Atlantic weather. Unable to continue, she was ordered to Lorient for repairs, arriving on the 19th, moved to Brest and finally returned to sea on the 28th. Commander von Stockhausen was subsequently decorated and in the following January was promoted to commander in chief of the 26 U Flottille. U-65 was handed over to a new commander named Hoppe, but he and his crew were destined to become another statistic in the Battle of the Atlantic. Fourteen months after she was first commissioned, U-65 was lost without survivors, sunk by the British submarine hunter HMS *Gladiolus* on 8 April 1941 at a position 60-04N, 15-45W, but not before dispatching 14 merchant ships to the bottom.

Fate continued to stalk everyone involved in the unusual voyage. Irish intelligence files[7] record that Commander von Stockhausen, accompanied by a Finnish naval attaché, was driving to Berlin when the car they were in was involved in an accident with a lorry-load of steel beams. Commander von Stockhausen was killed instantly, the Finnish attaché blinded. Another version of his death is to be found in the American intelligence files in Washington, which suggest that von Stockhausen was run down while crossing the road in Berlin. In whatever way he died, both versions agree on the date – 15 January 1943. Several sources have speculated that his death might not have been an accident but when one considers that von Stockhausen was a highly regarded naval commander who served with great distinction in the U-boat service, it is difficult initially to imagine why anyone in Germany should wish him dead. Certainly, many German ex-submariners still alive believe his death was nothing more than a tragic accident. For him to have been murdered would have meant somebody wanted him silenced: this could have been only for one reason. Apart from Ryan, who was dying anyway, von Stockhausen was the only person who could confirm the details of the secret voyage;

the murder of its commander would erase all trace. While it might seem incredible that anyone would go to such lengths, seen in the context of the extraordinary steps that were to be taken to hide many of the mysteries that involve the Duke, the murder of von Stockhausen might not be that surprising. If it was simply a road accident then it is curious that his death should be recorded in the files of at least two major intelligence services.

The failure of 'Operation Dove' was to end Frank Ryan's war. Returning to Germany he spent the rest of his life there and, after a number of painful illnesses, died in the sanatorium at Dresden Loschwitz on 10 June 1944. He lies buried in the cemetery there. His grave is marked with a simple wooden cross bearing his date of birth and that of his death under the name Francis Richards. The explanation for this can be found in a letter dated 16 January 1946 marked 'Secret' but now available in the Public Archives in Dublin. Written by the Department of Defence to Joe Walshe, the Secretary to the Department of External Affairs, it mentions among other things that Ryan used the aliases of Richards and Moloney while in Germany, but gives no reason why he used these aliases.

Whatever misfortunes overtook those on this fateful voyage, they were as nothing compared to the devastation felt by those who sent Russell to Ireland. His death brought to an end an incredible conspiracy, one that had it been successful could have placed the Duke of Windsor back on the throne of Britain.

Chapter Twenty-three

The Voyage that was Damned

BEFORE CONSIDERING WHAT the Nazis hoped to gain by sending Frank Ryan and Sean Russell to Ireland and deciding what was the objective of their mission, it is necessary to dispel several popular myths that surround the operation and which remain unchallenged for over half of a century. It might be helpful to recall what was known about the two men and how the impression that their return was of minor importance came to be believed. A re-examination of the previously reported facts soon establishes that the generally accepted view does not hold good in the light of the additional information now available. Clearly something vital was overlooked.

Frank Ryan left Ireland some time during early 1938 to take part in the Spanish Civil War. Wounded later that same year while an acting brigadier in the Lincoln Washington Brigade fighting in the Ebro Valley against the troops of General Franco, he was captured by a group of Italian 'Volunteers' that Mussolini had ordered to Spain with the motive of exchanging him for one of their officers captured by the Spanish. This was to prove fortuitous for Ryan; all the other members of the International Brigade captured by the Spanish were shot out of hand. What must have originally looked like misfortune turned out to have saved his life. Eventually they handed him over to the Spanish and he was imprisoned, but fortunately his fate was discovered by a group of American journalists who revealed the terrible conditions under which he was held. When news of his plight reached Ireland, it led to a clamour for his release. The Irish Government, who had adopted a policy of strict non-intervention in the Spanish Civil War, were placed in a dilemma. A 'Save Frank Ryan' campaign was mounted by several Irish newspapers of various political persuasions; they whipped up public opinion which brought pressure on Eamon De Valera, the *Taoiseach*, to do something. His response was to send several telegrams to General Franco urging him to release Ryan on humanitarian grounds, appealing as one Catholic and former freedom fighter to another. The requests were ignored. However, the newly formed Irish Red Cross, although initially unable to obtain news of Ryan, eventually located him and were appalled to discover that he was being held in a cell along with 18 other prisoners and that every morning nine were taken out and shot, to be replaced by a further nine to await the same fate. All this had a devastating effect on Ryan. Already wounded in the fighting, he was condemned to live in a world of silence, unable to speak or understand Spanish, his previous deafness becoming worse. There is little wonder his health deteriorated under this barbaric treatment.

With the end of the Civil War De Valera was able to act officially. He instructed the Irish Ambassador in Madrid to arrange for Ryan, who was being held on a charge of mass murder and arson, to be defended the cost to be borne by the State. This was more than generous – Ryan had frequently been involved in acts of terrorism during his period as leader of the IRA and was a self-confessed opponent of the elected Dublin Government. Had he remained in Ireland he would almost certainly have been arrested and interned together with most of the other members of the IRA.

Leopold Kerney, the Irish Ambassador in Madrid, arranged for a Señor Champourcin, considered one of the best lawyers in Spain, to conduct Ryan's defence, but the outcome was only partly successful. Ryan's death sentence was commuted to 30 years' imprisonment, but considering the conditions under which he found himself, this could not have come as much relief. A lifelong Communist, Ryan had friends in Germany and with the sort of irony of fate that dictates that when all else fails, it is the forces of opposition that provide a desperate man's salvation, the regime committed to destroying Communism came to his aid. The two men responsible for his release were Dr Jupp Hoven and Helmut Clissmann, who had become friendly with Ryan when they were students in Ireland and he was editor of *An Phoblacht*, a weekly left-wing Irish political newspaper. The two men were now working for the Abwehr monitoring events in Ireland; they explained Ryan's plight to Admiral Canaris and suggested it would be a propitious move to obtain his release, pointing out that not only would German intervention create a favourable impression in Ireland, but it would ensure that Ryan was available should Abwehr wish to make use of him. German intelligence was initially ambivalent about the potential value of Ryan, however Admiral Canaris was persuaded to make representations to the head of the Spanish police to secure his release. To Ryan's amazement this nearly deaf, frail, confused man found himself the guest of Nazi Germany, which must have seemed like some sort of miracle. The Abwehr arranged to have him handed over on 15 July 1940 at the frontier at Irun-Hendaye from where he was taken to Paris by Abwehr section leader Kurt Haller. Following a meal together at the Tour d'Argent, the well-known Paris restaurant, Haller wrote in his diary: 'Ryan was completely flabbergasted by the whole thing and thought he was dreaming.'

Irish intelligence records show that shortly after this they received information that Ryan was living in a flat in Berlin belonging to Helmut Clissmann and had been seen touring German prisoner-of-war camps trying to recruit Irish nationals captured while serving in the British army, offering to help them get back to Ireland. Later this was proved to be untrue when it was learned that it had been Russell who had been carrying out the recruiting. The Garda, still unaware that Russell had gone to Germany and not knowing where he was, learning that an Irishman was visiting the POW camps concluded it must be Frank Ryan. What the Nazis had in mind in trying to recruit ex-patriate Irishmen has never come to light, but the whole episode is reminiscent of a similar scheme carried out by Sir Roger Casement, the English supporter of the Irish movement who was arrested in 1918 when arriving in Southern Ireland by submarine from Germany. Following his arrest he was tried for treason, found guilty, stripped of his knighthood, executed and buried in Wandsworth Prison.

Ryan was a sick man. The time he spent in captivity in Spain had a devastating effect. However, he surprised the Nazis by recovering more quickly than expected. So impressed were they with his grasp of political matters that they decided to embark on what can only be regarded as a risky manoeuvre. They arranged for him to meet Sean Russell, who had arrived in Berlin on 3 May 1940.

It must have been a curious meeting. Several reports have revealed that they greeted each other like long-lost brothers, which is strange: the two men had never been close. Russell had fiercely opposed Ryan's left-wing views, while for his part Ryan had opposed the violence which marked Russell's time as Chief of Staff. This provides another curious insight into the strange business: Ryan was a well-known Communist and made no secret of his admiration for the regime in Russia – it seems incredible that the Nazis were prepared to help him. That they should help him return to Ireland is even more remarkable since the Nazis were engaged in hunting down and persecuting Jews and Communists all across Europe. That they were prepared to overlook his affiliation seems perplexing. It has been suggested that they were so impressed with Ryan that they were prepared to ignore his politics, that 'war makes for strange bedfellows', but this explanation defies credibility. Sending Ryan to Ireland carried a grave risk and could have proved an act of extreme folly had he landed. His presence in Ireland could have provided a rallying point for anti-Nazi feeling among the many left-wingers in the Republican movement which would have caused serious divisions. This in turn would have rendered what Russell was hoping to achieve difficult, if not impossible. Such fears were confirmed when Ryan returned to Germany later the same year and refused to write or speak on Germany's behalf. He was overjoyed when the Nazis invaded Russia, confidently predicting the defeat of Germany at the hands of the country he so admired. What seems such a puzzle is why they treated him with compassion – his contribution to the Nazis proved totally valueless.

Russell's arrival in Germany on the other hand was much more significant. When they were reunited he told Ryan that he was planning to return to Ireland and offered to take him along despite being perfectly aware that Ryan would be of little practical use. Ryan hadn't seen his homeland for well over two years and he had no first-hand knowledge of what was happening there. Russell's decision to take him along can only have been an act of charity. He was aware that Ryan was a very sick man; clearly the comradeship of Republicanism overruled his logic.

Without the advantage of knowing exactly in what Russell was involved, it is perhaps understandable that previous writers have seized upon and been led astray by a telegram that has been regarded as the reason Russell returned to Germany. At 16.55 on 24 January 1940, the Foreign Office in Berlin received a telegram from its Consul-General in Genoa. When this fell into Allied hands at the end of the war it appeared to clear up the mystery of Russell's leaving America. It read:

> John McCarthy, the ambassador of the Irish movement who has arrived from New York today, asked whether the German Government would be prepared to provide transport to Ireland for Sean Russell, Chief of Staff of the IRA who, unknown to the American Government, is still in New York. If this is possible he will make his way here by a new direct line from New York under an alias and be identified by McCarthy. The request is based on the fact that direct connection between America and Ireland has been suspended and the route via London appears impossible in view of

the risk of arrest. McCarthy, who leaves by sea today for Naples, would be grateful for a decision on his return from there on Saturday, 27 January.

(signed) Schmid.[1]

There is little doubt the telegram is genuine, but it now looks as if it too was part of the massive cover-up designed to draw attention away from Russell. The Nazis wanted to portray him as some unfortunate displaced person whom they were prepared to assist with no apparent ulterior motive other than that he was anti-British to explain why he chose to return via Germany. There has always been confusion about the identity of the man McCarthy. He was unknown to Irish and American intelligence and was never traced, then it was noticed that the address he was using in New York was that used by Russell. It is now believed they were one and the same person. This being so, it shows the telegram in a different light. It was probably a coded message from Russell to inform the Germans that he had already left America and that he had made his own arrangements to travel which we now know he did in April 1940. It is worth remembering that Italy did not declare war on Britain until June 1940; an American ship would have had no difficulty entering Genoa.

It is convenient at this point to examine the events that took place when Russell arrived in Germany. Apart from the entry recording his arrival, the next entry in the Abwehr War Diary on 20 May shows:

> Commenced instruction of Sean Russell in the use of sabotage materials. This instruction has been arranged at the request of Dr Veesenmeyer, the special representative of the Foreign Office, with whom constant contact is being maintained.[2]

The interesting part of this entry is the reference to Dr Veesenmeyer, who was the head of the Irish desk at the Foreign Office. He was one of the Nazi Party's most accomplished coup d'état specialists and was specially selected by Ribbentrop to foment rebellion in Ireland. He had proved his ruthless efficiency in liquidating Jews in Hungary and Czechoslovakia, for which he was later sentenced to seven years' imprisonment by the Nuremberg tribunal. He is known to have been a fervent advocate of using the IRA to foment a revolution in Ireland. It might seem strange that such a senior member of the Foreign Office should know about and ask to be kept informed about the training of

219

Russell, who, we are led to believe, was relatively unimportant. However, Russell was reported to be happy amusing himself learning the latest technology in the construction of bombs, taking the opportunity of gaining expertise in the laboratories of the Abwehr. Meanwhile, moves were taking place to decide his future. The next entry in the War Diary, by Major Marwede, on 23 May, states:

> Discussion has taken place in the office of Under Secretary of State Woerman in which Dr Veesenmeyer, Lahousen, Sean Russell and I took part. Subject to agreement of the naval staff it is planned to give Russell passage to Ireland by U-boat on 6 June and to place at his disposal the two operators trained by Abwehr II. Various questions with regard to delivery of radio apparatus, sabotage material and transport possibilities remain to be discussed with naval staff. In addition, discussion took place on Russell's employment in Ireland and on the possibilities of action against England.

Two days later another entry in the diary reads:

> Sean Russell's transport to Ireland, as required by Foreign Office, should be carried out by U-boat. The naval staff has indicated its agreement. U-boat will probably be available at ten days notice from 1 June. It is planned to land Russell at a suitable place and to bury the sabotage materials, wireless transmitter, etc. in suitable packing at a shallow spot. Russell will subsequently collect the buried equipment with the help of his IRA men.

It was to be close on six weeks before anything happened, then on 12 July the War Diary records:

> The Naval High Command has been requested in a memorandum dated 11 July to give approval in principle for the movement of two agents to Ireland by U-boat. The persons in question are the IRA leader Russell, whose transport to Ireland is at the request of the Foreign Office, and a Breton agent Abwehr II whom it was desired to land in Ireland before Russell in order to complete preparatory measures.

What emerges from these entries is that confusion was creeping in, either that or the Abwehr was trying to take over what had started as a Foreign Office operation. Having reported 'the Navy had indicated their agreement to the Foreign Office request' on 25

May, why were they writing a memorandum on 11 June to obtain the same approval?

It is at this point that the most incredible twist in this strange business was revealed. The following day there is another entry:

> Abwehr representative attached to German Embassy, Madrid, reports that Frank Ryan, an agent of Office 1 (West) whom it is planned to employ for the Irish movement, will be handed over at the Spanish frontier at Irun-Hendaye on July 14 or 15 under arrangements made with Abwehr II.

So there we have it. Ryan, it seemed, had become an Abwehr agent. The daring strategy of introducing Ryan to Russell begins to make sense. Russell's act of charity had played directly into the hands of Admiral Canaris by offering to take Ryan to Ireland. Ryan wasn't going, as was supposed, to help Russell, but to watch him, discover what he was doing and report back to the Abwehr.

What now seems clear is that during his negotiations in Spain, Admiral Canaris managed to 'turn' Ryan. This fervent Communist, with no previous contact with the Nazis and who was quite outspoken in his condemnation of the Third Reich, in a desire to get away from the terrible conditions under which he was being held, would probably have agreed to anything. It wouldn't have been difficult to recruit him and persuade him to work for the Abwehr. Telling him he wasn't required to spy on his own country, but only to discover what the German Foreign Office were planning in Ireland would have been a powerful incentive, the chance to return home even greater.

Discovering that Ryan was an Abwehr agent suggests that it wasn't the Abwehr who were sending Russell, but the Foreign Office. Why will be revealed later, but it now seems clear that Admiral Canaris realised that something important was being planned and very cleverly, aided by a stroke of luck, he managed to infiltrate it with one of his own agents.

That one Nazi department was prepared to spy on another should not come as any great surprise. One of the popular misconceptions widely held about Nazi Germany was that it was a totalitarian regime. Nothing could be further from the truth, in fact, it is probably wrong to describe it as a 'Government' in the conventional sense. Under the Nazis Germany bore more similarity to a feudal state owing allegiance to a medieval-type court. Democracy didn't exist under Fascism, the Nazis ruled through a collection of private organisations each controlled by a powerful figure responsible only to Hitler. There was never any attempt to co-ordinate any of these departments, even to carry out military action. All these various departments were, in effect, private armies fighting alongside each other for what was perceived as the common good. The only thing that showed any degree of centralisation concerned the formation of policy. This produced a system that was far from perfect; it lacked cohesion and produced jealousy and division between those in positions of power who were as anxious to discover what the other departments were doing as they were to manage their own. All leaders were constantly seeking ways to increase their sphere of influence. Hitler was very skilful in manipulating his patronage towards the various leaders, it enabled him to maintain his personal autocracy to the end. The main result of this system was to ensure that all the German leaders maintained their own private intelligence services to infiltrate, watch and report back on what the others were doing. H.R. Trevor Roper explains this clearly in his book *The Last Days of Hitler*:

> Total war, to the Nazis, did not mean, as it meant to us (and perhaps only to us), a concentration of all effort on the war, and a corresponding suspension of all inessential industry, for in Germany the production of many inessential luxuries was continued; it meant indiscriminate war by all methods and in all elements. In Nazi Germany neither war production, nor manpower, nor administration, nor intelligence was rationally centralised; and Ribbentrop's protest at Nuremberg that foreign intelligence was not supplied to the Foreign Minister but by thirty competing agencies is substantially true. The structure of German politics and administration instead of being, as the Nazis claimed, 'pyramidal' and 'monolithic' was in fact a confusion of private armies, and private intelligence services.

There are many recorded instances of where this fragmentation of effort worked to the Nazis' disadvantage. Many commentators have speculated that had the forces of Nazi Germany been totally behind him, there is little reason to suppose that Hitler would not have been triumphant. Fortunately this proved not to be the case.

The more we examine 'Operation Dove' and the voyage of the U-65, even confining ourselves to the evidence available in the late Seventies, the more it becomes clear that the events that surround it were not correctly understood or interpreted. For example, why did nobody bother to question the Nazis' decision to use a U-boat in this supposed unimportant and ill-fated mission? It seems strange that its use should not have raised a number of important questions that nobody seems to have addressed. With all other methods at their disposal why did the Nazis use a U-boat? There is no question that the facts that have been widely reported are substantially correct. Some minor details that have not previously been published have been supplied by the U-boat Archiv at Cuxhaven, but these only add to the original story that is recorded in the captured Nazi records. What seems so strange is that historians have never sought to question the obvious.

As has been seen, August 1940 was a difficult time for both the British and the Germans. The euphoria of Dunkirk was followed by a feeling of uncertainty, invasion was expected at any moment and, despite Churchill's brave attempts to rouse the morale of the people, few, aware of the country's dreadful position and lack of military preparedness, believed the outcome would be anything other than swift defeat. It has been suggested that Churchill's defiant stand was based on his certain knowledge that invasion was not the Germans' intention.[3] By this time the British had cracked the enemy Enigma codes and it is known that a copy of every transcript was sent to Downing Street as soon as it was encoded. Most of these are still classified as secret, so it can only remain speculation, for he failed to share his knowledge and reasons for optimism and belligerence. The battered army with most of its equipment abandoned in France desperately needed to be re-equipped. There were only two rifles for every three soldiers and the position regarding heavy guns and armour was even more desperate. The armament factories of Britain were working as never before and a great deal of munitions were being purchased in America, though much was failing to arrive due to the ravages of the U-boats.

The summer of 1940 proved a time of uneasy calm as both sides faced each other across the waters of the Channel with neither side quite sure what would happen next. When for almost two months the Luftwaffe failed to press home its advantage, the RAF used the time to re-group and turn itself into the fighting force it was eventually to become.

During this period there was only one theatre of war where the British and Germans were actively locked in conflict, that was at sea. The Battle of the Atlantic had begun and was developing into a bitter and hard-fought conflict which was going badly for Britain, who at best were only hanging on. Even the normally ebullient Churchill was later to admit: 'The U-boats were my greatest fear.' Shipping losses were growing alarmingly, many times outstripping the building programme. There was a growing fear that the German navy would succeed in starving the population of Britain into submission.

When the war was over and German records became available the fact that surprised many people was the relatively small number of U-boats that were responsible for the huge number of sinkings. The U-boats' killing rate was phenomenal. When Britain and France declared war in September 1939 Germany had only 37 submarines, including training boats, and despite their early effectiveness many were sunk. In the period prior to August 1940 the official records show that 27 were lost. Mid-1940 was a particularly bad time for the U-boat service; there were several times when as few as eight U-boats were operational.

During this period Hitler was still refusing to give orders to increase the size of the U-boat fleet, despite the protests from Doenitz who could demonstrate that he was close to forcing Britain into starvation, cutting off the vital supplies of food and munitions that would enable the enemy to regroup. Still Hitler vacillated.

Against this backdrop how can we believe that Doenitz would spare one of his deadly and most effective means of delivering the death blow to the enemy and to allow a U-boat, commanded by one of their most experienced and senior captains, to be diverted from the battle to be employed on a mission of little strategic importance? Can we really believe that Admiral Doenitz, desperate to keep his meagre fleet of submarines at sea to carry on the fight he was winning and which promised to deliver victory in a matter of months, would have allowed this to happen at a time when he was exhorting his crews that 'not a day shall pass without the sinking somewhere or other of a ship by one of the boats at sea'? How is it that earlier writers explained away this decision to spare one of Germany's precious fighting machines to deliver what they have persuaded us were a pair of less than important members of a small, illegal, discredited organisation to their home in a neutral country with no specific objective? To allow this at a time when every hour and every gallon of fuel spent at sea was vital?

Doenitz, the head of U-boat service, lived his life by what he described as his 'effective U-boat quotient'. When asked to explain what he meant, he replied: 'I mean the average sinkings per U-boat per day for all U-boats at sea.'[4] This measure of effectiveness shows that during mid-1940 these tonnages were: July 193, August 664 and September 758, which when translated into ships sunk by U-boats alone, amounted to 153, giving a total tonnage of 758,778. While it is accepted that U-65 was leaving on a normal offensive patrol, several days' endurance would have been lost through depletion of its fuel and food by this diversion to the coast of Galway. More than one British ship probably reached port that might otherwise have been destroyed.

Apart from the loss of potential killing power, the risk of sending a U-boat from its base in the Baltic to the west coast of Ireland cannot be underestimated. A study of the U-boat losses between September 1939 and August 1940 shows that of the 27 U-boats destroyed at sea, no less than 11 were lost between latitude 50 and 60 north, and zero and 15 degrees west, the very waters through which this curious and, so we have been asked to believe, relatively unimportant delivery trip would venture. The west coast of Ireland was a dangerous place for U-boats. The British had mined the waters of the St George's Channel which meant that its anti-submarine activities were concentrated around the Northern Channel between Ireland and Scotland, the sea area through which Russell's 'taxi' would pass, bringing it within range of anti-submarine aircraft based on the west of Britain and the Royal Navy ships that patrolled those waters. So effective had they become that Doenitz (who had previously referred to the area between 10 and 15 degrees west as 'the focal point of U-boat operations') was obliged during 1940 to restrict his U-boats from the area and force them to operate beyond 15 degrees west due to the increasing success of the Sunderland flying-boats based in Northern Ireland and Pembroke Dock in West Wales. The most westerly point of the bay of Galway is between nine and ten degrees west. To have approached a suitable beach for landing Russell would have meant going close to land, a dangerous manoeuvre for a submarine; if caught on the surface, lack of deep water would prevent it from diving to safety. All this supports the contention that U-65's mission was no casual delivery job but a dangerous and hazardous mission entrusted to a highly experienced officer. It was von Stockhausen, a former naval headquarters signals staff officer, who had interrupted Doenitz's daily staff conference the previous September to hand him a teleprinter message. The Admiral, clearly upset, paced up and down repeating to himself: 'Mein Gott! Also wieder Kregg gegen England!' (My God! So it's war with England again!)[5]

For this mission to have been sanctioned at all would have meant overruling Doenitz's objections. This supports the premise that somebody very powerful in the Nazi hierarchy was involved.

The more one tries to understand the reasons behind the voyage the more one is driven to seek its real purpose. The return of Russell was clearly important, the use of a valuable U-boat proves how important since there are plenty of other ways the Nazis could have sent him home. Only a month previously the Abwehr had employed Christian Nissen, a well-known Olympic yachtsman with the salty nickname of 'Hein Mueck', who was given a free hand to requisition any craft he wanted on the French coast. He chose a 35-foot sleek luxury yacht, the *Soiciz* belonging to a French colonel in Camberet-sur-Mer, and on the morning after a wild party set sail on 3 July, reporting on his return: 'After three days' sailing, I landed my passengers by dinghy under the cover of darkness in the gulf of Baltimore near the Fastnet Rock in the south-west extremity of Ireland.'[6]

Why did the Nazis not repeat this success? Why not use the *Soiciz* again? It would have been a far better way, probably safer, but more importantly it would have released a precious fighting ship to destroy enemy shipping. There can be only one explanation – this was no Abwehr operation. The use of the U-boat is explained by the need for total secrecy, not from the enemy, but from other members of the Nazi hierarchy in Germany.

Chapter Twenty-four

The Irish Adventure

ARE WE TO BELIEVE that Russell's journey was so secret, as has been suggested? Although some details can be found among the Abwehr records there is no indication of what the mission hoped to achieve and, more importantly, who was its sponsor. Not only is there evidence that Abwehr operations in Ireland had been banned but additional evidence that the Foreign Office was not directly involved, despite the involvement of Dr Veesenmeyer, is confirmed by learning the outcome of a meeting held on 5 August, three days before Russell was due to leave, and where he met Ribbentrop. Also present were Admiral Canaris, the head of the Abwehr, Lieutenant-Colonel Erwin Lahausen, head of Abwehr II, together with Dr Veesenmeyer of the German Foreign Office. Ribbentrop proved very offensive and expressed serious doubts that Russell would be of any use as an agent, adding that he 'disliked the Irish as a race' and did not think the proposed operation would provide anything of value. The purpose of this meeting is unclear. It is hardly likely to have been called to authorise the mission, it was too late for that, but it does confirm that either the venture did not have the backing of the German Foreign Office or that Ribbentrop was lying to protect its true purpose.[1]

The German High Command had long been suspicious of Admiral Canaris, who would eventually be uncovered as a traitor. In 1945 he would be involved in an attempt on Hitler's life after which he was taken to Flossenburg concentration camp, sentenced and hanged together with his former assistant, Colonel Oster. It has long been realised that one of Hitler's great failings was to underestimate the value of intelligence; it was also believed (correctly) that British intelligence had infiltrated the Abwehr and it was necessary to keep very sensitive information away from them. The purpose of the meeting with Ribbentrop seems to have been to persuade Canaris that the mission had not yet been sanctioned and that it was still under consideration, but as we now know Canaris had his own agent on board.

While it is relatively easy to establish that Russell's mission was not some low-key operation planned and controlled by the Abwehr, it has proved more difficult to discover what was planned, and exactly what he was going to do when he arrived.

An examination of the situation in Ireland dispels any idea that Russell had any real hope of rallying Republican support on the ground to embark on anything significant – a great deal of time would have to pass before the IRA would be seen as a force to be reckoned with. Of course, it could be argued that Hitler, or whoever was behind this special mission, believed the IRA was always prepared to believe it represented a real threat. In late 1939 Neville Chamberlain had written: 'There is no doubt that the IRA is powerful enough to take over the Government of Ireland.'[2]

What Chamberlain didn't know, or failed to take into consideration, was that following the outbreak of war the Irish army had been increased to 250,000, while at the same time support for the IRA was haemorrhaging away. There are various estimates of the IRA strength in 1939; they vary between 5,000 and 30,000 and whichever figure you use the probability of a successful insurrection in 1940 was remote. What the rest of the world had yet to learn was the success being enjoyed by the Ministry of the Interior under its newly appointed Assistant Secretary Bolan, the man De Valera entrusted with the job of defeating the IRA. Bolan effectively destroyed the IRA. Given more resources, his main success came from the introduction of the powerful weapon of internment that allowed members of the Garda, armed with lists of the IRA's active members, to swiftly round up and imprison them. So successful were they that at one point during 1940 it was believed that only one serving officer of the IRA had eluded capture. The main body of the IRA was interned in appalling conditions at either Portlaoighise prison or in the internment camps that had been set up at the Curragh.

Some writers have suggested that the Nazis regarded Russell as an important asset and believed that they saw in him their last chance to revive the IRA and mobilise it to influence events in their favour. Seen from Germany this might have had its attractions, but the reality was different. Why should anyone imagine that Russell would be successful in effecting a reversal in the misfortunes of the IRA when it was clear that it was under his leadership that the decline had started and accelerated to a point where its support had all but collapsed? All that remained in 1940 were small, isolated, dispirited groups with no coherent strategy. The IRA had effectively ceased to exist.

The purpose of Russell's trip has never been satisfactorily explained. Several people have advanced dubious theories, but all fall short of producing a reason why the Nazis should have employed considerable resources to help the two men return unless there was a motive. There seems little doubt that they were following some hidden agenda whose details were shared with only one or two top Nazis. Of course, there remains the possibility that Russell misled the Nazis, that he had successfully convinced them he could deliver something they were anxious to effect. However, this, too, is unlikely; to have made a promise he knew he couldn't deliver would have exposed himself and the IRA to the wrath of the Third Reich. Russell had seen the German military machine and the way the SS treated the people of the countries it had occupied at first hand, and to have misled the Nazis at a time when most of the world believed that Hitler was about to win the war would have been an act of extreme folly.

Most authors have suggested that his return was in some way connected with 'Operation Sealion', speculating that Russell's instructions were to remain under cover, await further orders from Germany and then instigate some sort of uprising to coincide with the landings on the south coast of England. The well-known story about how the signal would come when a red flower-pot was placed in a certain window of the German Embassy in Dublin has become part of the folklore that surrounds Russell and has no foundation. This explanation can be safely rejected. As we have seen, 'Operation Sealion' was simply a bluff to bring Britain to the negotiating table and with no real intention of mounting an invasion Hitler was hardly likely to have gone to the trouble of planning an uprising in Ireland to coincide with something he had no intention of embarking on. Another explanation must be found.

The clue lies in the inclusion of Ryan in the undertaking. As we know, he was politically astute: his understanding of the complex political situation in Ireland was what had attracted Helmut Clissmann and Dr Jupp Hoven to suggest his rescue from Spain and it might have been these two that suggested the mission in the first place. Irish politics have always been seen as something of a mystery by those outside Ireland – even those who live there often find it difficult to understand its complexity – and the political position in 1940 was as complicated as at any time in its long and troubled history. Ireland was still a member of the British Commonwealth, and held the distinction of being the only member never to declare war on Germany. The intention to remain neutral had been declared before Britain found herself at war. This was responsible for many curious anomalies: the advent of war had brought to an end the negotiations that were gradually cutting the links with Britain. For example, Ireland was still committed to having her foreign policy administered by the British and that produced the farcical situation that had Germany wanted to change its Minister Plenipotentiary Eduard Hempel in Dublin, the new appointee would have had to present his credentials to George VI in London, where presumably he would be interned. The reason that the *Taoiseach* Eamon De Valera opted for neutrality was not out of any wish to appear to support Fascism, nor was he fooled into believing that in the event of a German victory in neighbouring Britain he could expect to be left alone. Helmut Clissmann is reported to have confirmed this:

> Hitler would have sold Ireland down the river. I would have told the Irish that their freedom was coming. I would have been Lawrence of Arabia. It happened to several friends of mine, with the Bretons and the Walloons. Their freedom was promised, but then, when the Germans had what they wanted, the separatist groups were abandoned. Northern Ireland would be given to a Vichy-type Government in London.

Ireland's reason for neutrality was very simple: De Valera and his Fianna Fail party had spent the last two decades breaking the links with London and believed with good reason that if they joined in the common struggle against Germany they would be forced to re-establish many of them; this they were anxious to avoid. In the run-up to 1939 Britain and Ireland had been negotiating for more and more power to be devolved to Dublin and this had given rise to the contentious removal of the right to use the so-called 'Treaty Ports' in time of war. This had been given up by Neville Chamberlain in 1938 and was to prove a massive blunder. It caused Churchill to become almost apoplectic and sneer: 'A more feckless act it is hard to imagine. Why didn't he give away Malta while he was at it?'[3]

During July and August 1940, Ireland loomed large in many people's minds, the 'Irish back door', as it was called, would have made a perfect jumping-off ground for the invader to land on the lightly defended west coast of Britain and nobody was more alive to this possibility than Churchill. On 20 June he made a speech to a secret session of the House of Commons following the French collapse and in accordance with custom this speech has not been recorded, even for official or historical purposes, so no account exists, but fortunately the nine pages of notes, some having alterations in his own hand, have survived to give some indication of the matters on which he spoke:

> Question of Ireland
> > Greatly influenced by a great army developing here
> > Germans would fight in Ireland under great disadvantages
> > Much rather they break Irish neutrality than we.

Whatever Churchill said when he expanded on these brief notes is not known, but it shows that, in keeping with those responsible for defence, he was alive to the real danger posed by Irish neutrality and was known to have described Ireland's position as 'as at war, but skulking!'. His reference to the army is interesting – he was referring to the Irish army – and suggests that his fears about its expansion were not its ability to withstand a German invasion, but that it might be used for an entirely different purpose.

It can be safely assumed that Russell and Ryan's mission had nothing to do with espionage or the possibility of causing an insurrection involving the IRA. Hitler was playing for much bigger stakes and it is much more likely that this motive in sending the two men was to suggest that the army in the South be mobilised to invade the North. We learn from *Modern Ireland 1600–1972* by R.F. Foster that:

> Germany ruled out the option of a direct Irish attack early on, after drawing up detailed plans (and considering the destabilising invasion of Northern Ireland, imaginatively suggested by Hitler for the twenty-fifth anniversary of Easter 1916).

Hitler and Hess would have been aware that De Valera and his Fianna Fail party were former freedom fighters who had come to power in 1920 following the armed uprising of 1919 and were strongly committed to the aims of Irish unity. They would also have known that Russell and Ryan were former comrades in arms in that struggle and were not only known to those in power but understood the minds and aspirations that had set the foundations of a free and independent Ireland. Hitler would have been encouraged by the fact that Fianna Fail had come to life as a result of insurrection and murder, it was the kind of politics he understood.

It now seems clear that Russell and Ryan were emissaries whose aim was to try and persuade the legitimate Government of

Ireland to insurrection, pointing out that there would never be a better time to rise up and claim back the seven counties in the North which the South always maintained should be part of a unified Ireland. This was later confirmed by Colonel Erwin Lahausen who at his trial at Nuremberg confirmed that Russell's mission was to foment an uprising and to ensure that the British did not get their hands on the 'Treaty Ports'. If such a move had been successful the Irish could have expected considerable support from Germany and there is more than sufficient evidence to support the contention. We know that Captain Hermann Goertz, the best known of the Nazi spies working in Ireland, had landed in May 1940 with the task of finding a suitable site for a parachute landing and he had selected a site near Waterford, and it is also known that British intelligence were intercepting all his reports. In his book, *Mirror of Deception*, Gunter Pies describes how Goertz was in touch with the well-known double agent Arthur Owen and was passing the information to Owen to send back to Germany. He tells how a Roman Catholic priest, a member of the Nationalist organisation, travelled to London several times a month with documents sewn in his shirt. He had exact instructions how to get rid of them. When he left Ireland the Abwehr agent sent a radio message to Owen (and of course to British intelligence) who were alerted that the important documents were to arrive at Brompton Oratory. There Owen, under the watchful eye of two SIS men, would approach the priest who would be sitting at the end of a pew and ask him if he would hear his confession. 'Of course, my son,' the Irishman would reply and lead German agent 3504 to the confessional where British intelligence would take possession of the material Hauptmann Goertz was sending to Germany. When the war was over Goertz remained in Ireland and wrote a series of articles for the *Irish Times* about his mission before he committed suicide rather than face trial in Germany. It has also been revealed that Clissmann had been sending messages to assure the Irish of Hitler's benign intentions and his promises to reunite the North and South. But the final proof must be the letter that was discovered when the Justice File S253/4 was released in 1993 in Dublin. Its contents have not hitherto been made public. This letter, written to the Minister of the Interior by Chief Superintendent P. Carroll of Crime Branch 3 of the Garda Siochana, states:

I am directed by the Commissioner to state that information received indicates that the IRA in Northern Ireland have been warned through Sean Russell who is stated to be in Germany that the Germans will invade this country by air with parachutists, gliders, etc between the 14th and 17th March 1941.

P. Carroll, Chief Superintendent.

The Minister, apart from initialling it on 20 February 1941, seems to have done nothing – which seems remarkable.

Nobody except the Nazis knew of Russell's death. The Irish were the first of the others to know, and it would be later that summer before they learned, so a message purporting to come from Russell should have been taken seriously. March 1941 was the 25th anniversary of the Easter rising. Goertz was sending back messages regarding suitable landing sites for paratroops and gliders and yet nobody seems to have taken much interest in this extraordinary piece of intelligence. There is no record that they passed the information on to British intelligence and it seems incredible if they were unaware that Russell was coming with proposals to drive the British out of Ireland that no action was taken and they appear to have been so relaxed about news of the impending invasion.

It now seems clear that Russell's untimely death put paid to something that might well have changed the direction of the war – an Irish civil war using the Irish army backed with Nazi paratroops must have been Churchill's worst nightmare. A united Ireland, still a member of the British Commonwealth and with massive support in America for a negotiated peace, could not have given Hitler a more suitable opportunity to employ the Duke of Windsor and explains why almost up to the moment when Russell was due to leave, Hitler was urging those in Portugal to have him kept available. As a mediator for peace, the role in which the Duke seems to have cast himself, he would have attracted much more support across the world and in particular in Britain where there was still a large body of opinion in favour of a pact with Hitler, and who believed that an alliance between a now powerful force based in Germany and the declining British Empire was a great stabilising force for world peace and prosperity rather than the present debilitating conflict that would leave both sides to face years of austerity. This dream, which first surfaced in *Mein Kampf* back in 1926, was one in which Hitler never stopped believing or trying to attain.

Chapter Twenty-five

A Curious Postscript

THERE WERE SUFFICIENT MYSTERIES surrounding Russell, and particularly the mission that cost him his life, to encourage a re-examination but gradually, in view of the limited information that was available, it began to look as if the study would produce nothing but questions and that the latter part of his life was destined to remain obscure. Investigating Russell's life proves fascinating – the more you explore the more mysteries you discover and, like everything else connected with Irish politics, it has proved not to be without its touch of humour. During the search for an explanation of what Russell was planning, several strange stories came to light.

The *Irish Times* of 21 August 1951 carried a photograph of a statue that had been erected in Fairview Park, Dublin, as a memorial to Sean Russell, and announced that it was to be formally unveiled on Sunday, 9 September. Surprisingly, the ceremony was allowed to go ahead. Instead of trying to stop it, the Garda seemed content to simply monitor and record what took place. A secret report produced for the Ministry of the Interior dated 10 September and signed by Detective Inspector 1761, John F. Flaherty, gives a curious but amusing account of what had taken place on the previous day. His report describes how a procession gathered in O'Connell Street, an assembly it would have been difficult for the Garda to have ignored. In attendance were the City of Dublin Girl Piper Band, the Pomeray Accordion Band, the Transport Workers Band and Joe McKelvey's Pipe Band, which led a march that set off across O'Connell Street Bridge for the unveiling ceremony. Clearly this was no covert or secret gathering, in fact it must have been quite a noisy affair. The report contains several lists which classified the marchers into 'active members of the IRA', the 'ex-members of the IRA' and 'fellow travellers'. The names of those identified were recorded. The report concludes that the remainder, some of whom had travelled from various parts of the 26 counties, were probably only there out of curiosity. With typical Irish frankness the report draws attention to the fact that the crowd would probably have been greater had the IRA supporters from Mayo and Kerry turned out. However, it explains that they were otherwise engaged, attending the replay of the All Ireland football final taking place at the same time. It notes that three volleys of shots were fired at the unveiling ceremony from 'what appeared to be new revolvers' and estimates that of the 1,500 or so who were present only 150 were IRA activists, adding the somewhat cryptic rider that 'this does not include the members of the various bands in attendance'.

Even making allowance for the vagaries of Irish politics it is still difficult to understand what was going on. Why was this march permitted? Why did the Government allow a statue dedicated to a well-known enemy of the State to be erected in full view of the world? Equally intriguing is the reason why the IRA felt obliged to erect a memorial at all. Russell's period as Chief of Staff was brief, just 28 months, of which more than 16 were spent either in America or in Germany with little or no evidence that he was working on behalf of the IRA. Under his leadership, the IRA was plunged into total disarray. Russell achieved nothing of significance to advance the cause of Republicanism. Rather he abandoned its members at a time when they were being hunted down and imprisoned. Nothing has been revealed in the period since his death to warrant him being singularly honoured; his record prior to becoming Chief of Staff wasn't particularly successful either. An article published in the *Belfast News Letter* on 24 June 1940 drew attention to the danger of co-operation between the IRA and the Nazis. It estimated of the total number of IRA sympathisers, both North and South of the border, at 5,000, of which 4,000 were without arms. What arms there were had been those left over from the days of 1921, supplemented by a few Tommy-guns imported from America.

The report of this strange incident presents us with a dilemma. Do we simply dismiss Russell in the way of previous writers, or does it indicate that maybe his true involvement has, somehow, been missed? What explanation can there be for affording him this special honour? No other leader of the IRA has ever had a statue erected to their memory. Michael Collins is remembered by a rather grand tombstone near where he was assassinated; several leaders have a road, one even has a railway station, named after them. Even those leaders of the IRA shot by firing squad in Dublin following the 1923 Civil War are only remembered by a small plaque on a wall. So what did Russell do to be treated as a hero? Is it possible that all those who have previously studied his life have missed something? If so, the almost casual way history has treated his fatal attempt to return in U-65 may also be wrong. To have achieved such status, fêted by his fellow Republicans while the Government he devoted his life to opposing turned a blind eye, begs the question, what exactly did Russell do?

Fairview Park was owned by the local authority: someone must have given permission. His statue is maintained, even to this day, from the public purse. Fifty-four years after his death nobody, including the IRA, can satisfactorily explain why it was erected. Whatever Hitler and those close to him hoped to achieve with Russell's mission has never been revealed – it is highly unlikely that the Irish Government or the IRA ever knew. Whatever it was it seemed destined to remain another intriguing secret.

The strange business of why the Dublin Government allowed the monument to be erected in a public park defies explanation; the reason, if it could be discovered, might hold the key to many other matters. It is worth noting that Eamon De Valera and his Fianna Fail party had only two months before been re-elected to power after a defeat in February 1948. Fianna Fail has always openly opposed the IRA despite its formation from the same origins, and still this illegal march went ahead. The monument stood unattended for 18 days after its photograph appeared in the press. Those in authority couldn't very well pretend they didn't know what was going on, neither can the Garda claim they didn't intervene to avoid trouble, or explain it away by saying they wanted to wait to see who turned up. The IRA was an illegal organisation, marches and public demonstrations had been banned in the Republic since 1939, so how can we explain the Government's thinking behind its apparent acquiescence to what happened? Nobody in Ireland, despite vigorous enquiries, can explain why the Dublin Government appears to have colluded in honouring an enemy of the State that history has tried to persuade us didn't do very much for the cause and even less for his country. In drawing up the lists of who was there, the police clearly demonstrated that they knew perfectly well who the current members of the IRA were. Any they didn't recognise were dismissed as onlookers.

There is a curious footnote to this strange business. Some time after the statue had been dedicated it was defaced. The right arm, raised in salute, was sawn off by right-wing extremists who believed it was raised in a Communist and not in an oratorial pose. Russell, a lifelong opponent of Communism, might well have enjoyed the irony. The statue still stands but looks somewhat incongruous as the substitute arm that now rests across his chest is smaller than that of the original. The erection of the statue, which remains a mystery in Ireland, even caused controversy in America. Clan-na-Gael, the sister organisation of the IRA whose members are traditionally drawn from Republican ex-patriate Irish living there, and responsible for raising most of the funds and arms for the IRA, was itself in trouble. Due to the efforts of the FBI it virtually ceased to exist between 1939 and 1945. But, following a convention, it was reformed in 1946. During the war it had accumulated close on $30,000 and many of the members wanted the money used to build a monument to Russell in Dublin. There were others who disagreed, who wanted the money to remain against the day when the IRA would again rise in Ireland and be used to finance terrorism. Such was the disagreement that it caused a split, a common enough occurrence in anything to do with the Irish Republican movement. The pro-statue faction led by James Conaty and Joseph Stynes won and promptly expelled those opposed to the building of the statue. The IRA in Dublin sent a man named Monaghan to try and heal the rift but he failed. In the manner of pro-republican politics both anti-statue and those groups in support were later to split following disagreements unconnected with this issue. The fact that it appears to be American-based supporters of the IRA who originally raised the question of the memorial is interesting. It provides a clue to why Russell was given this honour and confirms that whatever Russell found himself involved in, it emanated from the time when he was in the United States. Russell has been dead for well over half a century, forgotten; even those who remember his name are convinced that the truth of whatever he was involved in had died with him. Several generations of children have played in Fairview Park without knowing or caring who Russell was, or why he stands there staring into the distance. Then just as the mists of time were settling over Russell, there was a dramatic development, an exciting revelation. Fifty-four years after his curious death Russell hit the headlines.

The front page of *The Sunday Times* of 3 January 1993 carried the eye-catching headline 'IRA PLOT TO KILL KING AND QUEEN' and revealed that a Department of Justice file containing details of a plot to assassinate King George VI and Queen Elizabeth during their state visit to Canada and America during the summer of 1939 had been declassified by the Irish Government and contained information that suggested that Russell was involved in a plot to murder the Royal couple. Sadly the information was, by and large, only a confirmation of intelligence available in America.

Russell's somewhat obscure tracks finally led to the discovery of his part in the more important conspiracy, a strange story of political intrigue that involves many of the leading players on the international stage during the early days of the Second World War. Following Russell's trail since he left Ireland in 1939 until his fateful return has offered an understanding of several other mysterious matters that successive Governments have gone to great lengths to suppress.

Another curious story came to light that may have some bearing on what has been suggested. In his book *King of Fools*, John Parker relates a story that he obtained following a discussion he had with the Duke of Grantmesnil, the former Kenneth De Courcy, who was a friend of the Duke of Windsor and who was later to be accused by Maitre Blum, the Duke and Duchess's French lawyer, of being concerned with removing many of the Duke's papers from his safe, acting on the instructions of Earl Mountbatten who was working on behalf of the Royal Family. Grantmesnil reveals that the Duke of Windsor invited him to visit at La Croë. When he arrived the Duke of Windsor asked that he carry out a delicate mission on his behalf, to contact De Valera and to ask him if it would be possible for the Duke and Duchess to settle in Southern Ireland. The suggestion at first seems highly unlikely: that Ireland is a beautiful country is beyond question, but it is no accident that the British nobility have been attracted to the French Riviera because of its wonderful climate; life in winter in Ireland cannot compare with the life the Duke enjoyed for over a quarter of a century on the Côte d'Azur where he mixed with many of his former friends who either had houses there or went there on holiday. What possible motive could he have for wanting to exchange that for a house in Ireland?

Grantmesnil recalls how he wrote from La Croë on Windsor notepaper to Eamon De Valera to ask if he could go and see him 'on an urgent and confidential matter', revealing:

> I had never met him, but he knew my family. It was my brother who helped him escape prison during the IRA troubles. I returned to England and was duly invited to Dublin. I took off by private plane and went to De Valera's office. I was shown into an ante-room to await his arrival and explained the purpose of my visit: the Duke of Windsor wishes to take up permanent residence in his country.

De Valera sat back in his chair and said nothing for what seemed like a minute or two. Then he leaned forward and said: 'You saw me arrive in this building, did you not? You saw that my car was surrounded by security, that I was protected through every step I made to my office? My life is in constant danger and I can say it would be the same, even much worse, for your former King. There would be political uproar if he were to move here. I cannot believe that he would want to lead the sort of life he would be subjected to.'

Does the fact that the Duke showed an interest in Ireland suggest that he had developed a nostalgic feeling for the country? If he did, it is strange, for he had never shown any previous interest in that part of his kingdom while Duke of Windsor or as Edward VIII. Is it possible that having been involved in a Nazi plan to unite the country by insurrection he thought that in post-war Ireland he stood a chance of doing it alone? The British people, who were by now thoroughly disenchanted with him, would never have allowed him to return. His image had changed: he was now seen as a foolish adventurer who threw away everything in pursuit of a misplaced ideal. His current unpopularity had more to do with a growing affection for the Royal Family who had become closer to the people, having shared the dangers and possibility of defeat, rather than any awareness of the Duke's chequered recent past. If he saw Ireland as a possible base for a reverse of his fortunes he was thwarted again. He returned to Paris to live out his life with a woman who never returned the affection he showed for her, and to reflect on a life that might have been.

Chapter Twenty-six

Hess: the Enduring Mystery

IT IS NOT POSSIBLE to conclude an examination of the events involving the Duke of Windsor and to trace his co-operation with the Nazis without studying the crucial and central part played by Rudolf Hess. The connection that is known to have begun when the two men met in Munich in the early Thirties and was to culminate when they met in Lisbon in July 1940 was a great deal more significant than is generally realised.

It is unfortunate that the mysterious flight Hess made to Scotland in May 1941, and all the attention it inevitably attracted, has overshadowed the part he played in the formation of Nazi Germany, and the effect it had on the way in which the war developed. While it was untrue, it is easy to understand why it suited both sides to portray Hess as a weak-minded, confused figure whose mission to Scotland was of no real importance, something of an aberration on his part to achieve a peaceful outcome to what he believed would be a costly and long-drawn-out conflict that would leave the two countries economically weak. He genuinely believed that the peoples of both countries were violently opposed to a damaging war, and he was correct, but by the time he came to Britain the mood had changed and his flight became a strange diversion that has been turned into a mystery simply because of the British Government's refusal to divulge the truth. The picture this has left in most people's minds is that of the tragic figure of an old man alone in Spandau prison in Berlin who refused to explain what he had hoped to achieve, and who, despite the efforts of his family and many influential people who regarded his treatment as barbaric, was destined to die alone. The Governments of the nations responsible for his incarceration refused to show any compassion and allow his release. This picture helps to cloud the former activities of Hess who was a force to be reckoned with in the Nazi hierarchy.

Hess was one of the first members of the Nazi Party and from the very beginning was a fervent supporter and admirer of Hitler and as he and the party grew, so did Hess. Constantly to be found standing at Hitler's elbow, he was finally rewarded. Hitler signed a decree on 21 April 1933: 'I appoint the director of the Political Central Commission, Rudolf Hess, as my deputy and authorise him to decide all matters concerning the directions of the party in my name.'

By 1936 he had begun to be overshadowed by Martin Bormann, and this might explain why Bormann accompanied Hess to the meeting at the Hotel Meurice; it also lends credence to its importance. As early as 1931 Hess had been concerned with foreign affairs. Hitler had made him responsible for Germans abroad and he had assumed control of the intelligence services and was able to monitor the gathering of information. There is no doubt that it was Hess who kept Hitler informed of what was going on, and we are reminded of this when we learn of his complicity in the 'Night of the Long Knives'. On 30 June 1934 Hess and Bormann supervised the arrest of 110 people Hitler had decided to eliminate. While the number was eventually reduced, it was Hess who read out over the telephone the names of those who were to be murdered by firing squad, in the belief that they were more loyal to President Hindenburg than to the ambitious Hitler who was making his bid for outright control. By remaining in the background, Hess was able to conceal his willing participation and was thus never regarded as being as 'bloodthirsty' as were many of the other Nazi leaders; but there is no doubt that his commitment to violence was just as strong.

To help him gain understanding of the political situation in other countries, Hess was to be heavily influenced by his former tutor and friend, Major-General Professor Karl Haushofer, but as time went on it was Haushofer's son Albrecht who took over the role and whose influence on both Hitler and Hess was considerable. They were both to rely on his knowledge of foreign affairs that he had gained on several important overseas missions, including several to Britain, which he is know to have visited regularly. Haushofer was a German patriot whose origins were partly Jewish and who passionately advocated peace between Britain and Germany. In his frequent reports he stressed that it was fundamental that Nazi Germany remained in a state of peaceful co-existence with Britain. Writing in *Zeitschrift fur Geopolitik* in April 1935 he decided somewhat prophetically that: 'The final decision on the fate of Europe – as was the case at the turn of the century – is in the hands of Britain.'

This belief was long established and came initially from the elder Haushofer who had successfully convinced his pupil of the danger of Bolshevism which, if it was to be halted, would need the military might of the whole of Western Europe. Hess was not only convinced but he was also able to impress this view upon Hitler to such an extent that it became official Nazi policy and is to be found outlined in *Mein Kampf*. It was one of the overriding reasons for the Nazi fascination with the Duke of Windsor who, they believed, could bring it about.

There is now little dispute among those who have studied what took place in Portugal in July 1940 that the hand of the deputy Führer can be detected in the plot to persuade the Duke and Duchess to return and take up residence in Spain. Hess went to Lisbon in a last desperate effort in what has come to be regarded as a 'tug of war' to keep the Duke on the Iberian peninsula. As the events in Lisbon were coming to a climax, a telegram from Stohrer, the German Ambassador, to Ribbentrop revealed: 'Victor is expected.' A few days later in another telegram that was also discovered among the captured German papers, Schellenberg confirmed that 'Victor was with Willi'.

In his book *The Crown and the Swastika*, Peter Allen traces the identity of the mystery man called 'Victor' who is referred to in several German documents of the time, and makes a convincing case that 'Victor' was Hess and that his reason for going to Lisbon was to see the Duke. Several other authors have revealed that the 'Willi' mentioned was the Duke of Windsor. The distinguished author Michael Block, who has written extensively about the Duke and Duchess, having had a unique access to their papers through the law firm in Paris that acted for them, chose *Operation Willi* as the title for his book about the Windsors' escapades in Spain and Portugal in 1940. There is now no serious doubt that 'Victor' was Hess and 'Willi' was the Duke.

Later the following year, when Hess flew to Scotland in the Messerschmitt 110, the plane he had been known to fly on a number of previous occasions, we know that it carried the identification letters VJ-OQ and it has been revealed that he always used the call sign 'V for Victor', which seems more than coincidence and almost certainly explains where the codename 'Victor' originated.[1]

It is relatively easy to trace the connection between Hess and the Duke that began in the early Thirties and lasted until the Duke seems either to have lost his nerve in the face of threatened action initiated by Churchill or, with a great deal more perception than he had hitherto shown, decided that Germany was not going to win the war and severed his past connections. The former is more likely. We know that Walter Monckton was sent to Lisbon and spelled out in no uncertain terms to his client the action Britain would take if he did not comply with his orders and go to the Bahamas. The dream that the Duke and the Nazis shared was beginning to falter. Hitler even played what he must have thought was his ace: he told Ribbentrop that the Nazis were prepared to pay three million dollars into a Swiss bank for the Duke, hinting that more might be made available, if the Duke would stay. Knowing the Duke's reputation for meanness and his affection for money they expected this to provide a powerful attraction, but the fright he had received from Churchill seems to have proved a greater deterrent. The Duke sailed, but in an effort to keep a foot in both camps he sent the message quoted in a previous chapter.

Knowing it would not prove too difficult to bring him back, the Nazis saw his departure on 1 August as only a temporary setback. They had already put plans in place to keep tabs on him in the Bahamas. What they could never have foreseen was that the operation in which they intended to include the Duke would end in failure. With the death of Russell everything collapsed.

The effect this had on Hitler is not difficult to trace. Five days later – 17 August – he declared all the waters around Britain a war zone. This included the waters around Ireland, and he warned that U-boats would sink any vessel that sailed there, including ships of neutral countries. He turned his attention to and began to give serious consideration to 'Operation Sealion' and held several meetings with his Chiefs of Staff. Instead of regarding it as a ploy to frighten the British, he allowed the planning to be intensified and, more importantly, gave Goering the chance to fulfil his arrogant boast that he could defeat the Royal Air Force in a matter of weeks. All overtures for peace were forgotten. Hitler concentrated his mind on the prospect of all-out war with the 'old enemy'.

Hess, on the other hand, refused to accept that the hope of some form of alliance with Britain had faded. He continued to believe that the course of action being adopted was a mistake. Not only did he believe that to invade England successfully was impossible, but he saw the danger of ditching a policy that had been fundamental since he and Hitler had first discussed it in Landsdorf Prison back in 1920 and had vowed never to find themselves fighting on two fronts at the same time. He remained convinced that most of the informed thinking in Britain still wanted peace, and began to make plans that would culminate in his flight to Scotland in May 1941.

The reason behind Hess's flight remains one of the unsolved mysteries of the war, but only for one simple reason: the British Government's refusal to tell the truth about what happened. Despite the Government's promise to release the remainder of the material in 2017, there is no discernible reason why they have to wait that long. Not only is it inexplicable, but it is about as disgraceful as conspiring to keep a sick, old man alone in a crumbling prison and waiting for him to die before demolishing his prison in an attempt to make the world forget the scene of such inhumanity. What explanation can there be for expending the vast amount of money it cost to keep him imprisoned? To have done it at a time when British and American Governments were sanctimoniously lecturing the countries of the Third World about their record on human rights was nothing less than duplicitous.

For many years the British and American governments attributed the reason for Hess's continuing imprisonment to Russian intransigence. On a number of occasions, following pressure from the West German Government and Amnesty International, Western governments maintained that they would be happy to release him, but the Soviets would not agree. This is a fairly transparent excuse, the real reason was that while Hess remained in prison anything he said or wrote could be suppressed. The Soviet authorities were more anxious than most to discover the reason behind Hess's flight to Scotland, they have always suspected that the British and the Nazis had been plotting against Russia in 1941 and if Hess were released and confirmed this it would have had considerable propaganda value during the 'cold war' period.

It is generally accepted that when the information is released it will prove little, if anything, that is not already known. Files previously placed in the public records office are known to have been removed and 'edited'. All this secrecy has achieved is to keep alive the memory of a Nazi war criminal who would otherwise have been forgotten. Already neo-Nazi elements have erected a memorial to his memory near the spot where he landed, and this has been torn up by Anti-Nazi League members. In making a secret of the affair the Government has turned Hess into some sort of martyr, and by allowing a memorial to be erected on British soil to a convicted war criminal the British Government has given tacit support to the growing spread of neo-Nazi organisations across Europe.

Much of the research over the last decade has gradually answered most of the questions. The suggestion that Hess's plane had insufficient fuel to reach Scotland has been resolved: Helmut

Kaden, Messerschmitt's chief test pilot, has provided incontrovertible evidence that not only could the Messerschmitt 110 reach the point it did, but could have gone a great deal further. The various arguments about the identity of the plane have been resolved, although why this became the subject for debate is difficult to understand – the remains of the plane have been on public display for over half a century and are to be found at the Imperial War Museum at Duxford in Cambridgeshire still bearing the original numbers.

A great deal of interest was generated in the Hess story with the publication in 1984 of Hugh Thomas's *Murder of Rudolf Hess*, in which it is suggested that the man who had landed in Scotland was not Hess but a 'doppelganger'. It was an ingenious and meticulously constructed conspiracy theory that produced a great deal of fact that had not previously been revealed. This version was given added authority by being based on the medical evidence of a non-existent bullet wound. Hugh Thomas had been a former army surgeon who had served in Northern Ireland and is regarded as an acknowledged expert in bullet wounds and his allegation that the man who flew to Scotland did not have any, when it was known that Hess did, made for an argument that was initially hard to challenge. However, several examinations of Hess's body following his death have produced the official line that the man in Spandau had evidence of an old bullet wound and thus was Hess. Lord James Douglas-Hamilton, who had previously written *Motive for a Mission*, first published in 1971 and updated in 1979, and *The Truth about Rudolf Hess*, published in 1993, demolishes much of the conspiracy theory and takes the more conventional line drawing on a great deal of material available through Government sources and those held by his family.

What has never been satisfactorily explained – and it is common to all the many and various accounts, and it does not matter which version of events the reader chooses to believe – is why did Hess or his 'double' choose to try and make contact with the Duke of Hamilton?

On this question the evidence is very speculative. There is not, nor ever has been, any suggestion that the Duke of Hamilton was anything other than an honest, straightforward and likeable RAF officer whose patriotism was beyond question. Much has been made of the Duke of Hamilton's prowess as a pilot – he gained considerable fame when as chief pilot of the Mount Everest Flight Expedition of 1933 he successfully flew over the mountain, a considerable achievement considering the type of aircraft available

– and while Hess, who was also a pilot of some skill, would have been impressed, to suggest this should have persuaded Hess to select him as a go-between for the Governments of Britain and Germany to negotiate an armistice cannot be taken seriously. It has also been revealed that the Duke of Hamilton visited Germany before the war and did in fact attend a large dinner party hosted by Hitler, at which Hess was present, at the time of the 1936 Olympic Games in Berlin but several people who were also there have stated that the two men never met. Most accounts have explained that the Duke of Hamilton was acquainted with the Haushofers and reveal how contact was made with the Duke of Hamilton by letter that came via Lisbon and was intercepted by MI6. It is at this point that the various interpretations fail to provide a satisfactory reason why anyone in Germany should imagine that the Duke of Hamilton should want to help his country's enemies. The only explanation that remains, and the one that seems to have gained the most credence, is that Hess was the victim of a plot by British intelligence, who had fooled him into believing that the Duke of Hamilton was powerful enough to influence the King and the War Cabinet to sue for peace and had led him into believing that if he came he could persuade the Duke that this was in the best interests of the British. Sadly, we will probably never know. If British intelligence was responsible it is difficult to see a motive; if the intelligence services were working on behalf of the War Cabinet the next question has to be – to what end? It was not to use Hess for propaganda purposes: not only did they do precious little with him after he arrived, but his presence seems to have been more of an embarrassment to the British than it was to the Nazis, who simply dismissed the incident saying Hess was mad. Had the initiative been Hess's alone, it is easy to dismiss him as, if not simple, very gullible and having a great deal of misplaced optimism that he had never previously shown.

However, there is another suggestion that has not been developed. Two aspects of the Hess flight have been overlooked by the various later historians but are relevant to this book which directs the reader to consider affairs that happened in Ireland and America.

When Hess landed there was a certain amount of scepticism that he might not be Hess, but an imposter. Anxious to find out, Churchill discussed the matter with Anthony Eden, the Foreign Secretary, who in turn handed the task to Sir Ivone Kirkpatrick, the Foreign Office expert on Germany who had previously met Hess. Kirkpatrick was instructed to carry out the initial interrogation mainly to ascertain if indeed it was the deputy Führer who had arrived.

Kirkpatrick is reported to have spent several hours interrogating Hess and much of what was discussed has been revealed and is well known, but one aspect of the discussions is a very curious remark which surely needs some explanation. Kirkpatrick recorded:

> I then threw a fly over him about Ireland. He said that in all his talks with Hitler, the subject of Ireland had never been mentioned incidentally. Ireland had done nothing for Germany in this war and it was therefore to be supposed that Hitler would not concern himself in Anglo-Irish relations. We had some little conversation about the difficulty of reconciling the wishes of the South and the North and from this we passed on to American interest in Ireland, and so to America.[2]

Hess was lying. Even ignoring what has been suggested in previous chapters and accepting that Hess had not been part of the plot to send Russell back to Ireland, it is clear that he would have known about it and the many other initiatives mounted by the Nazis. This is not particularly important, but the fact that Kirkpatrick should have tried to discover what was being planned for Ireland is a great deal more revealing. We have already discovered that Irish intelligence had received information about a planned invasion of Northern Ireland two months previously. This titbit of information leads us to believe that British intelligence was also aware of it. It all adds support to the conclusions drawn about 'Operation Dove' and its importance.

However, when examining the part played by Bedaux, Flynn and the Duke of Windsor in the conspiracy a rather startling piece of information came to light. In his highly acclaimed book, *Trading With The Enemy*, Charles Higham revealed much of the illegal co-operation that existed between American industrial companies and the Nazis. There is a remarkable suggestion that owes its origin to a file discovered among the information that has become available from the Department of the Army at Fort Meade in Maryland. Higham states:

> In the summer of 1937, according to MI6 files in the Ministry of Defence, London, Bedaux met with the Duke of Windsor, Bedaux's close friend Errol Flynn, Rudolf Hess and Martin Bormann in a secret encounter at the Hotel Meurice in Paris. At this meeting the

Duke promised to help Hess contact the Duke of Hamilton, who had a direct link with Himmler and Kurt von Schroder to the Schroder Bank and the Worms Bank through their common membership in Frank Buchman's Moral Rearmament Movement. Hess was determined to insure an alliance with Great Britain that would continue despite Hitler's conquest. Bedaux was the instrument and Errol Flynn was the glamorous accomplice. The plan was postponed; efforts were made by Hess to meet with Hamilton on several further occasions, which finally led to Hess's dramatic landing on the Hamilton estate in 1941.

Can it really be that the reason why Hess came to Scotland was as a result of the meeting in the Hotel Meurice? It certainly looks as if it might be, and if this is the case then it could offer a justification for the Government's reluctance to come clean over the Hess affair. Could it be that simple? To explain the premise behind the Hess mission would inevitably lead to the Duke of Windsor's duplicity. It is simply another part of the attempt to hide the story that has been suppressed by successive Cabinets since 1936 and has given rise to a cover-up that involved Sir Anthony Blunt and Sir Owen Morehouse, both of whom were knighted as a reward for their services to the Crown, Earl Mountbatten, who is believed to have also taken information from the Duke's safe following his death, and 'Fruity' Metcalfe, who is known to have collected a great deal of material held by the Bank of England and handed it over to the Royal Family.

Half a century has passed. All the members of the intelligence services who played a part have kept their oath of secrecy; most have taken the information to the grave. The only way that this story will ever come to light will be if the monarchy falls and the new republic that would replace it chooses to make the information available. This would be the supreme irony, for the Duke of Windsor gave an interview to the *Daily Herald* in 1938 in which it was reported: 'If the Labour Party wished and were in a position to offer it he would be prepared to be President of the English Republic.' The article was banned by the censor.

If there was a ghost watching while the Treaty of Rome which united Western Europe was signed then it would surely have been Hitler's; he would have smiled as he saw his dream fulfilled. Similarly, if an Act making Britain a republic is ever signed, there will be a slightly built couple watching with a quiet smile of satisfaction on their faces.

Sources

Introduction

1 David Sinclair, *Queen and Country*, 1979
2 Captured German Documents, Volume X Series D
3 Duchess of Windsor, *The Heart has its Reasons*, 1956
4 David Sinclair, *Queen and Country*, 1979
5 Ibid
6 Peter Wright, *Spycatcher*, (Australia) 1987

Chapter 1

1 Peter Allen, *The Crown and The Swastika*, 1983
2 Lord Templewood, *Nine Troubled Years*, 1954

Chapter 2

1 This letter was published in *The Times* in 1956
2 Duchess of Windsor, *The Heart has its Reasons*, 1956
3 Michael Block (Ed.), *Wallis and Edward Letters 1931–1937*, 1986
4 John Parker, *King of Fools*, 198ε
5 John Parker, *King of Fools*, 1988
6 George V to Baldwin, revealed in Andrew Sinclair, *Last of the Best*, 1969

Chapter 3

1 Stephen Birmingham, *Duchess, Wallis Warfield Windsor*, 1981
2 J. Bryan III and Charles J.V. Murphy, *The Windsor Story*, 1979
3 Discussion with Baldwin and later reported by Baldwin
4 This telegram is pictured in Frances Donaldson's *Edward VIII, The Road to Abdication*, 1974
5 Charles Higham, *Wallis, Secret Life of the Duchess of Windsor*, 1988
6 John Parker, *King of Fools*, 1988

Chapter 4

1 Captured German Documents
2 Halifax Diaries
3 J. Bryan III and Charles J.V. Murphy, *The Windsor Story*, 1979
4 Lady Helen Hardinge, *Loyal to Three Kings*, 1967
5 Kenneth Rose, *George V*, 1983

Chapter 5

1 Diana Mosley, *The Duchess of Windsor*, 1980
2 Ladislas Farago, *The Game of The Foxes*, 1972
3 Captured German Documents, Volume X Series D
4 Ladislas Farago, *The Game of The Foxes*, 1972
5 Michael Block, *Ribbentrop*, 1992
6 Sir Henry Channon, *Diaries of Sir Henry Channon*, 1967

Chapter 6

1 Report on interrogation of Nazi war criminals, National Archives, Washington
2 Davidson, J.C.C. (1st Viscount), *Memoirs of a Conservative*, 1969

Chapter 7

1 Sir Henry Channon, *Diaries of Sir Henry Channon*, 1967
2 Michael Block (Ed.), *Wallis and Edward Letters 1931–1937*, 1986
3 Ibid
4 John Parker, *King of Fools*, 1988
5 Fruity Metcalfe's letters to his wife are an important source. They were later made available to Frances Donaldson; most commentators have relied upon this source.

Chapter 8

1 Stephen Birmingham, *Duchess, The Story of Wallis Warfield Windsor*, 1981

SOURCES

Chapter 9

1 Captured German Records, Volume X Series D
2 Michael Block (Ed.), *Wallis and Edward Letters 1931–1937*, 1986

Chapter 10

1 Duke of Windsor, *A King's Story*, 1951
2 Declassified State Department Files, Washington
3 Captured German Documents, Foreign Policy Documents

Chapter 11

1 Errol Flynn, *My Wicked Wicked Ways*, 1936

Chapter 13

1 Charles Higham, *Errol Flynn The Untold Story*, 1980
2 Bowyer Bell, *The Secret Army, The IRA 1916–1979*

Chapter 14

1 Public Records Office, London
2 National Archives, Dublin

Chapter 15

1 Father Coughlin, *American Swastika and Modern Ireland*
2 Article *Sunday Times*, 3 January 1993
3 National Archives, Dublin, File No. S253/40

Chapter 16

1 Captured German Documents, Volume X Series D, Documents of Foreign Policy released in 1957
2 Bernard Edwards, *They Sank the Red Dragon*, 1987
3 Enno Stephan, *Spies in Ireland*, Berlin 1963

Chapter 17

1 Ladislas Farago, *The Game of The Foxes*, 1972

Chapter 18

1 Captured German Documents, Volume X Series D
2 J. Bryan III and Charles J.V. Murphy, *The Windsor Story*, 1979
3 Duke of Windsor, *A King's Story*, 1947
4 William Morrow inc., *Book of Lists*, New York 1977
5 J. Bryan III and Charles J.V. Murphy, *The Windsor Story*, 1979

Chapter 19

1 Ladislas Farago, *The Game of The Foxes*, 1972

Chapter 21

1 Lord Templewood, *Nine Troubled Years*, 1954
2 Captured German Documents, Volume X Series D
3 Michael Block, *Duke of Windsor's War*, 1982
4 Sir Winston Churchill, *Great War Speeches*
5 Captured German Records, Volume X Series D
6 *Ibid*

Chapter 22

1 Lord Templewood, *Nine Troubled Years*, 1954
2 Sefton Delmer, *Black Boomerang*
3 U-Boat Archive, Cuxhaven
4 Declassified State Department Files, Washington
5 National Archives, Dublin File No. S253/40
6 Ladislas Farago, *The Game of The Foxes*, 1972
7 National Archives Dublin and Washington. Several sources have revealed details of Ryan's time in Spain. Later details after leaving Spain are to be found in captured Abwehr documents.

Chapter 23

1 Captured German Documents, Volume X Series D
2 Abwehr War Diary in Washington
3 F.W. Winterbottom, *The Ultra Secret*, 1974
4 John Terraine, *Business in Great Waters. U Boat War 1916–1949*, 1989
5 *Ibid*
6 Enno Stephan, *Spies in Ireland*, Berlin 1963

Chapter 24

1 Enno Stephan, *Spies in Ireland*, Berlin 1963
2 Richard Collier, *The World in Flames*, 1979
3 R.F. Foster, *Modern Ireland 1600–1972*, 1989

Chapter 26

1 James Douglas-Hamilton, *The Truth about Rudolf Hess*, 1994
2 Sir Ivone Kirkpatrick, *Inner Circle*, 1959

Bibliography

Allen, Peter, *The Crown and the Swastika* (Robert Hale, London, 1983).

Andrew, Christopher, *Secret Service, the Making of the British Intelligence Community* (William Heinemann, London, 1985).

Bell, J. Bowyer, *The Secret Army: the IRA 1919 to 1979* (Poolbeg Press, Dublin, 1970).

Bishop, Patrick, and Mallie, Eamonn, *Provisional IRA* (William Heinemann, London, 1985).

Block, Michael (editor), *Wallis and Edward Letters 1931–1937* (Weidenfeld & Nicolson, London, 1986).

Block, Michael, *Ribbentrop* (Transworld, London, 1992).

Block, Michael, *Operation Willi* (Weidenfeld & Nicolson, London, 1984).

Boyle, Andrew, *Climate of Treason* (Hutchinson, London, 1979).

Bradford, Sarah, *George VI* (Weidenfeld & Nicolson, London, 1989).

Breuer, William B., *The Secret War with Germany* (Airlife, England, 1988).

Bryan, J. III, and Murphy, Charles J.V., *The Windsor Story* (Granada, London, 1979).

Bryant, Arthur, *The Turn of the Tide* (Collins, London, 1957).

Canedy, Susan, *America's Nazis* (Mark Grath Publications, USA, 1990).

Churchill, Sir Winston, *Great War Speeches* (Corgi, London, 1957).

Collier, Richard, *The World in Flames* (Hamish Hamilton, London, 1979).

Conrad, Earl, *Errol Flynn: a Memoir* (Robert Hale, London, 1979).

Coogan, Tim Pat, *The IRA* (Pall Mall Press, Dublin, 1970).

Costello, John, *Mask of Treachery* (William Morrow, New York, 1988).

Deacon, Richard, *A History of the British Secret Service* (Frederick Muller, London, 1969).

Douglas-Hamilton, James, *The Truth about Rudolf Hess* (Mainstream, Edinburgh, 1993).

Douglas-Hamilton, James, *Motive for a Mission: the story Behind Rudolf Hess's Flight to Britain* (Mainstream, Edinburgh, 1979).

Duggan, John P., *Neutral Ireland and the Third Reich* (Gill & MacMillan, Dublin, 1975).

Edwards, Bernard, *They Sank the Red Dragon* (University of Wales Press, Cardiff, 1987).

Farago, Ladislas, *The Game of The Foxes* (Hodder & Stoughton, London, 1972).

Fleming, Peter, *Invasion 1940* (Rupert Hart Davis, London, 1957).

251

BIBLIOGRAPHY

Flynn, Errol, *My Wicked, Wicked Ways* (William Heinemann, London, 1960).
Foster, R.F., *Modern Ireland 1600–1972* (Allen Lane, Penguin Press, 1988).
Hess, Wolf Rudiger, *My Father Rudolf Hess* (W.H. Allen, London, 1986).
Higham, Charles, *American Swastika* (Doubleday, New York, 1985).
Higham, Charles, *Trading with the Enemy* (Robert Hale, London 1983).
Higham, Charles, *Errol Flynn: the Untold Story* (Granada, London, 1980).
Higham, Charles, *Wallis* (Sidgwick & Jackson, London, 1988).
Hitler, Adolf, *Mein Kampf* (Hurst & Blackett, England, 1933).
Hough, Richard, *Former Naval Person Churchill and the Wars at Sea* (Weidenfeld & Nicolson, London, 1985).
Hoyt, Edwin P., *Goering's War* (Robert Hale, London, 1990).
Hoyt, Edwin P., *Hitler's War* (Robert Hale, London, 1989).
Huff, David, *Queen Mary* (Collins, London, 1985).
Inglis, Brian, *Roger Casement* (Hodder & Stoughton, London, 1973).
Irving, David, *Hess: the Missing Years 1941–1945* (Macmillan, London, 1987).
Lane, Peter, *The Queen* (Robert Hale, London, 1979).
Lang, von Jochem, *The Secretary: Martin Bormann – the man who Manipulated Hitler* (Deutsche Verglas-Anstalt, Berlin, 1977).
Mosley, Diana, *The Duchess of Windsor* (Sidgwick & Jackson, London, 1980).
Mosley, Sir Oswald, *My Life* (Nelson, London, 1968).
Neave, Airey, *Nuremburg* (Hodder & Stoughton, London, 1978).
Padfield, Peter, *Flight for the Führer* (Weidenfeld & Nicolson, London, 1991).
Parker, John, *King of Fools* (Macdonald, London, 1988).
Pies, Gunter, *The Mirror of Deception* (Weidenfeld & Nicolson, London, 1977).
Pincher, Chapman, *Web of Deception* (Sidgwick & Jackson, London, 1987).
Roberts, Andrew, *Eminent Churchillians* (Weidenfeld & Nicolson, London, 1994).
Rose, Kenneth, *King George V* (Weidenfeld & Nicolson, London, 1983).
Schenk, Peter, *Invasion of England* (*Landung in England*) (Oberbaum Verlag, Berlin, 1987).
Schwarzwaller, Wulf, *Rudolf Hess the Deputy* (Quartet Books, London, 1988).
Shirer, William, *The Rise and Fall of the Third Reich* (Secker & Warburg, London, 1960).
Sinclair, David, *Queen and Country* (J.M. Dent & Sons, London, 1979).
Stephan, Enno, *Spies in Ireland* (Macdonald, London, 1963).
Stone, Norman, *Hitler* (Hodder & Stoughton, London, 1980).
Terraine, John, *Business in Great Waters: the U-boat War 1916–1945* (Leo Cooper, London, 1989).
Thomas, Hugh, *The Murder of Rudolf Hess* (Hodder & Stoughton, London, 1979).
Thomas, Hugh, *Hess: the Tale of Two Murders* (Hodder & Stoughton, London, 1988).
Trevor Roper, H.R., *The Last Days of Hitler* (Macmillan, London, 1947).
Warwick, Christopher, *King George VI and Queen Elizabeth: a Portrait* (Sidgwick & Jackson, London, 1985).
West, Nigel, *MI5* (Bodley Head, London, 1981).
Winterbotham, F.W., *The Ultra Secret* (Weidenfeld & Nicolson, London, 1974).
Wright, Peter, *Spycatcher* (William Heinemann, Australia, 1987).
Ziegler, Phillip, *King Edward VIII* (Collins, London, 1990).

Index